HUNT FOR WOLVERINE
WEAPON LOST

HUNT FOR WOLVERINE #1

WRITER **Charles Soule**

"SECRETS AND LIES"

ARTIST **David Marquez**

COLOR ARTIST **Rachelle Rosenberg**

"HUNTER'S PRYDE"

PENCILER **Paulo Siqueira**

INKER **Walden Wong**

COLOR ARTIST **Ruth Redmond**

COVER ART **Steve McNiven, Jay Leisten & Laura Martin**

WEAPON LOST #1-4

WRITER **Charles Soule**

ARTIST **Matteo Buffagni**

COLOR ARTIST **Jim Charalampidis**

COVER ART **Greg Land, Jay Leisten &
Romulo Fajardo Jr.** (#1-2);
**Giuseppe Camuncoli, Roberto Poggi &
Dean White** (#3); AND **Giuseppe Camuncoli,
Roberto Poggi & Federico Blee** (#4)

LETTERER **VC's Joe Sabino**

ASSISTANT EDITORS **Annalise Bissa & Christina Harrington**

EDITORS **Mark Paniccia & Jordan D. White**

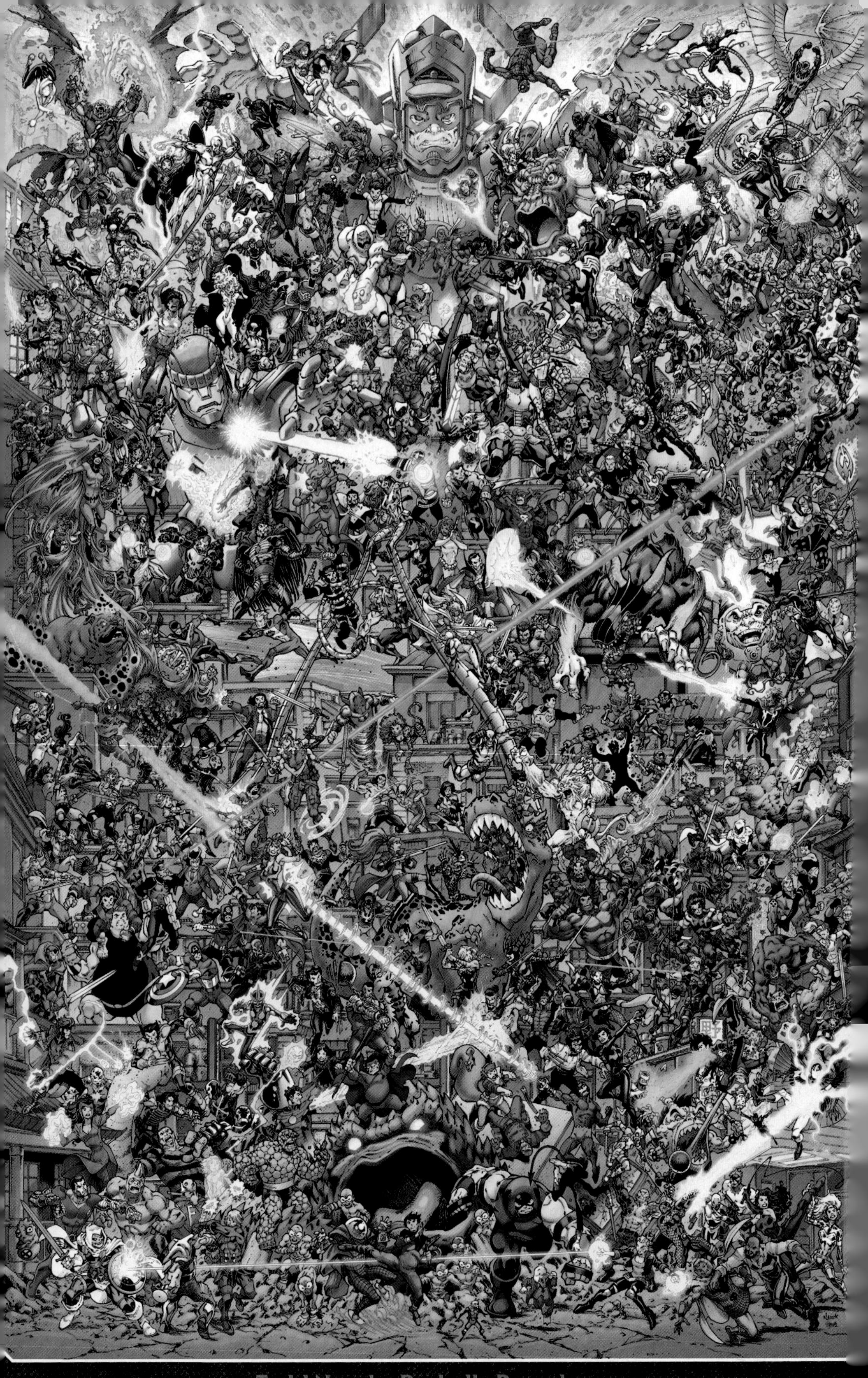

Todd Nauck & Rachelle Rosenberg

WEAPON LOST #1, ADAMANTIUM AGENDA #1, CLAWS OF A KILLER #1 & MYSTERY IN MADRIPOOR #1 CONNECTING VARIANTS

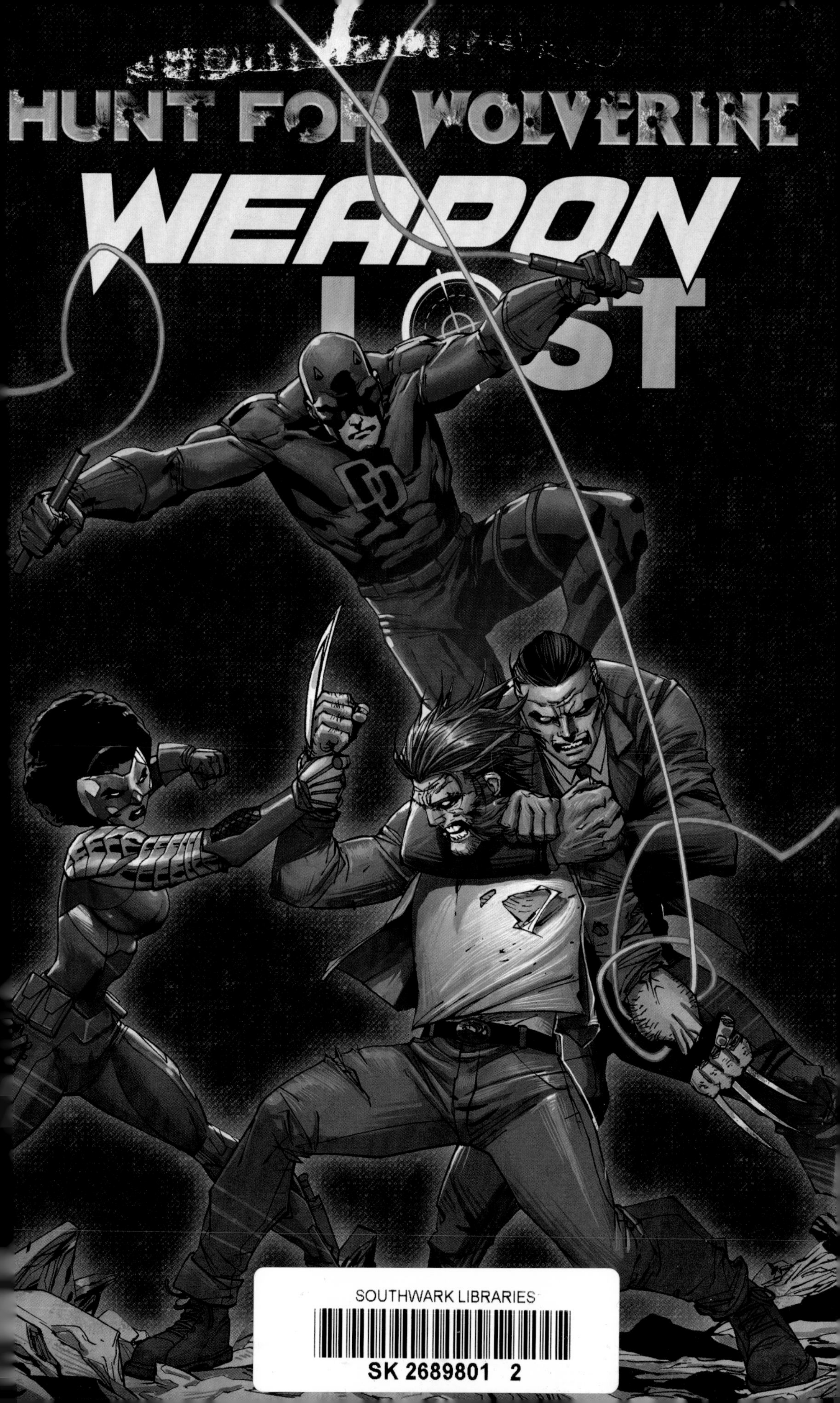
HUNT FOR WOLVERINE
WEAPON LOST

COLLECTION EDITOR **Jennifer Grünwald**
ASSISTANT EDITOR **Caitlin O'Connell**
ASSOCIATE MANAGING EDITOR **Kateri Woody**
EDITOR, SPECIAL PROJECTS **Mark D. Beazley**
VP PRODUCTION & SPECIAL PROJECTS **Jeff Youngquist**
SVP PRINT, SALES & MARKETING **David Gabriel**

BOOK DESIGNER **Adam Del Re**

EDITOR IN CHIEF **C.B. Cebulski**
CHIEF CREATIVE OFFICER **Joe Quesada**
PRESIDENT **Dan Buckley**
EXECUTIVE PRODUCER **Alan Fine**

HUNT FOR WOLVERINE: WEAPON LOST. Contains material originally published in magazine form as HUNT FOR WOLVERINE #1 and HUNT FOR WOLVERINE: WEAPON LOST #1-4. First printing 2018. ISBN 9
1-302-91302-1. Published by MARVEL WORLDWIDE, INC., a subsidiary of MARVEL ENTERTAINMENT, LLC. OFFICE OF PUBLICATION: 135 West 50th Street, New York, NY 10020. Copyright © 2018 MARVEL
similarity between any of the names, characters, persons, and/or institutions in this magazine with those of any living or dead person or institution is intended, and any such similarity which may exist is pu
coincidental. **Printed in Canada.** DAN BUCKLEY, President, Marvel Entertainment; JOHN NEE, Publisher; JOE QUESADA, Chief Creative Officer; TOM BREVOORT, SVP of Publishing; DAVID BOGART, SVP of Busi
Affairs & Operations, Publishing & Partnership; DAVID GABRIEL, SVP of Sales & Marketing, Publishing; JEFF YOUNGQUIST, VP of Production & Special Projects; DAN CARR, Executive Director of Publishing Technol
ALEX MORALES, Director of Publishing Operations; DAN EDINGTON, Managing Editor; SUSAN CRESPI, Production Manager; STAN LEE, Chairman Emeritus. For information regarding advertising in Marvel Co
or on Marvel.com, please contact Vit DeBellis, Custom Solutions & Integrated Advertising Manager, at vdebellis@marvel.com. For Marvel subscription inquiries, please call 888-511-5480. **Manufactured betw**
10/12/2018 and 11/13/2018 by SOLISCO PRINTERS, SCOTT, QC, CANADA.

10 9 8 7 6 5 4 3 2 1

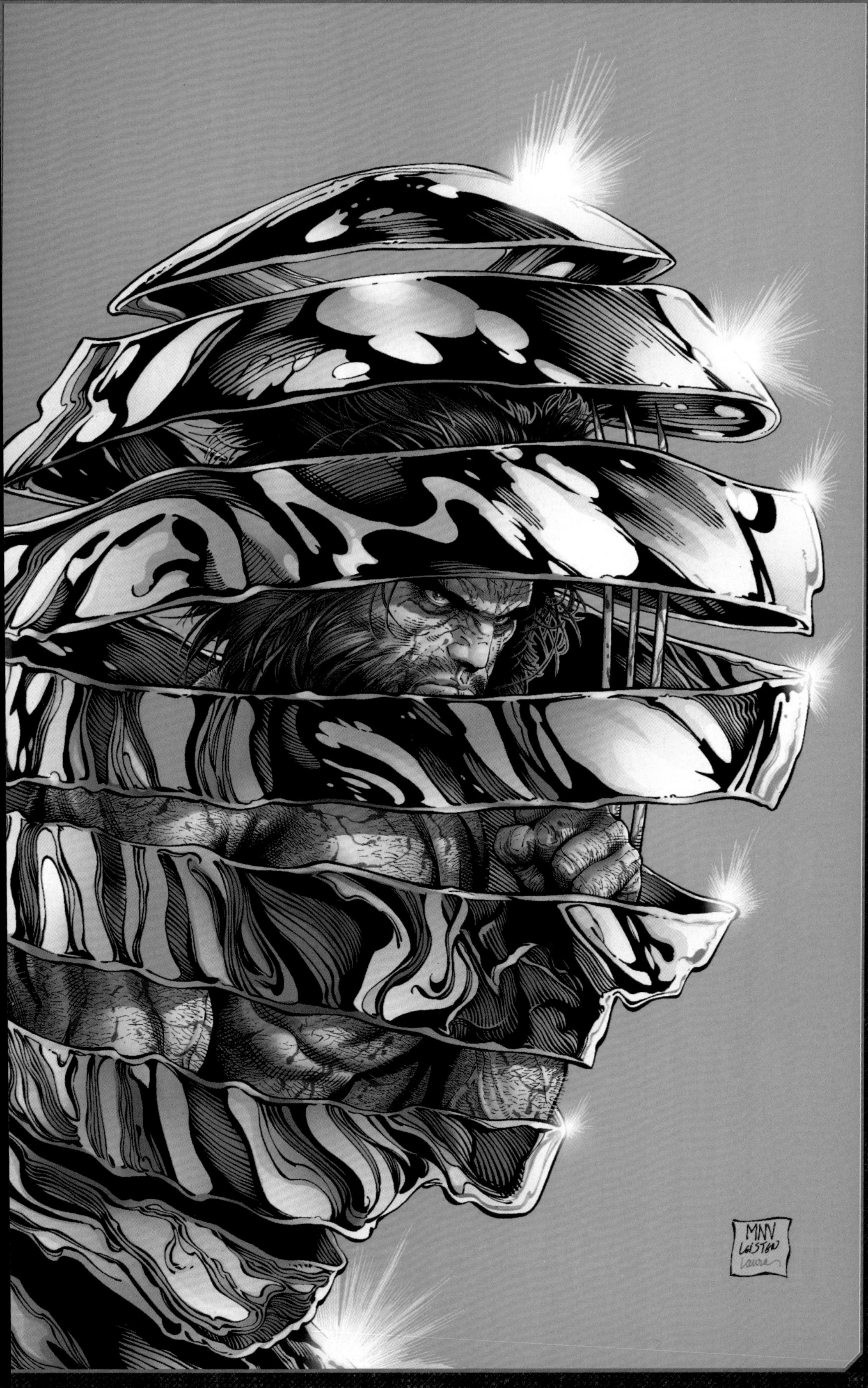

HUNT FOR WOLVERINE 1

WOLVERINE DIED,
ENTOMBED IN
MOLTEN ADAMANTIUM.

THE X-MEN TOOK HIS
METAL-ENCASED BODY
AND HID IT AWAY,
KEEPING ITS LOCATION SECRET.

BUT NOTHING STAYS BURIED.

IT WAS ONLY A MATTER OF TIME.

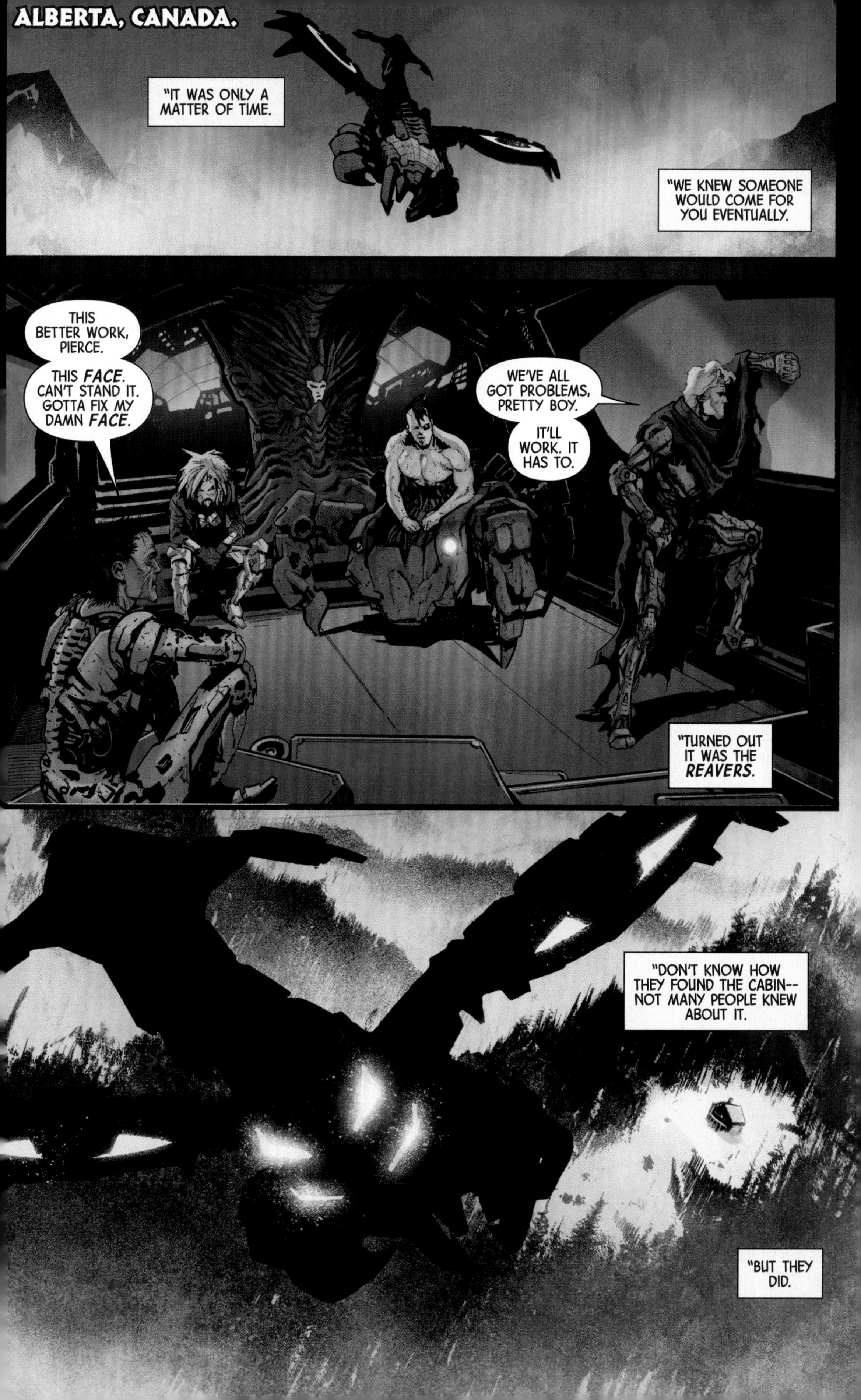

ALBERTA, CANADA.
"IT WAS ONLY A MATTER OF TIME.
"WE KNEW SOMEONE WOULD COME FOR YOU EVENTUALLY.
THIS BETTER WORK, PIERCE.
THIS FACE. CAN'T STAND IT. GOTTA FIX MY DAMN FACE.
WE'VE ALL GOT PROBLEMS, PRETTY BOY.
IT'LL WORK. IT HAS TO.
"TURNED OUT IT WAS THE REAVERS.
"DON'T KNOW HOW THEY FOUND THE CABIN-- NOT MANY PEOPLE KNEW ABOUT IT.
"BUT THEY DID.

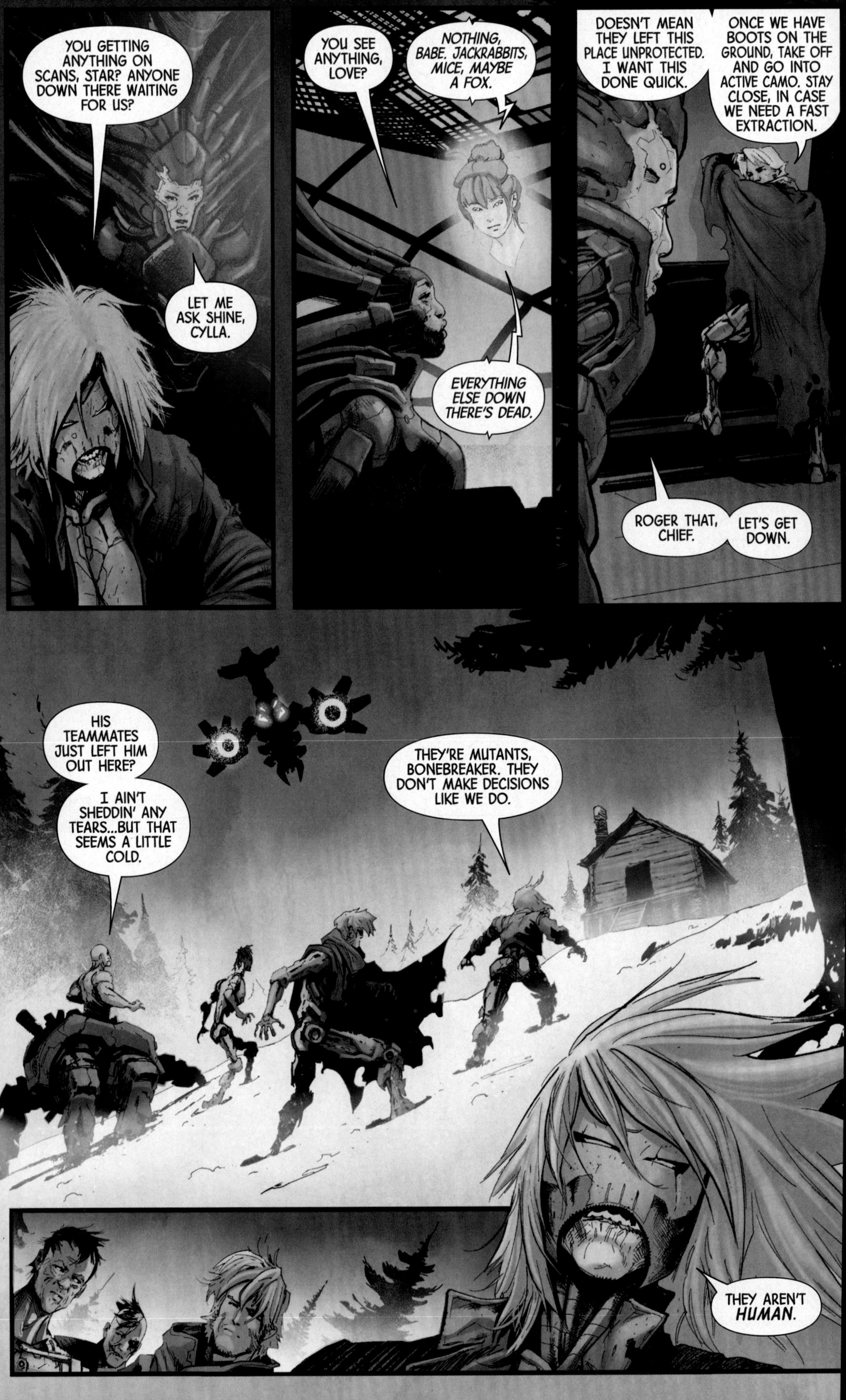
YOU GETTING ANYTHING ON SCANS, STAR? ANYONE DOWN THERE WAITING FOR US?
LET ME ASK SHINE, CYLLA.
YOU SEE ANYTHING, LOVE?
NOTHING, BABE. JACKRABBITS, MICE, MAYBE A FOX.
EVERYTHING ELSE DOWN THERE'S DEAD.
DOESN'T MEAN THEY LEFT THIS PLACE UNPROTECTED. I WANT THIS DONE QUICK.
ONCE WE HAVE BOOTS ON THE GROUND, TAKE OFF AND GO INTO ACTIVE CAMO. STAY CLOSE, IN CASE WE NEED A FAST EXTRACTION.
ROGER THAT, CHIEF.
LET'S GET DOWN.
HIS TEAMMATES JUST LEFT HIM OUT HERE?
I AIN'T SHEDDIN' ANY TEARS...BUT THAT SEEMS A LITTLE COLD.
THEY'RE MUTANTS, BONEBREAKER. THEY DON'T MAKE DECISIONS LIKE WE DO.
THEY AREN'T *HUMAN*.

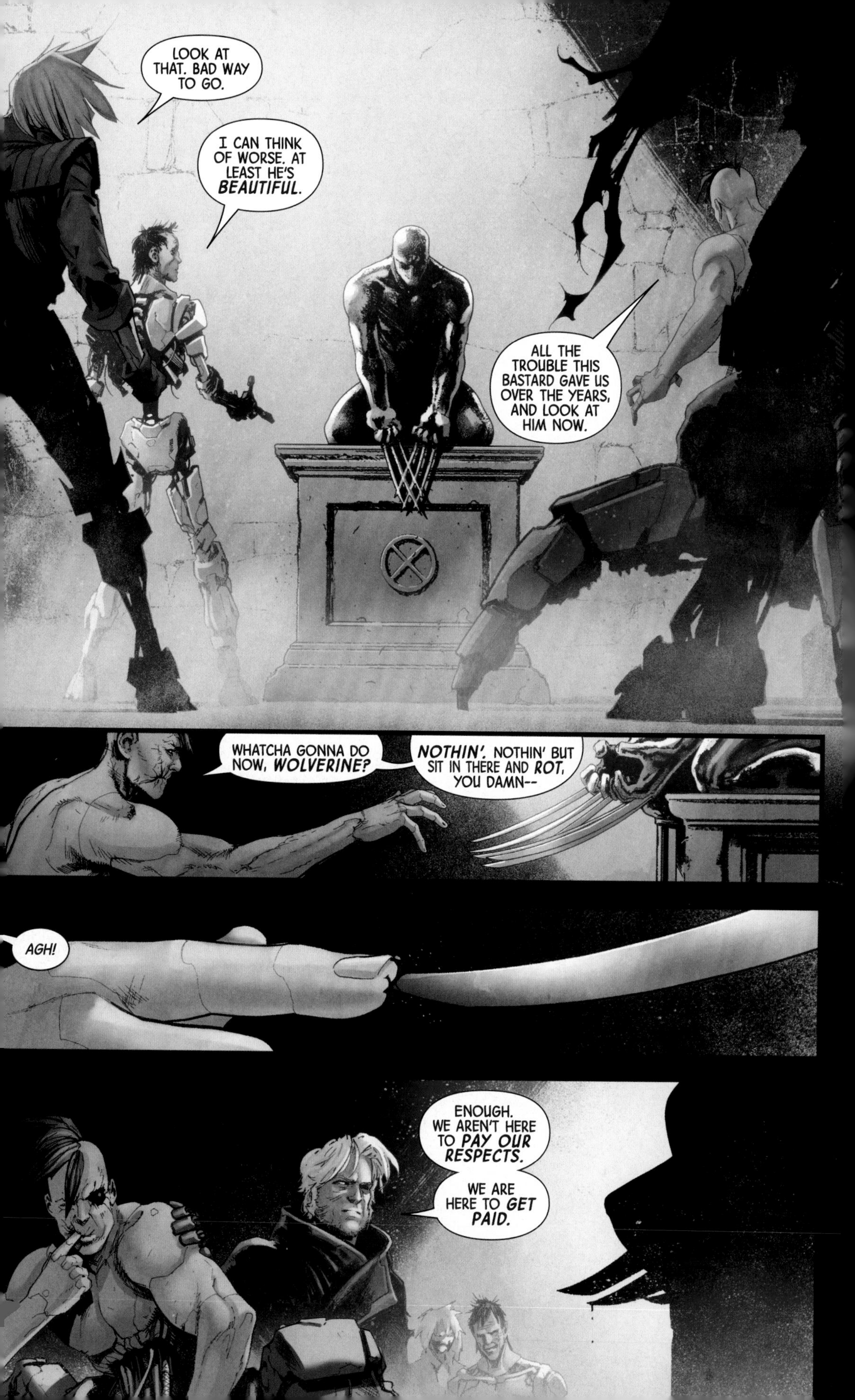
LOOK AT THAT. BAD WAY TO GO.
I CAN THINK OF WORSE. AT LEAST HE'S *BEAUTIFUL*.
ALL THE TROUBLE THIS BASTARD GAVE US OVER THE YEARS, AND LOOK AT HIM NOW.
WHATCHA GONNA DO NOW, *WOLVERINE?*
NOTHIN'. NOTHIN' BUT SIT IN THERE AND *ROT*, YOU DAMN--
AGH!
ENOUGH. WE AREN'T HERE TO *PAY OUR RESPECTS*.
WE ARE HERE TO *GET PAID*.

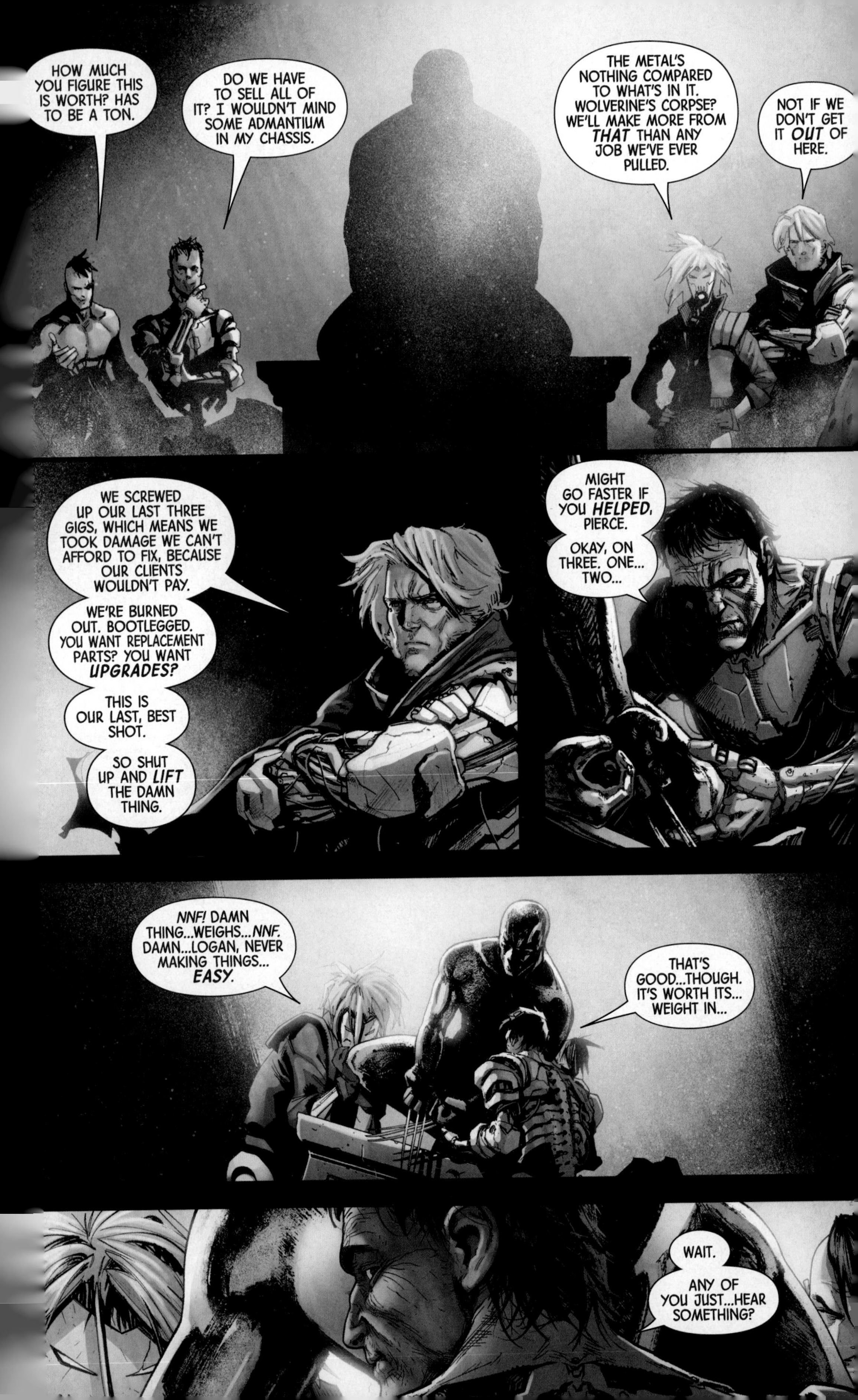
HOW MUCH YOU FIGURE THIS IS WORTH? HAS TO BE A TON.
DO WE HAVE TO SELL ALL OF IT? I WOULDN'T MIND SOME ADMANTIUM IN MY CHASSIS.
THE METAL'S NOTHING COMPARED TO WHAT'S IN IT. WOLVERINE'S CORPSE? WE'LL MAKE MORE FROM *THAT* THAN ANY JOB WE'VE EVER PULLED.
NOT IF WE DON'T GET IT *OUT* OF HERE.
WE SCREWED UP OUR LAST THREE GIGS, WHICH MEANS WE TOOK DAMAGE WE CAN'T AFFORD TO FIX, BECAUSE OUR CLIENTS WOULDN'T PAY.
WE'RE BURNED OUT. BOOTLEGGED. YOU WANT REPLACEMENT PARTS? YOU WANT *UPGRADES?*
THIS IS OUR LAST, BEST SHOT.
SO SHUT UP AND *LIFT* THE DAMN THING.
MIGHT GO FASTER IF YOU *HELPED*, PIERCE.
OKAY, ON THREE. ONE... TWO...
NNF! DAMN THING...WEIGHS...*NNF.* DAMN...LOGAN, NEVER MAKING THINGS... *EASY*.
THAT'S GOOD...THOUGH. IT'S WORTH ITS... WEIGHT IN...
WAIT.
ANY OF YOU JUST...HEAR SOMETHING?

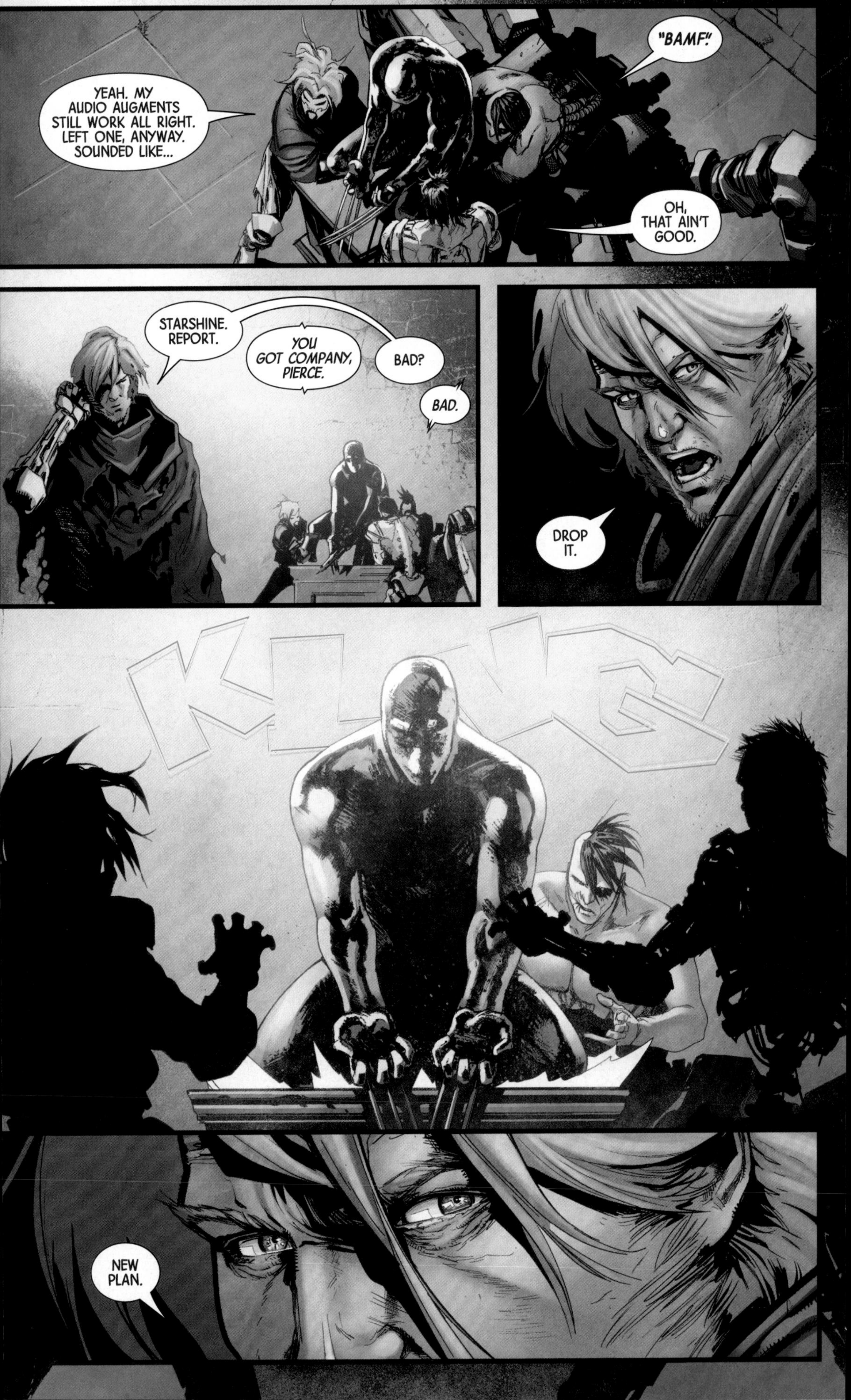
YEAH. MY AUDIO AUGMENTS STILL WORK ALL RIGHT. LEFT ONE, ANYWAY. SOUNDED LIKE...
"BAMF."
OH, THAT AIN'T GOOD.
STARSHINE. REPORT.
YOU GOT COMPANY, PIERCE.
BAD?
BAD.
DROP IT.
KLANG
NEW PLAN.

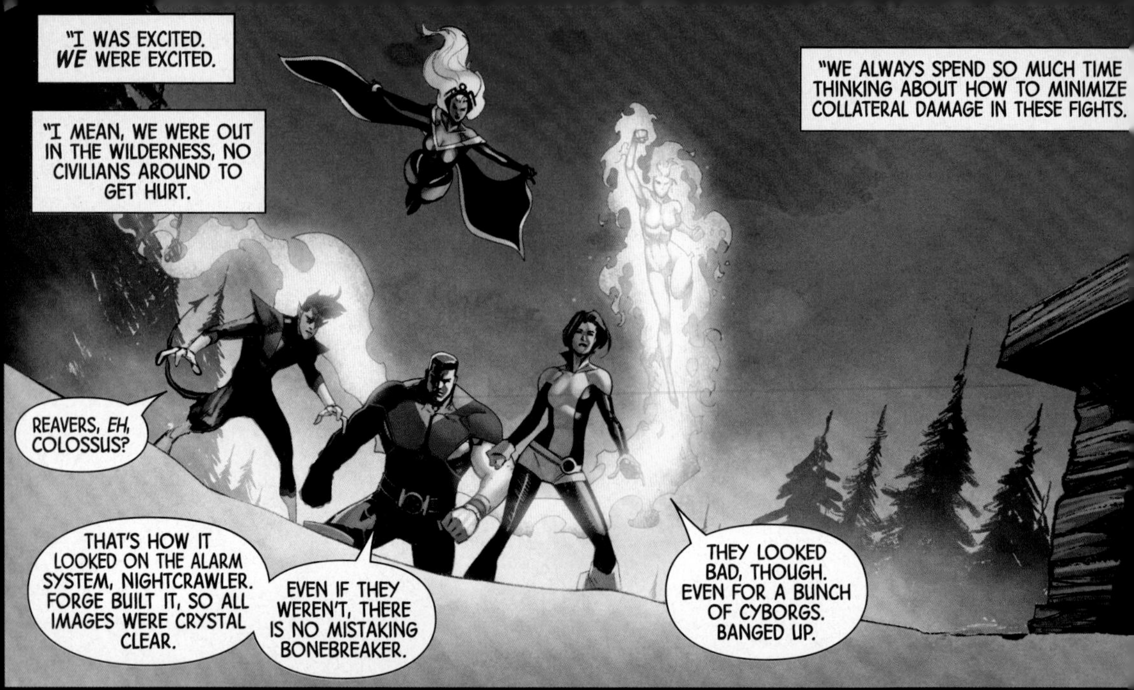
"I WAS EXCITED. *WE* WERE EXCITED.
"I MEAN, WE WERE OUT IN THE WILDERNESS, NO CIVILIANS AROUND TO GET HURT.
"WE ALWAYS SPEND SO MUCH TIME THINKING ABOUT HOW TO MINIMIZE COLLATERAL DAMAGE IN THESE FIGHTS.
REAVERS, *EH*, COLOSSUS?
THAT'S HOW IT LOOKED ON THE ALARM SYSTEM, NIGHTCRAWLER. FORGE BUILT IT, SO ALL IMAGES WERE CRYSTAL CLEAR.
EVEN IF THEY WEREN'T, THERE IS NO MISTAKING BONEBREAKER.
THEY LOOKED BAD, THOUGH. EVEN FOR A BUNCH OF CYBORGS. BANGED UP.

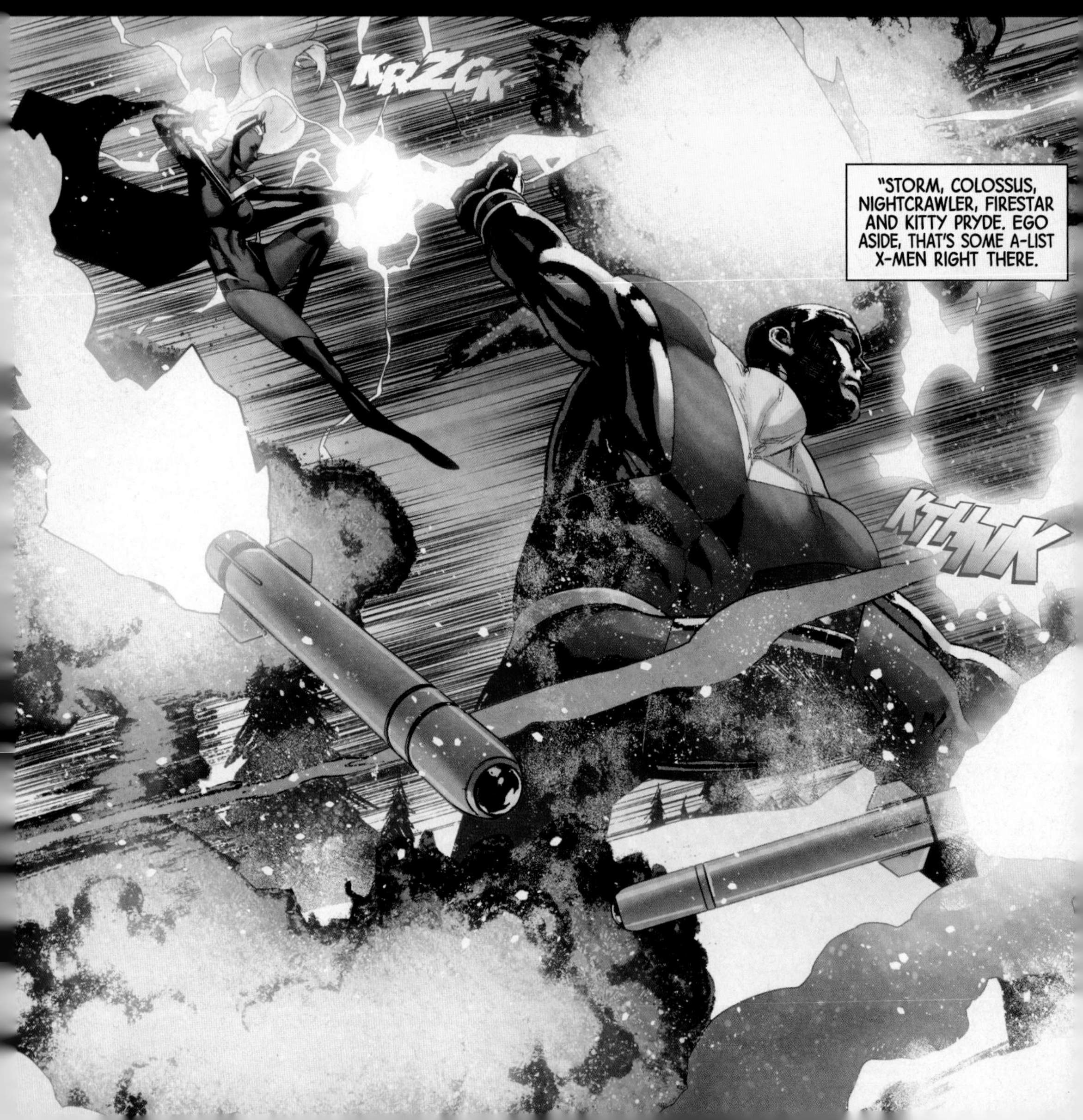
KRZCK
"STORM, COLOSSUS, NIGHTCRAWLER, FIRESTAR AND KITTY PRYDE. EGO ASIDE, THAT'S SOME A-LIST X-MEN RIGHT THERE.
KTHVK

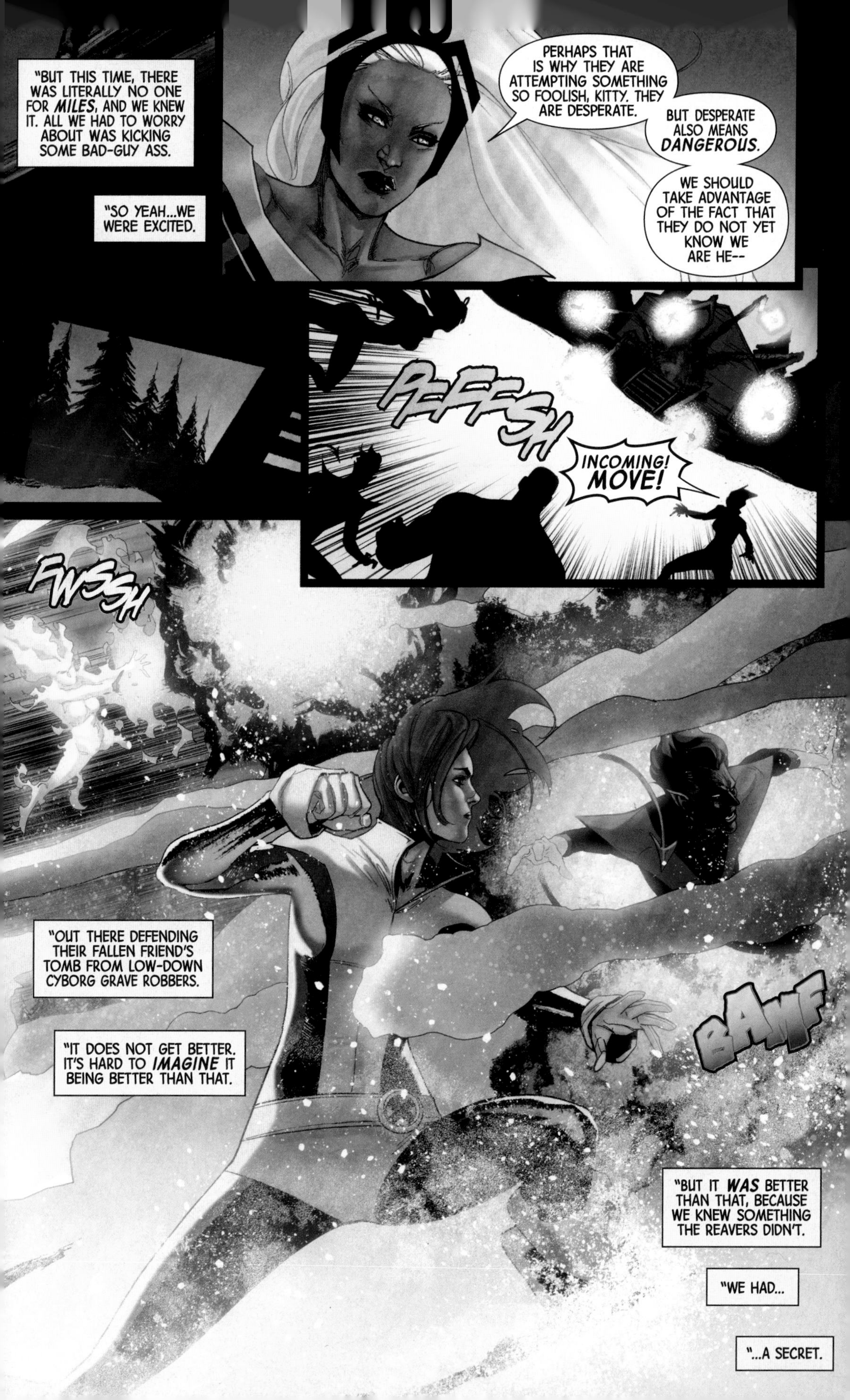

"BUT THIS TIME, THERE WAS LITERALLY NO ONE FOR MILES, AND WE KNEW IT. ALL WE HAD TO WORRY ABOUT WAS KICKING SOME BAD-GUY ASS.
"SO YEAH...WE WERE EXCITED.
PERHAPS THAT IS WHY THEY ARE ATTEMPTING SOMETHING SO FOOLISH, KITTY. THEY ARE DESPERATE.
BUT DESPERATE ALSO MEANS DANGEROUS.
WE SHOULD TAKE ADVANTAGE OF THE FACT THAT THEY DO NOT YET KNOW WE ARE HE--
PFFFSH
INCOMING! MOVE!
FWSSH
"OUT THERE DEFENDING THEIR FALLEN FRIEND'S TOMB FROM LOW-DOWN CYBORG GRAVE ROBBERS.
"IT DOES NOT GET BETTER. IT'S HARD TO IMAGINE IT BEING BETTER THAN THAT.
BAMF
"BUT IT WAS BETTER THAN THAT, BECAUSE WE KNEW SOMETHING THE REAVERS DIDN'T.
"WE HAD...
"...A SECRET.

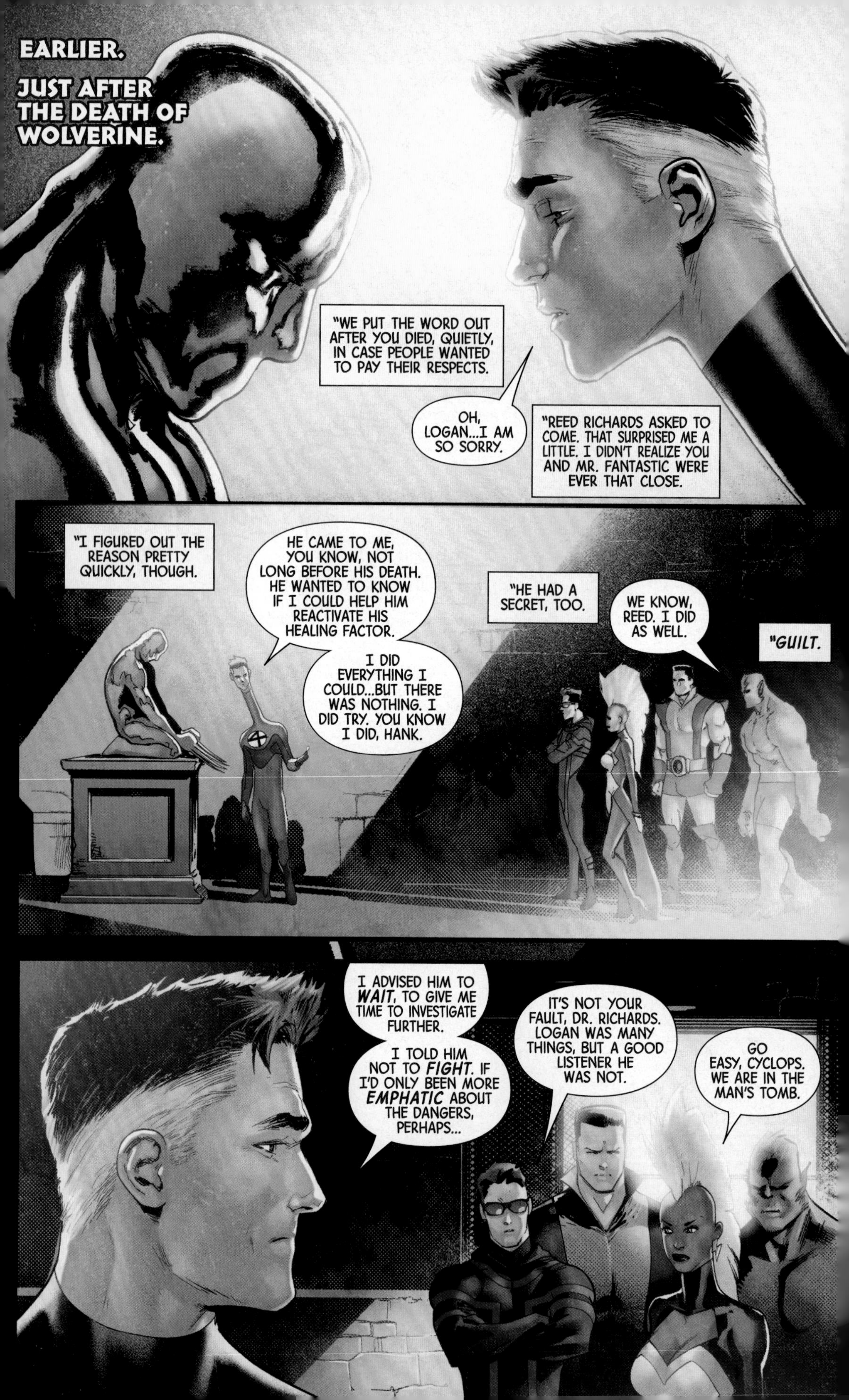
EARLIER.
JUST AFTER THE DEATH OF WOLVERINE.
"WE PUT THE WORD OUT AFTER YOU DIED, QUIETLY, IN CASE PEOPLE WANTED TO PAY THEIR RESPECTS.
OH, LOGAN...I AM SO SORRY.
"REED RICHARDS ASKED TO COME. THAT SURPRISED ME A LITTLE. I DIDN'T REALIZE YOU AND MR. FANTASTIC WERE EVER THAT CLOSE.
"I FIGURED OUT THE REASON PRETTY QUICKLY, THOUGH.
HE CAME TO ME, YOU KNOW, NOT LONG BEFORE HIS DEATH. HE WANTED TO KNOW IF I COULD HELP HIM REACTIVATE HIS HEALING FACTOR.
I DID EVERYTHING I COULD...BUT THERE WAS NOTHING. I DID TRY. YOU KNOW I DID, HANK.
"HE HAD A SECRET, TOO.
WE KNOW, REED. I DID AS WELL.
"GUILT.
I ADVISED HIM TO WAIT, TO GIVE ME TIME TO INVESTIGATE FURTHER.
I TOLD HIM NOT TO FIGHT. IF I'D ONLY BEEN MORE EMPHATIC ABOUT THE DANGERS, PERHAPS...
IT'S NOT YOUR FAULT, DR. RICHARDS. LOGAN WAS MANY THINGS, BUT A GOOD LISTENER HE WAS NOT.
GO EASY, CYCLOPS. WE ARE IN THE MAN'S TOMB.

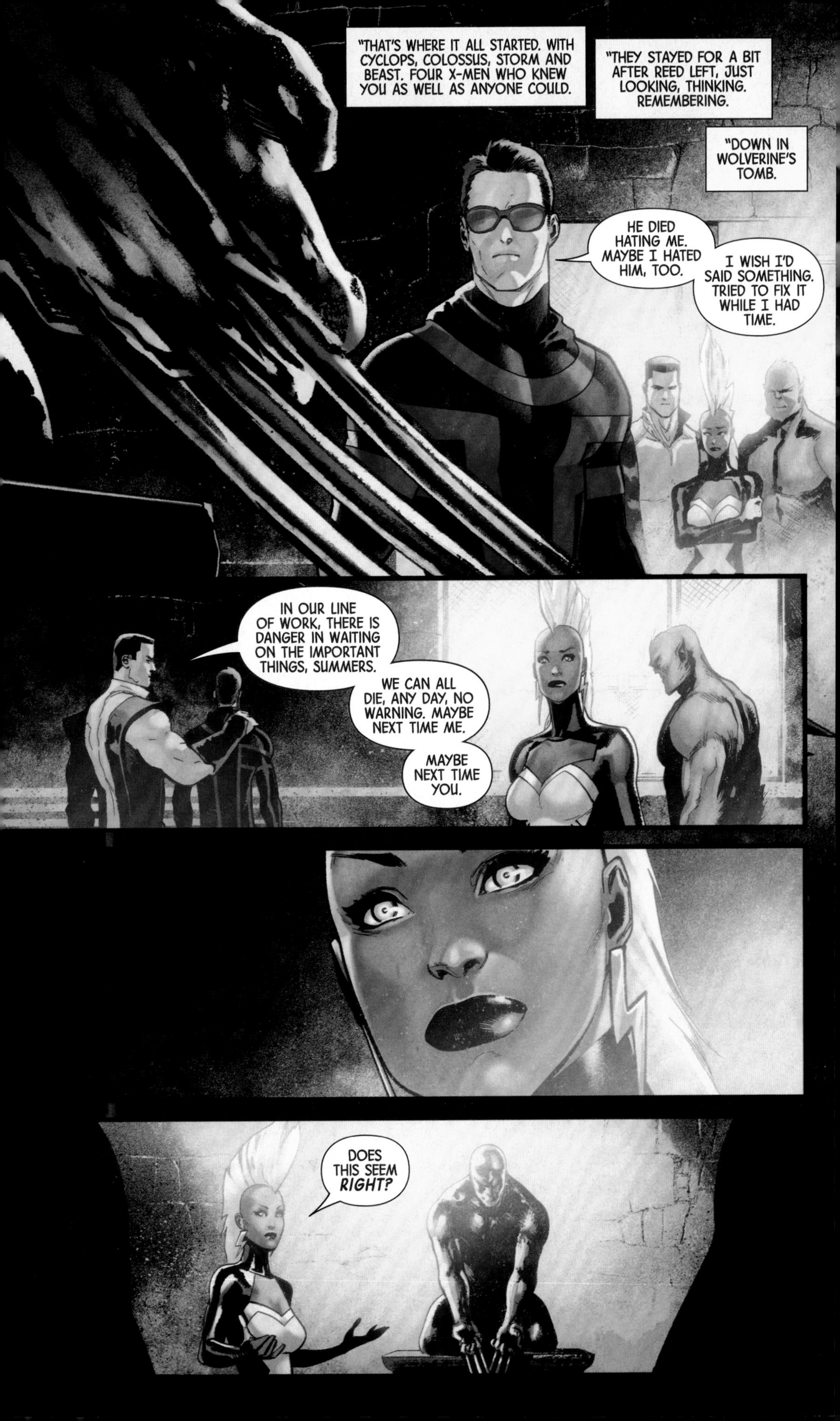
"THAT'S WHERE IT ALL STARTED. WITH CYCLOPS, COLOSSUS, STORM AND BEAST. FOUR X-MEN WHO KNEW YOU AS WELL AS ANYONE COULD.
"THEY STAYED FOR A BIT AFTER REED LEFT, JUST LOOKING, THINKING. REMEMBERING.
"DOWN IN WOLVERINE'S TOMB.
HE DIED HATING ME. MAYBE I HATED HIM, TOO.
I WISH I'D SAID SOMETHING. TRIED TO FIX IT WHILE I HAD TIME.
IN OUR LINE OF WORK, THERE IS DANGER IN WAITING ON THE IMPORTANT THINGS, SUMMERS.
WE CAN ALL DIE, ANY DAY, NO WARNING. MAYBE NEXT TIME ME.
MAYBE NEXT TIME YOU.
DOES THIS SEEM *RIGHT?*

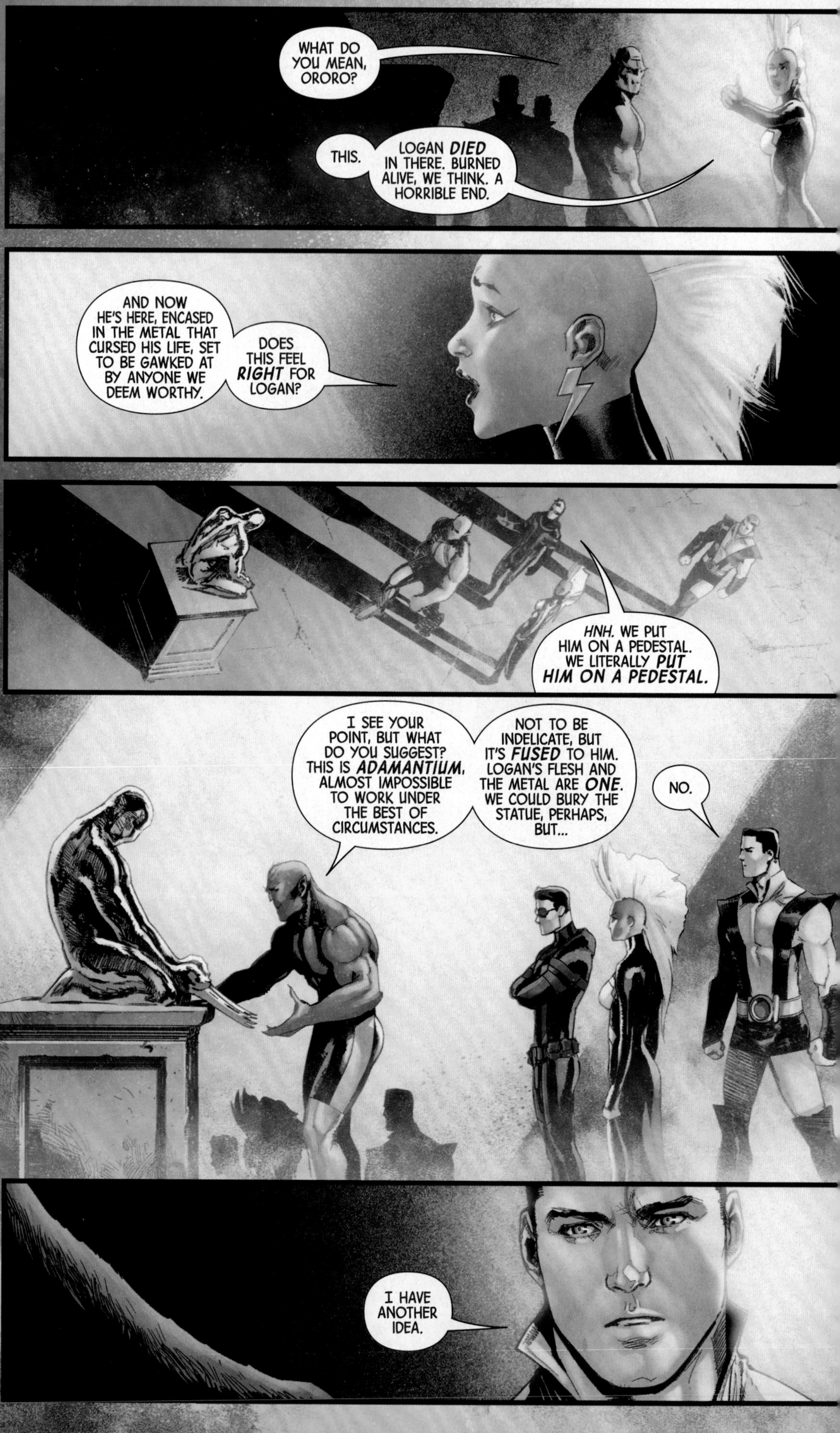

WHAT DO YOU MEAN, ORORO?
THIS.
LOGAN DIED IN THERE. BURNED ALIVE, WE THINK. A HORRIBLE END.
AND NOW HE'S HERE, ENCASED IN THE METAL THAT CURSED HIS LIFE, SET TO BE GAWKED AT BY ANYONE WE DEEM WORTHY.
DOES THIS FEEL RIGHT FOR LOGAN?
HNH. WE PUT HIM ON A PEDESTAL. WE LITERALLY PUT HIM ON A PEDESTAL.
I SEE YOUR POINT, BUT WHAT DO YOU SUGGEST? THIS IS ADAMANTIUM, ALMOST IMPOSSIBLE TO WORK UNDER THE BEST OF CIRCUMSTANCES.
NOT TO BE INDELICATE, BUT IT'S FUSED TO HIM. LOGAN'S FLESH AND THE METAL ARE ONE. WE COULD BURY THE STATUE, PERHAPS, BUT...
NO.
I HAVE ANOTHER IDEA.

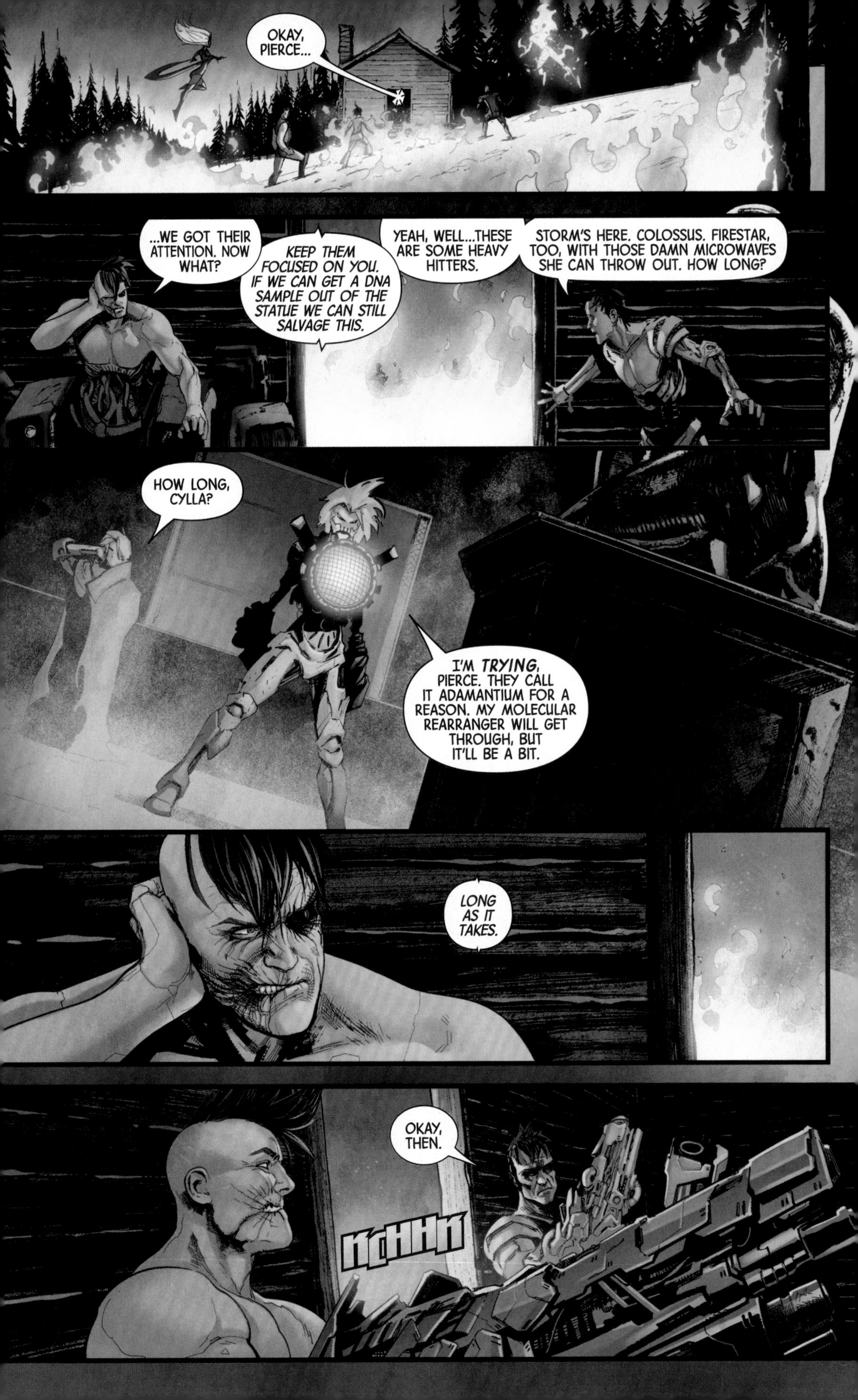
OKAY, PIERCE...
...WE GOT THEIR ATTENTION. NOW WHAT?
KEEP THEM FOCUSED ON YOU. IF WE CAN GET A DNA SAMPLE OUT OF THE STATUE WE CAN STILL SALVAGE THIS.
YEAH, WELL...THESE ARE SOME HEAVY HITTERS.
STORM'S HERE. COLOSSUS. FIRESTAR, TOO, WITH THOSE DAMN MICROWAVES SHE CAN THROW OUT. HOW LONG?
HOW LONG, CYLLA?
I'M TRYING, PIERCE. THEY CALL IT ADAMANTIUM FOR A REASON. MY MOLECULAR REARRANGER WILL GET THROUGH, BUT IT'LL BE A BIT.
LONG AS IT TAKES.
OKAY, THEN.
KCHHK

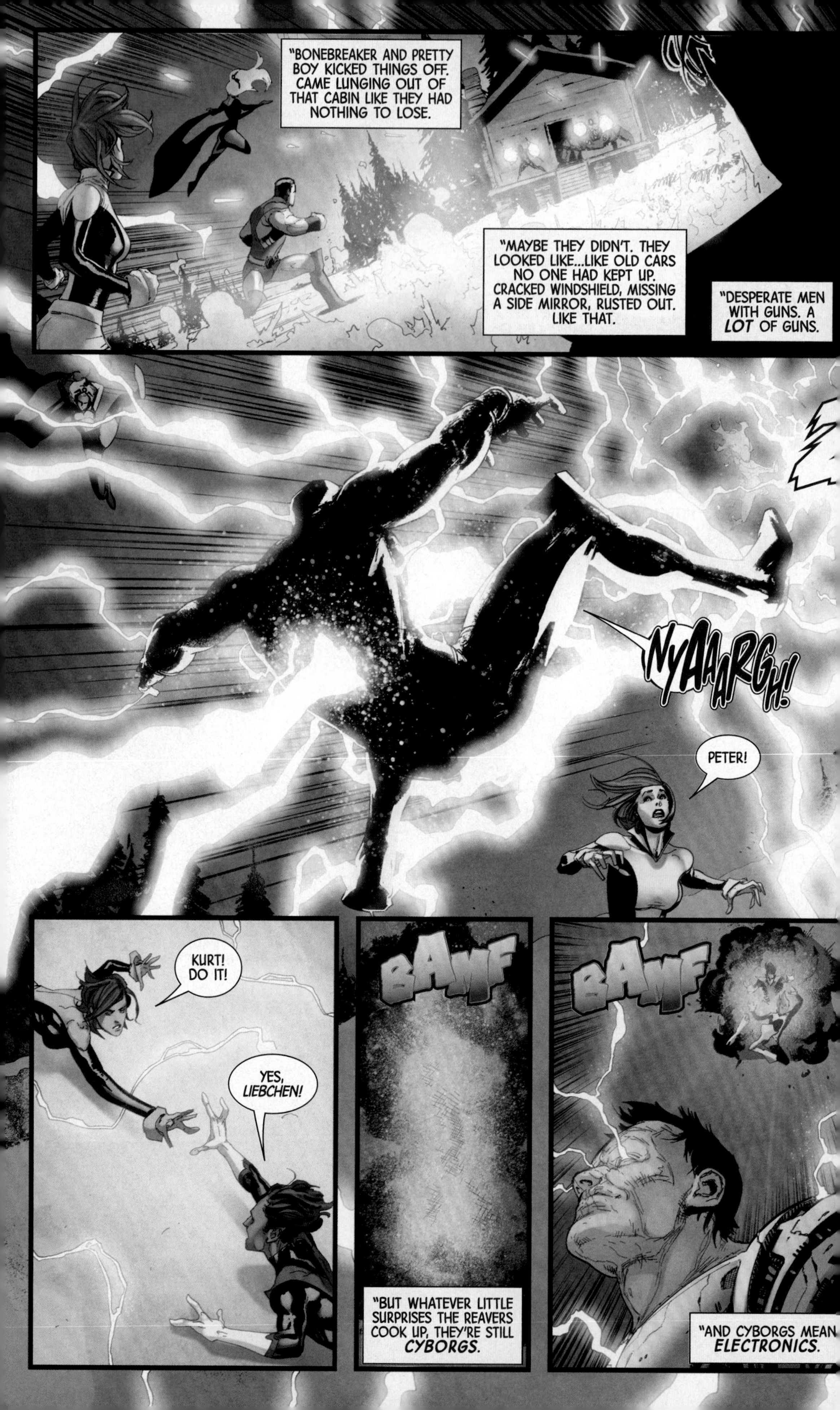
"BONEBREAKER AND PRETTY BOY KICKED THINGS OFF. CAME LUNGING OUT OF THAT CABIN LIKE THEY HAD NOTHING TO LOSE.
"MAYBE THEY DIDN'T. THEY LOOKED LIKE...LIKE OLD CARS NO ONE HAD KEPT UP. CRACKED WINDSHIELD, MISSING A SIDE MIRROR, RUSTED OUT. LIKE THAT.
"DESPERATE MEN WITH GUNS. A LOT OF GUNS.
NYAAARGH!
PETER!
KURT! DO IT!
YES, LIEBCHEN!
BAMF
"BUT WHATEVER LITTLE SURPRISES THE REAVERS COOK UP, THEY'RE STILL CYBORGS.
BAMF
"AND CYBORGS MEAN ELECTRONICS.

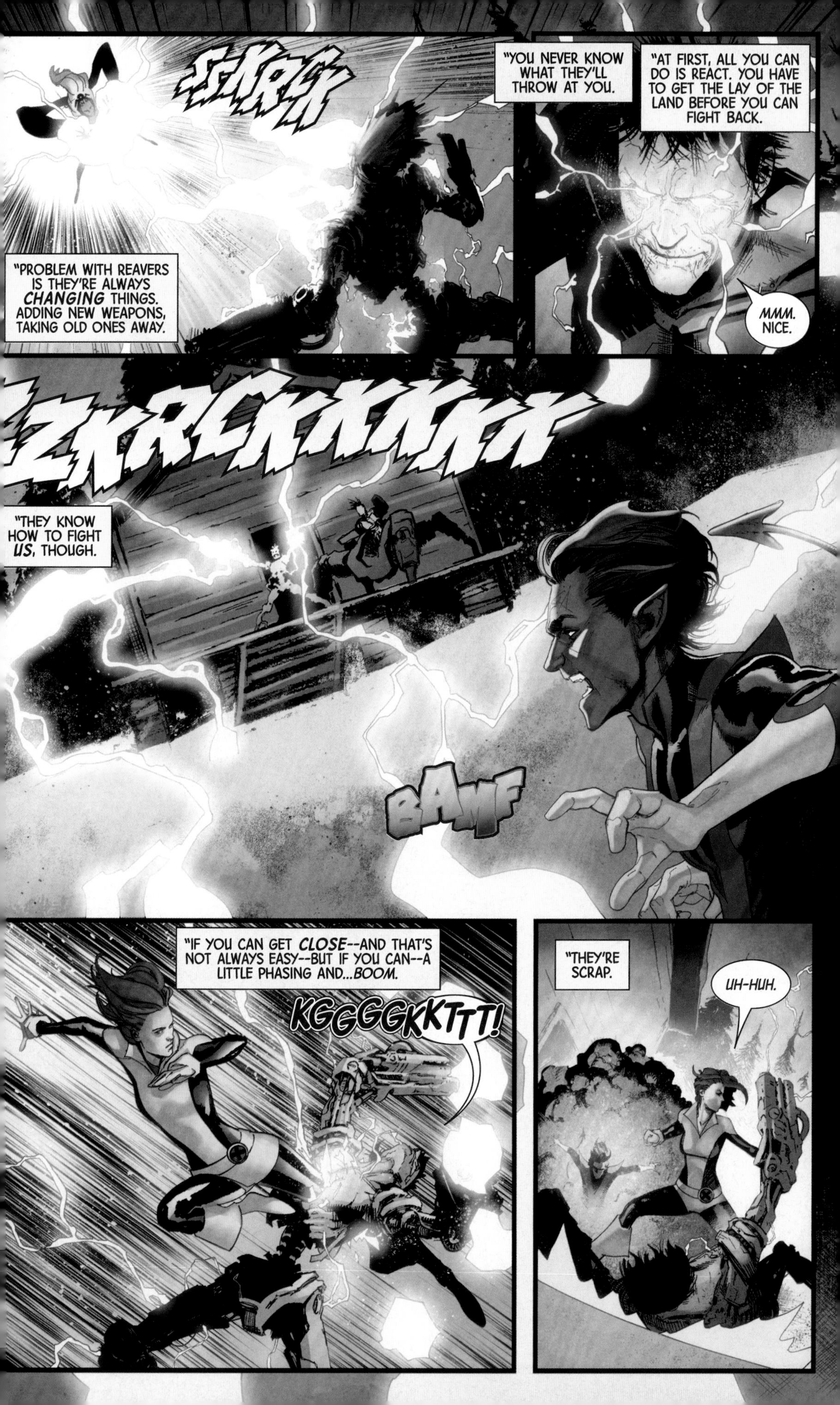
SKRAK
"YOU NEVER KNOW WHAT THEY'LL THROW AT YOU.
"AT FIRST, ALL YOU CAN DO IS REACT. YOU HAVE TO GET THE LAY OF THE LAND BEFORE YOU CAN FIGHT BACK.
"PROBLEM WITH REAVERS IS THEY'RE ALWAYS *CHANGING* THINGS. ADDING NEW WEAPONS, TAKING OLD ONES AWAY.
MMM. NICE.
ZKRACKKKKK
"THEY KNOW HOW TO FIGHT *US*, THOUGH.
BAMF
"IF YOU CAN GET *CLOSE*--AND THAT'S NOT ALWAYS EASY--BUT IF YOU CAN--A LITTLE PHASING AND...*BOOM.*
KGGGGKKTTT!
"THEY'RE SCRAP.
UH-HUH.

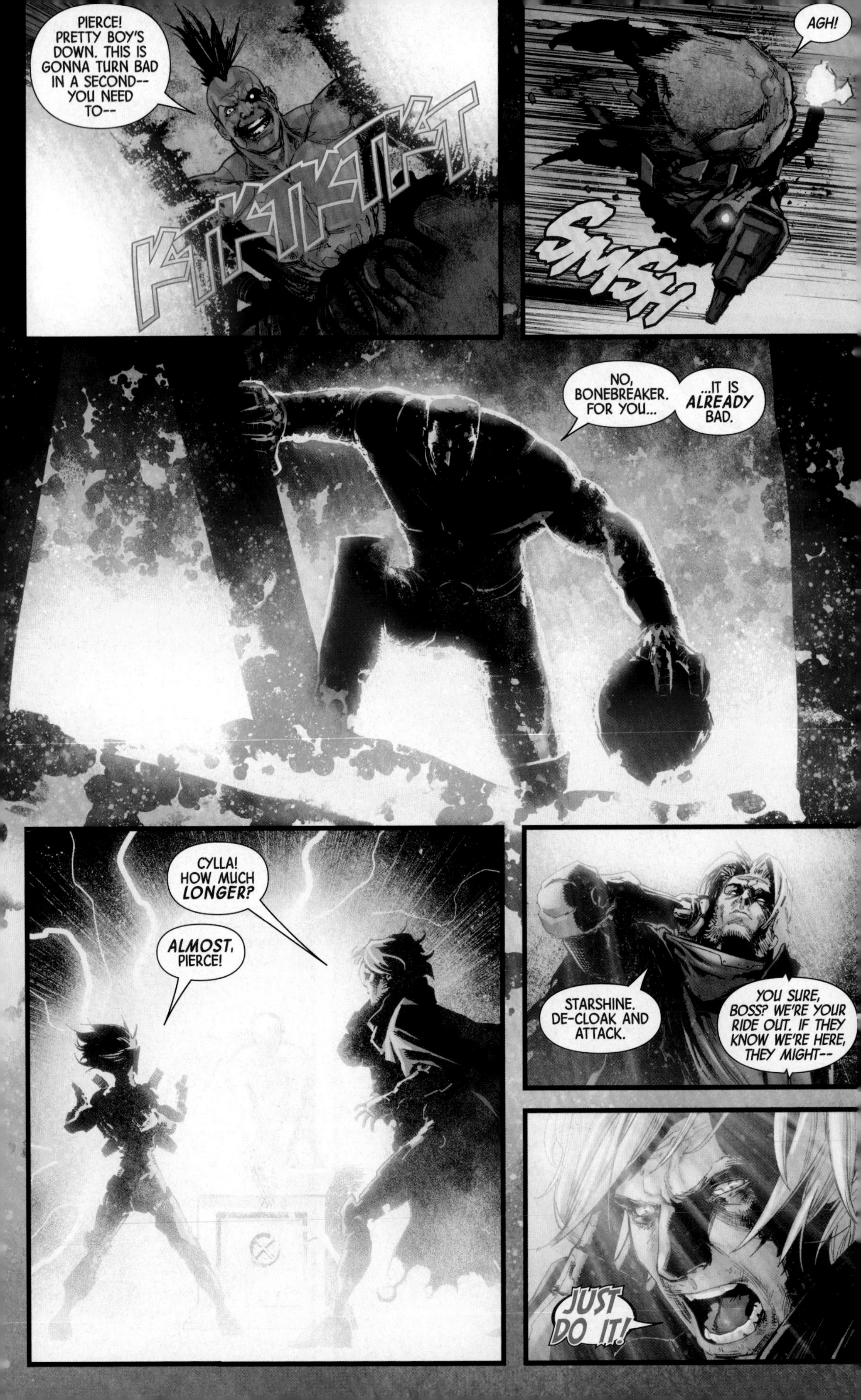
PIERCE! PRETTY BOY'S DOWN. THIS IS GONNA TURN BAD IN A SECOND-- YOU NEED TO--
KTKTKTKT
AGH!
SMSH
NO, BONEBREAKER. FOR YOU...
...IT IS ALREADY BAD.
CYLLA! HOW MUCH LONGER?
ALMOST, PIERCE!
STARSHINE. DE-CLOAK AND ATTACK.
YOU SURE, BOSS? WE'RE YOUR RIDE OUT. IF THEY KNOW WE'RE HERE, THEY MIGHT--
JUST DO IT!

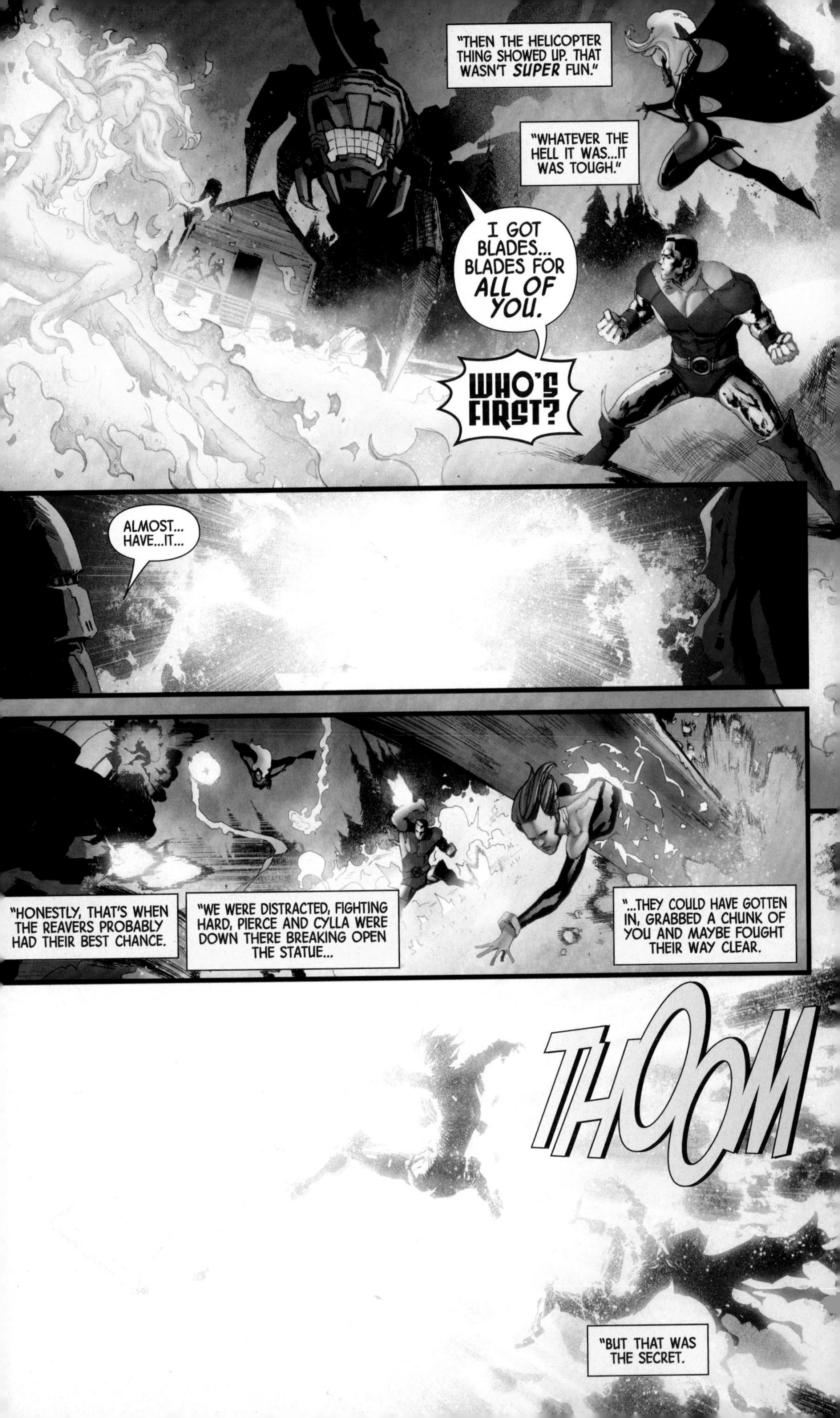
"THEN THE HELICOPTER THING SHOWED UP. THAT WASN'T SUPER FUN."
"WHATEVER THE HELL IT WAS...IT WAS TOUGH."
I GOT BLADES... BLADES FOR ALL OF YOU.
WHO'S FIRST?
ALMOST... HAVE...IT...
"HONESTLY, THAT'S WHEN THE REAVERS PROBABLY HAD THEIR BEST CHANCE.
"WE WERE DISTRACTED, FIGHTING HARD, PIERCE AND CYLLA WERE DOWN THERE BREAKING OPEN THE STATUE...
"...THEY COULD HAVE GOTTEN IN, GRABBED A CHUNK OF YOU AND MAYBE FOUGHT THEIR WAY CLEAR.
THOOM
"BUT THAT WAS THE SECRET.

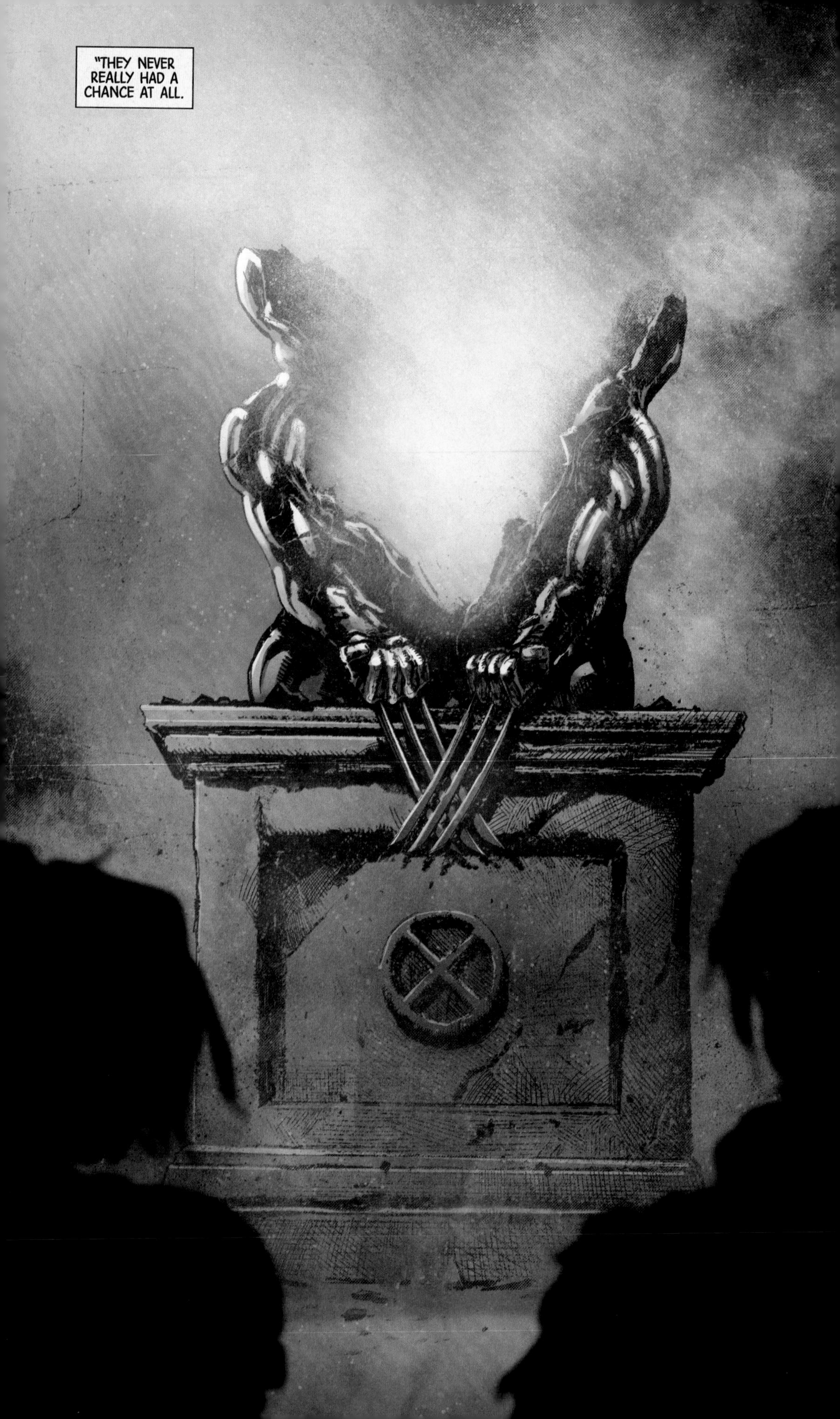
"THEY NEVER REALLY HAD A CHANCE AT ALL.

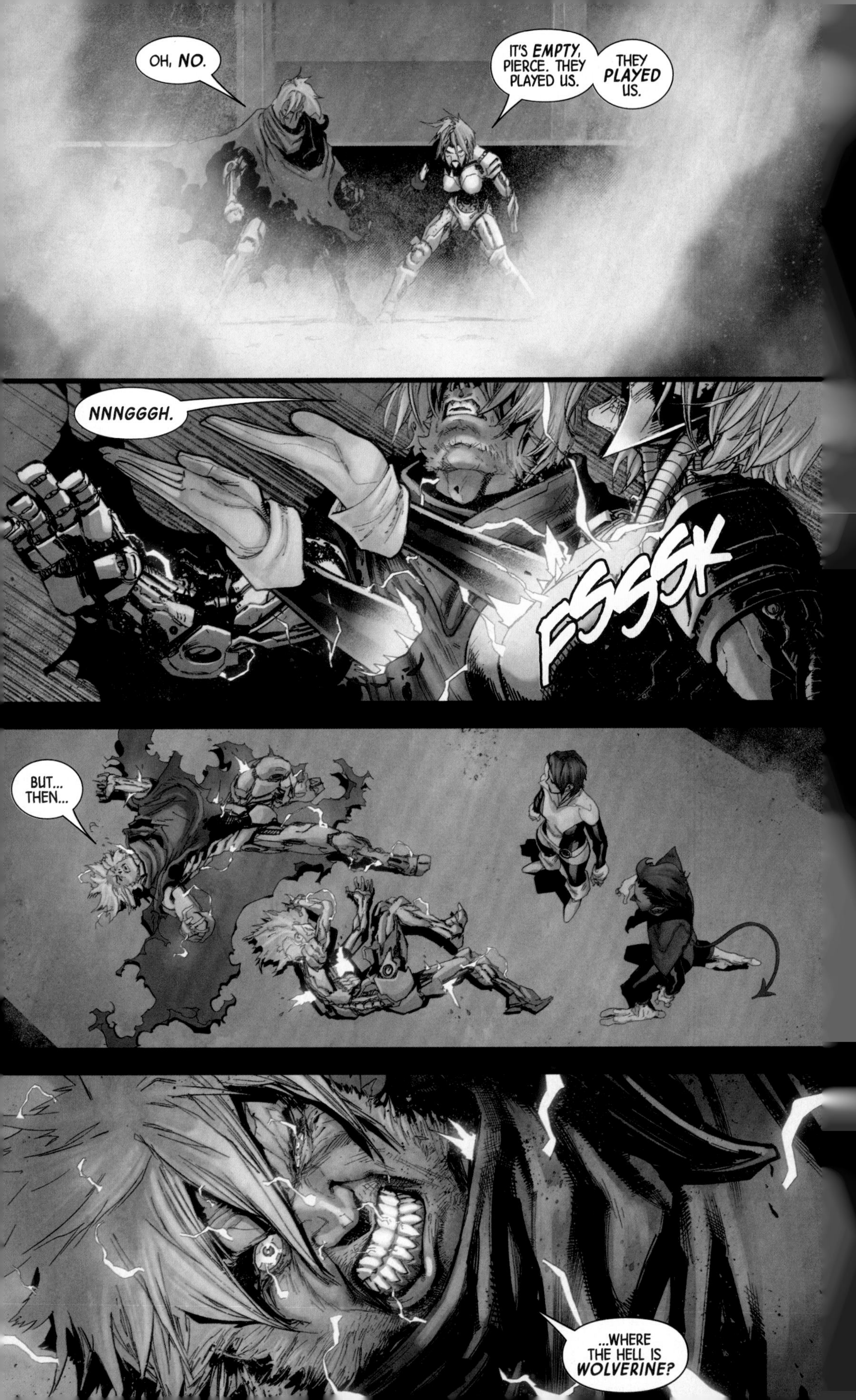
OH, NO.
IT'S EMPTY, PIERCE. THEY PLAYED US.
THEY PLAYED US.
NNNGGGH.
ESSSK
BUT... THEN...
...WHERE THE HELL IS WOLVERINE?

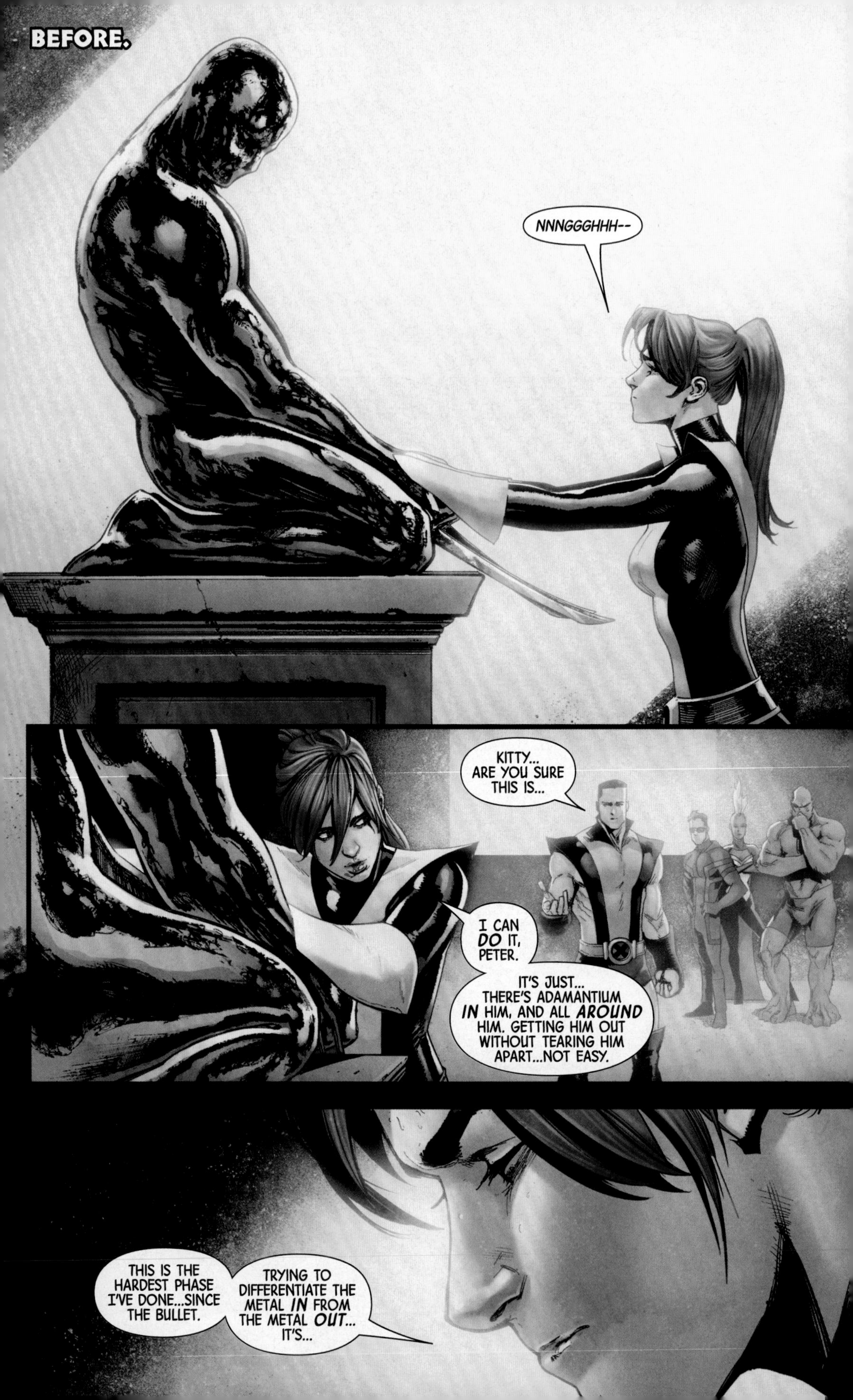
BEFORE.
NNNGGGHHH--
KITTY... ARE YOU SURE THIS IS...
I CAN DO IT, PETER.
IT'S JUST... THERE'S ADAMANTIUM IN HIM, AND ALL AROUND HIM. GETTING HIM OUT WITHOUT TEARING HIM APART...NOT EASY.
THIS IS THE HARDEST PHASE I'VE DONE...SINCE THE BULLET.
TRYING TO DIFFERENTIATE THE METAL IN FROM THE METAL OUT... IT'S...

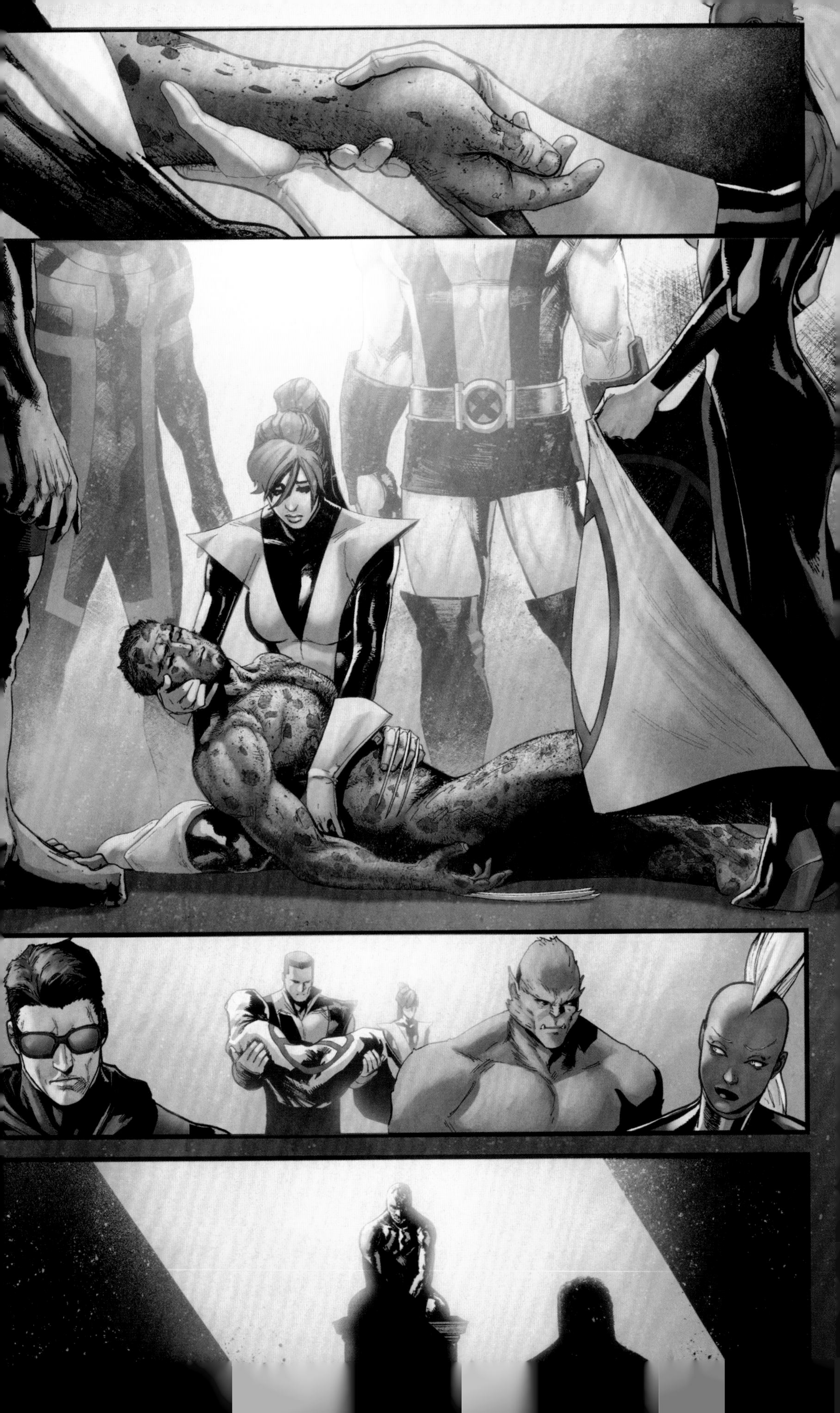

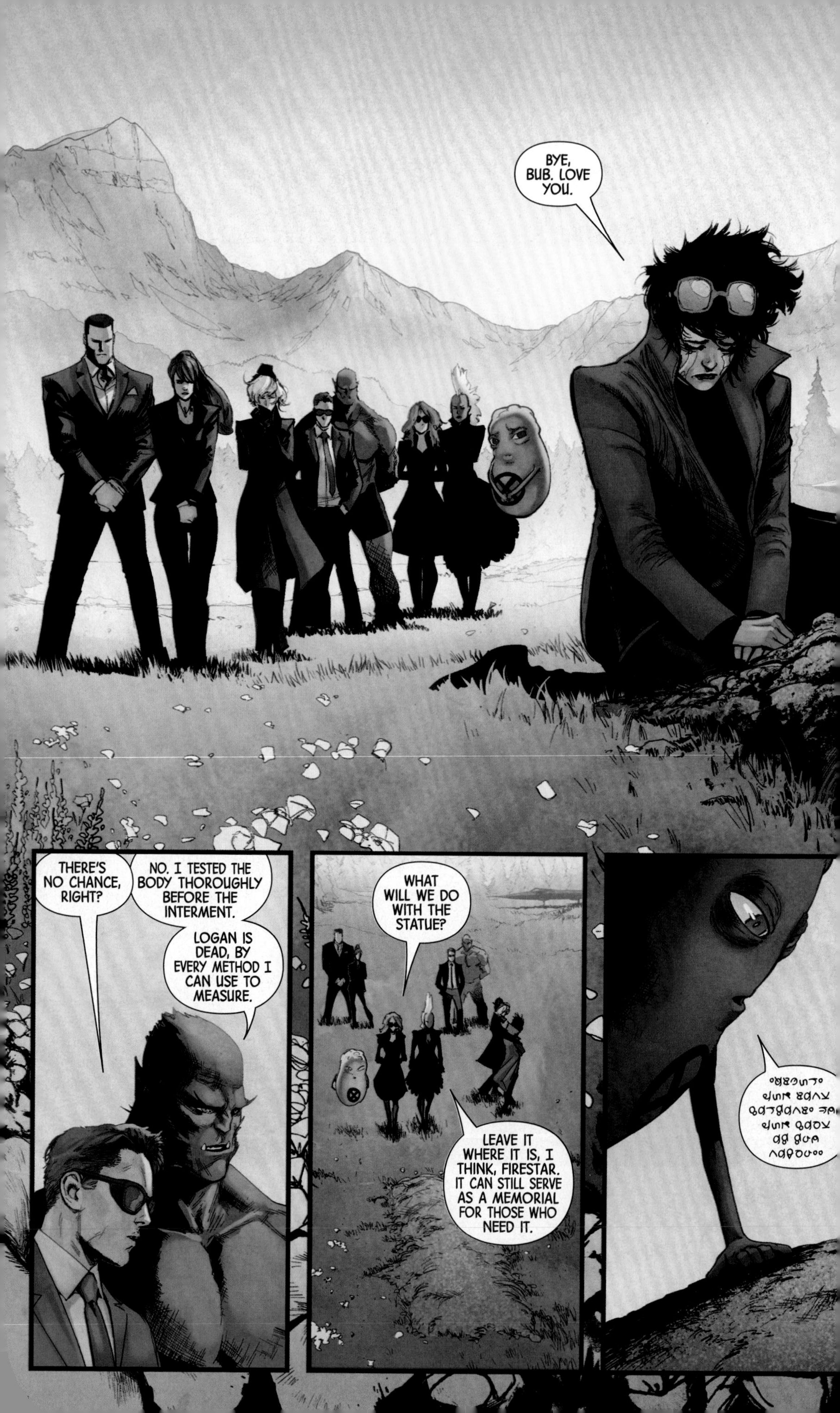
BYE, BUB. LOVE YOU.
THERE'S NO CHANCE, RIGHT?
NO. I TESTED THE BODY THOROUGHLY BEFORE THE INTERMENT.
LOGAN IS DEAD, BY EVERY METHOD I CAN USE TO MEASURE.
WHAT WILL WE DO WITH THE STATUE?
LEAVE IT WHERE IT IS, I THINK, FIRESTAR. IT CAN STILL SERVE AS A MEMORIAL FOR THOSE WHO NEED IT.

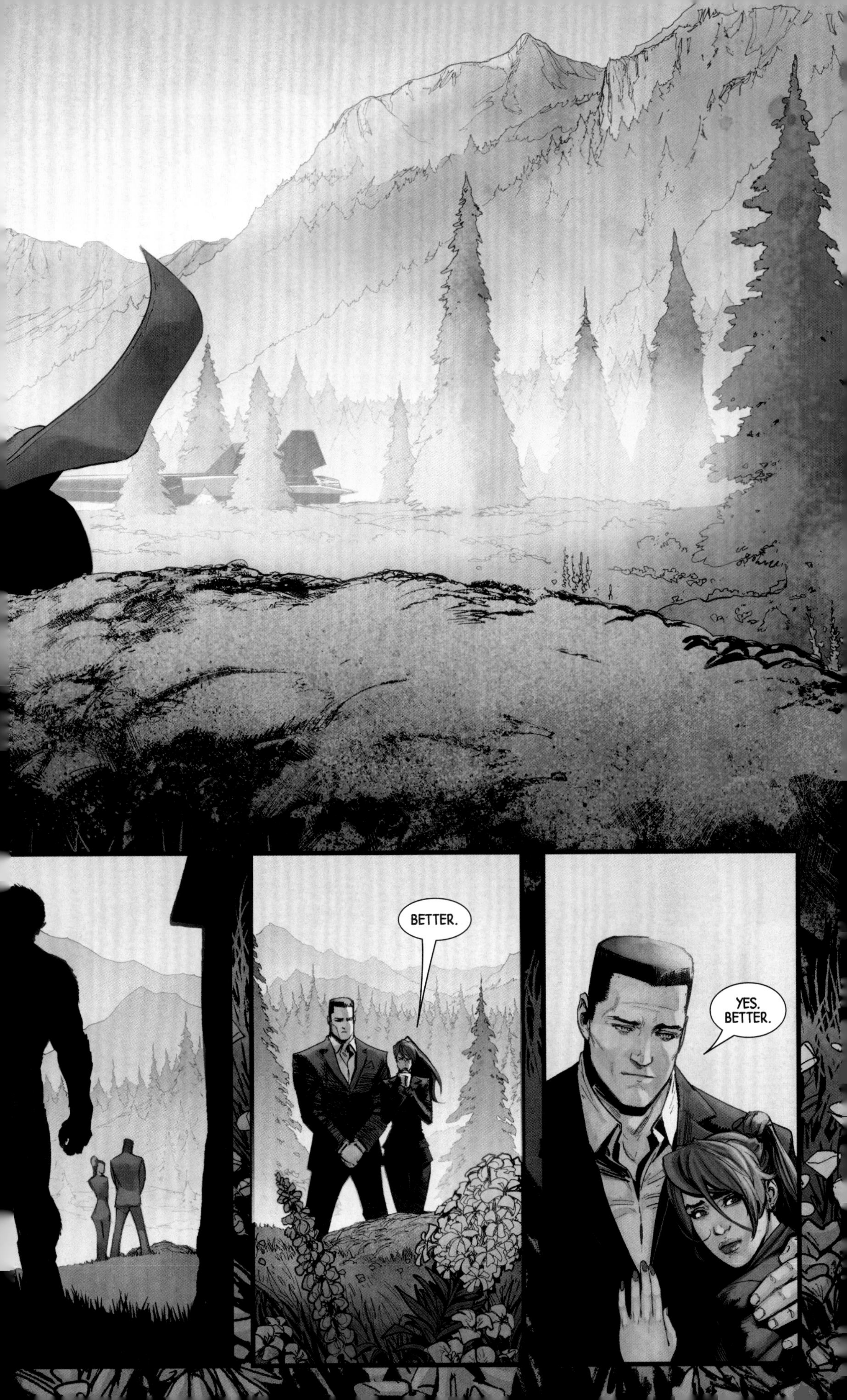
BETTER.
YES. BETTER.

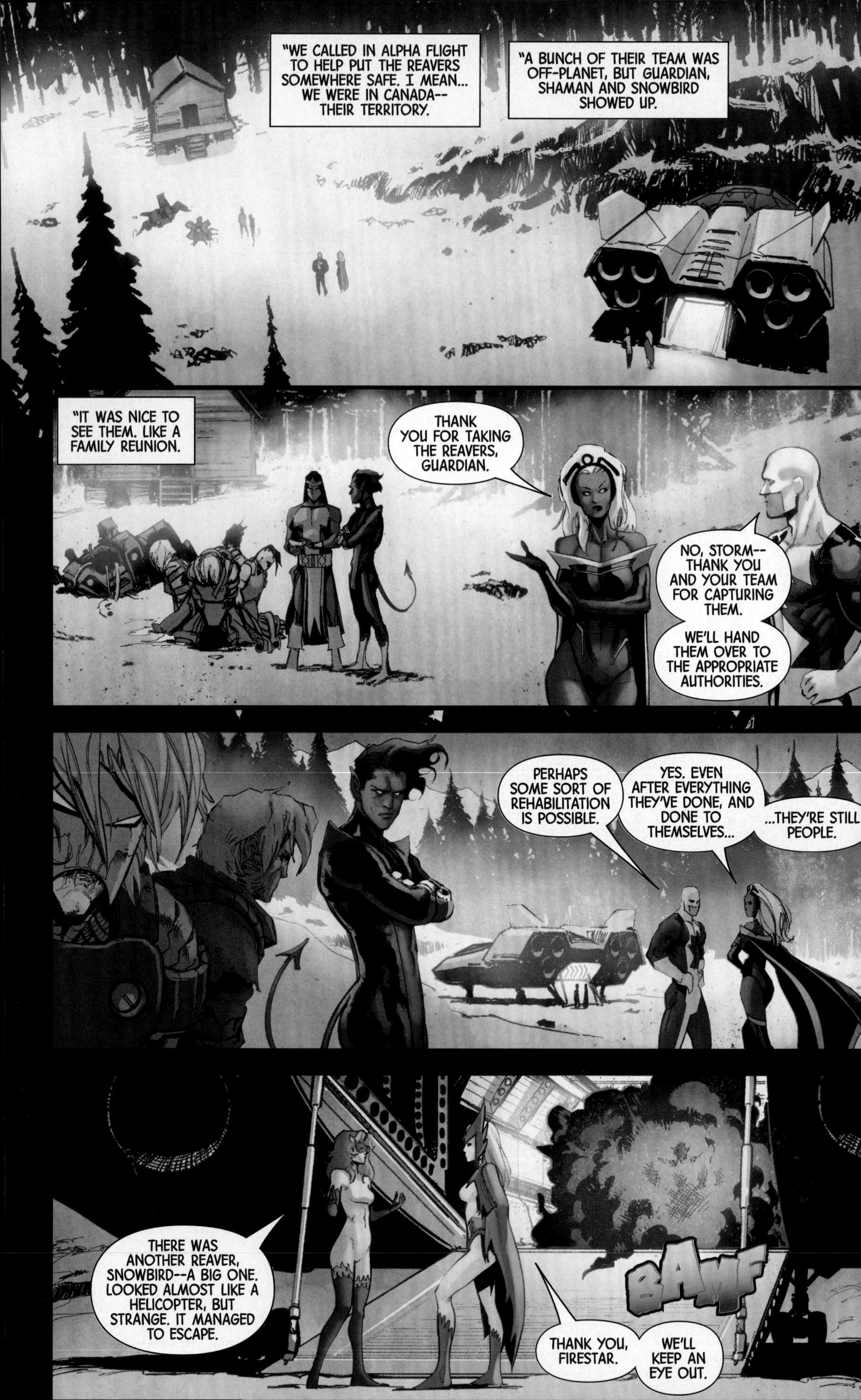
"WE CALLED IN ALPHA FLIGHT TO HELP PUT THE REAVERS SOMEWHERE SAFE. I MEAN... WE WERE IN CANADA-- THEIR TERRITORY.
"A BUNCH OF THEIR TEAM WAS OFF-PLANET, BUT GUARDIAN, SHAMAN AND SNOWBIRD SHOWED UP.
"IT WAS NICE TO SEE THEM. LIKE A FAMILY REUNION.
THANK YOU FOR TAKING THE REAVERS, GUARDIAN.
NO, STORM-- THANK YOU AND YOUR TEAM FOR CAPTURING THEM.
WE'LL HAND THEM OVER TO THE APPROPRIATE AUTHORITIES.
PERHAPS SOME SORT OF REHABILITATION IS POSSIBLE.
YES. EVEN AFTER EVERYTHING THEY'VE DONE, AND DONE TO THEMSELVES...
...THEY'RE STILL PEOPLE.
THERE WAS ANOTHER REAVER, SNOWBIRD--A BIG ONE. LOOKED ALMOST LIKE A HELICOPTER, BUT STRANGE. IT MANAGED TO ESCAPE.
BAMF
THANK YOU, FIRESTAR.
WE'LL KEEP AN EYE OUT.

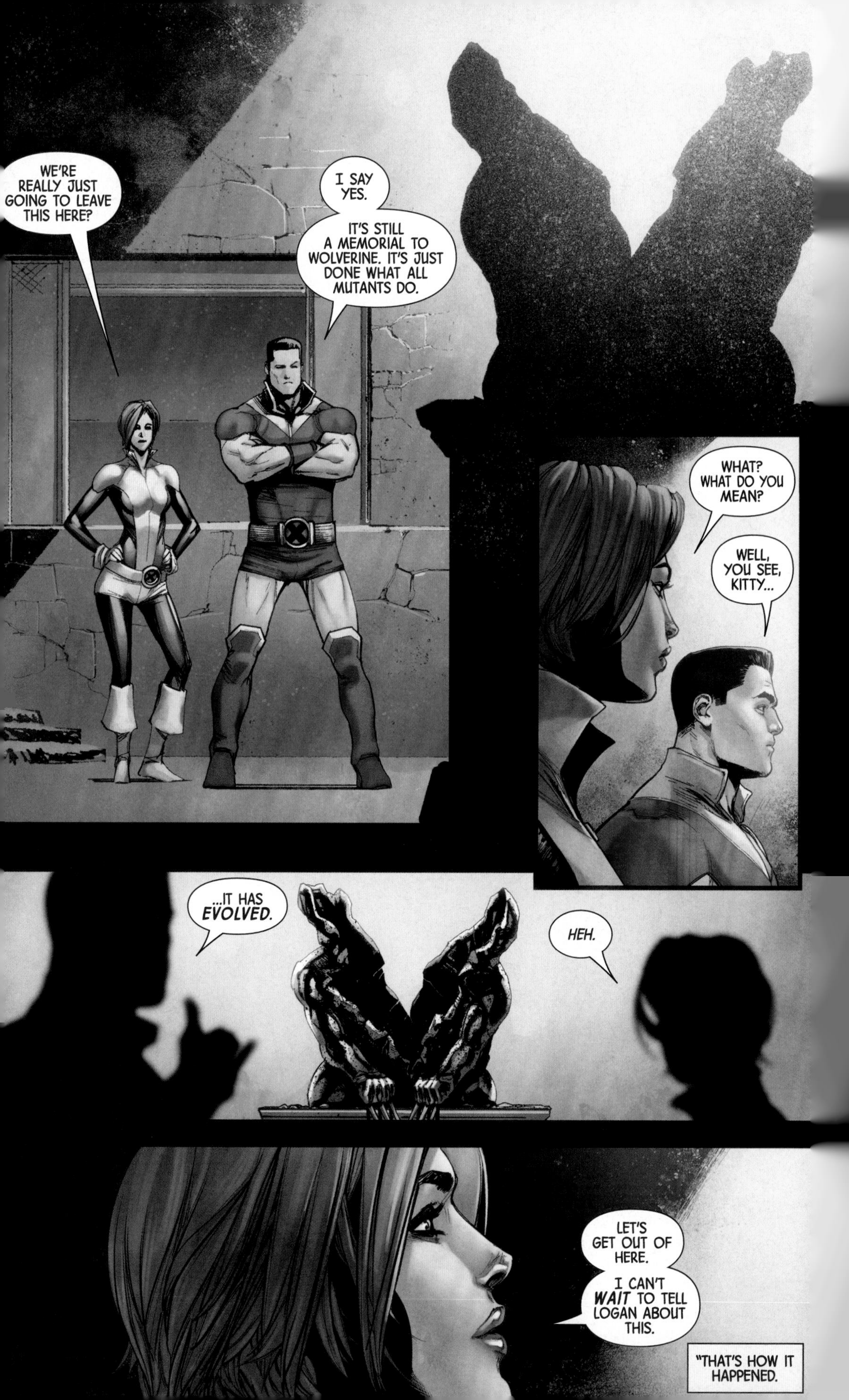
WE'RE REALLY JUST GOING TO LEAVE THIS HERE?
I SAY YES.
IT'S STILL A MEMORIAL TO WOLVERINE. IT'S JUST DONE WHAT ALL MUTANTS DO.
WHAT? WHAT DO YOU MEAN?
WELL, YOU SEE, KITTY...
...IT HAS EVOLVED.
HEH.
LET'S GET OUT OF HERE.
I CAN'T WAIT TO TELL LOGAN ABOUT THIS.
"THAT'S HOW IT HAPPENED.

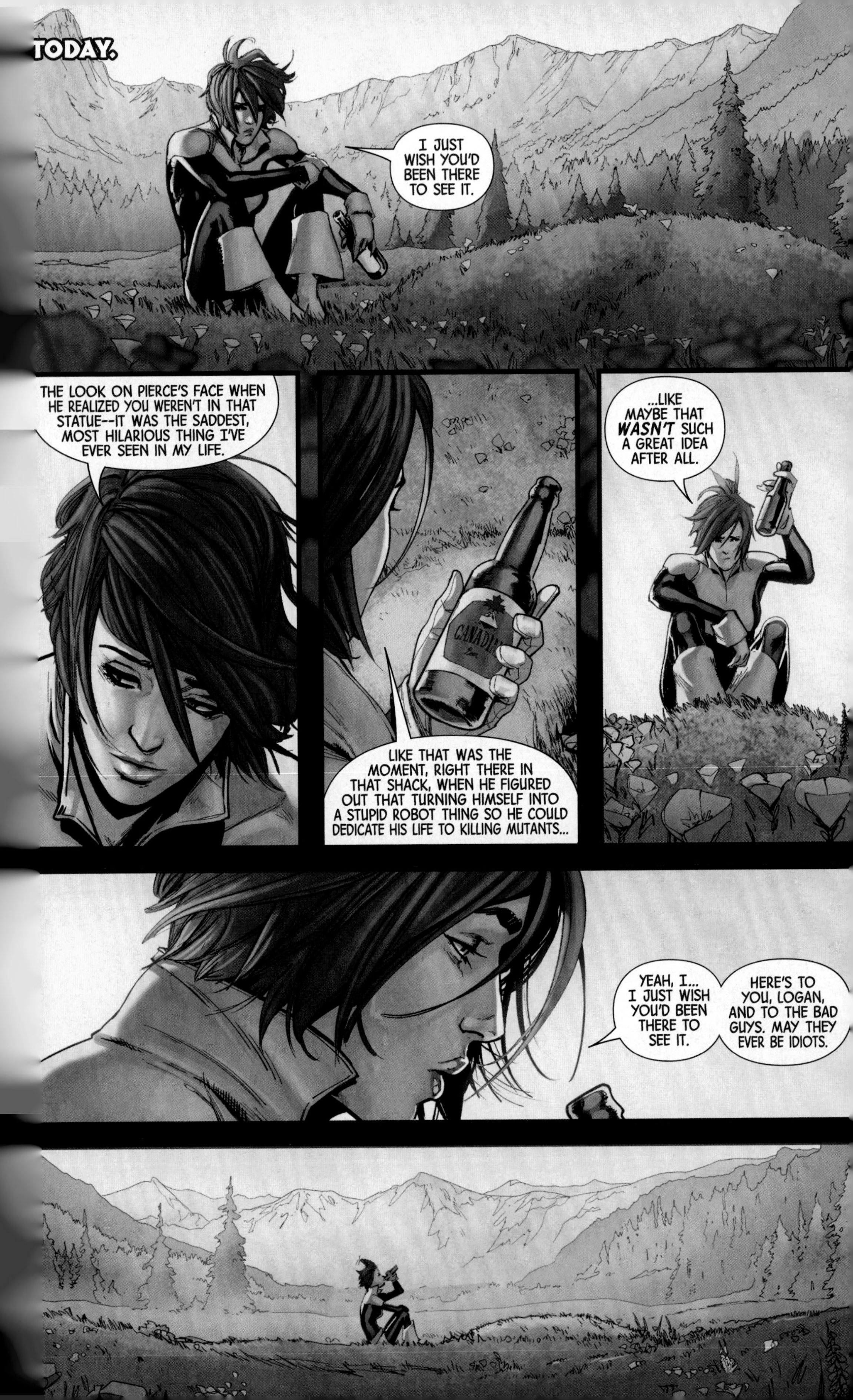
TODAY.
I JUST WISH YOU'D BEEN THERE TO SEE IT.
THE LOOK ON PIERCE'S FACE WHEN HE REALIZED YOU WEREN'T IN THAT STATUE--IT WAS THE SADDEST, MOST HILARIOUS THING I'VE EVER SEEN IN MY LIFE.
CANADIAN
LIKE THAT WAS THE MOMENT, RIGHT THERE IN THAT SHACK, WHEN HE FIGURED OUT THAT TURNING HIMSELF INTO A STUPID ROBOT THING SO HE COULD DEDICATE HIS LIFE TO KILLING MUTANTS...
...LIKE MAYBE THAT WASN'T SUCH A GREAT IDEA AFTER ALL.
YEAH, I... I JUST WISH YOU'D BEEN THERE TO SEE IT.
HERE'S TO YOU, LOGAN, AND TO THE BAD GUYS. MAY THEY EVER BE IDIOTS.

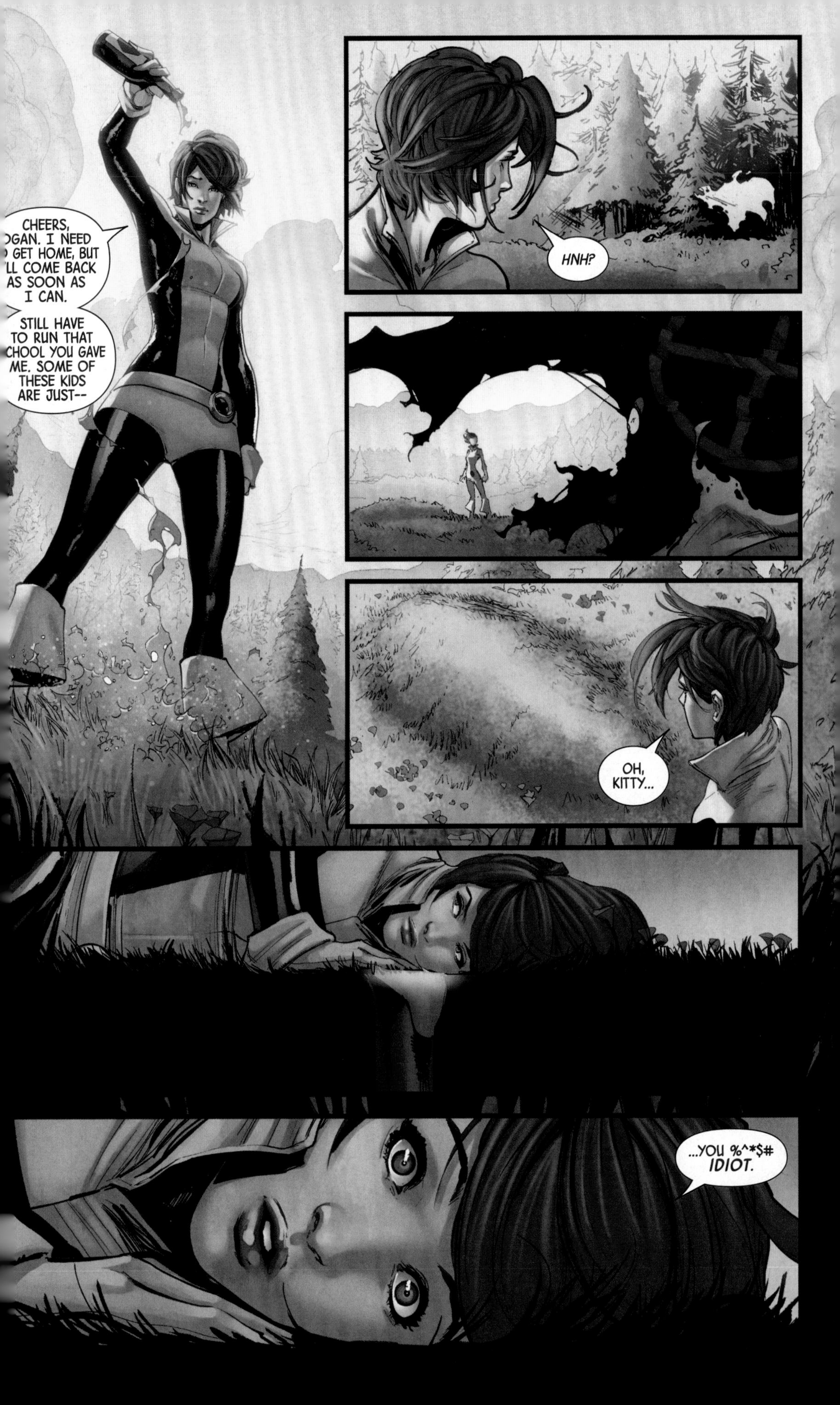
CHEERS, OGAN. I NEED GET HOME, BUT LL COME BACK AS SOON AS I CAN.
STILL HAVE TO RUN THAT CHOOL YOU GAVE ME. SOME OF THESE KIDS ARE JUST--
HNH?
OH, KITTY...
...YOU %^*$# IDIOT.

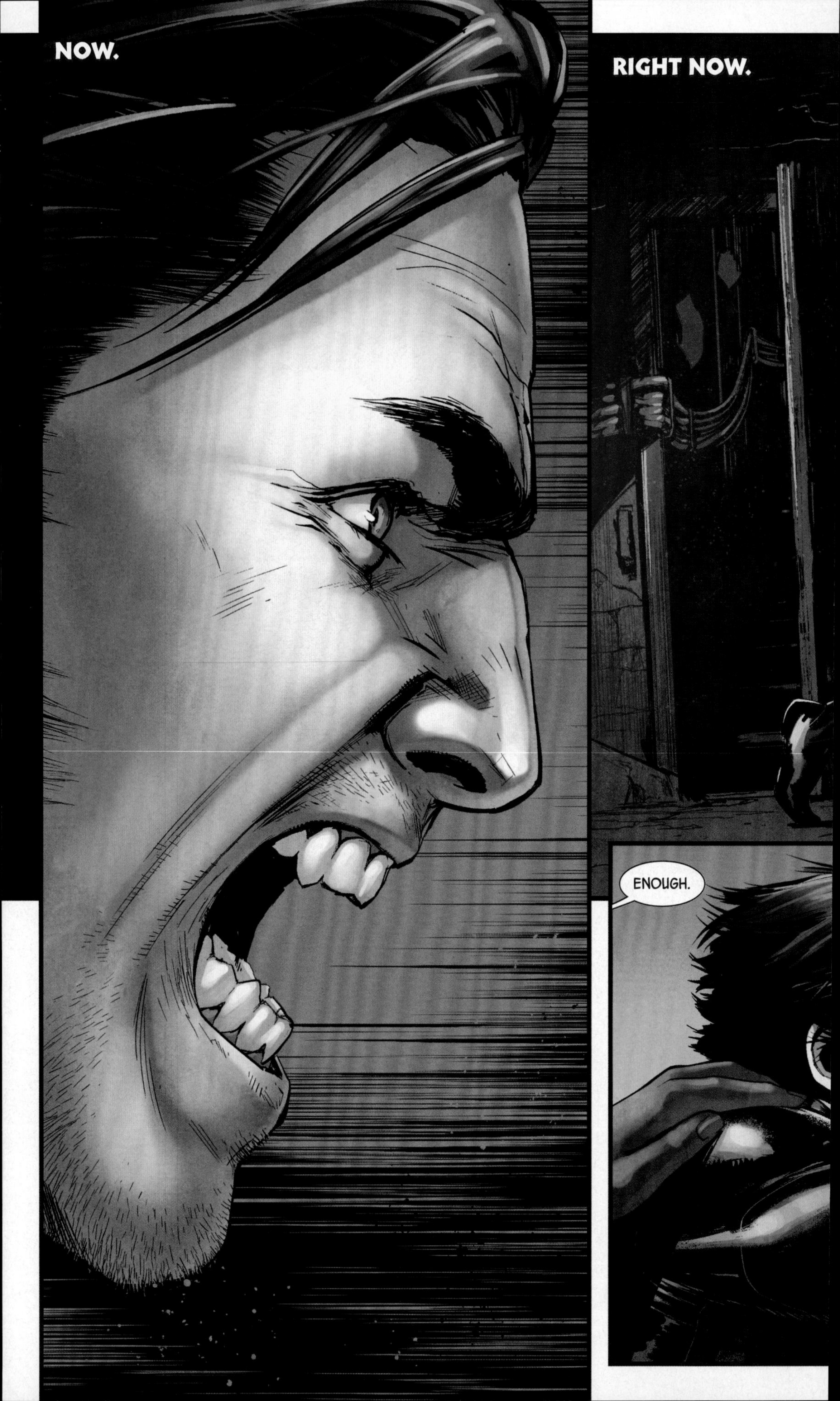
NOW.
RIGHT NOW.
ENOUGH.

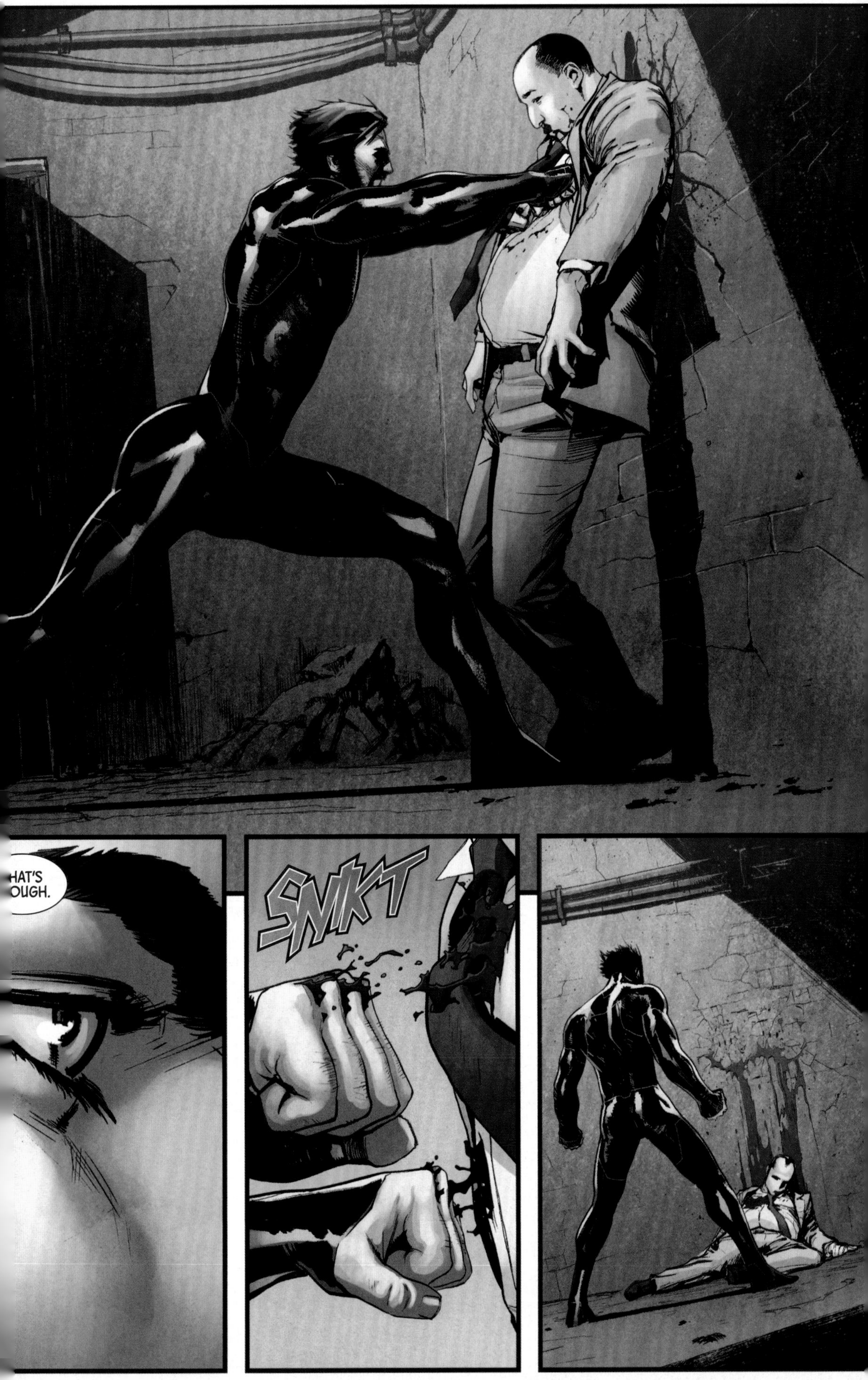
HAT'S
OUGH.
SNIKT

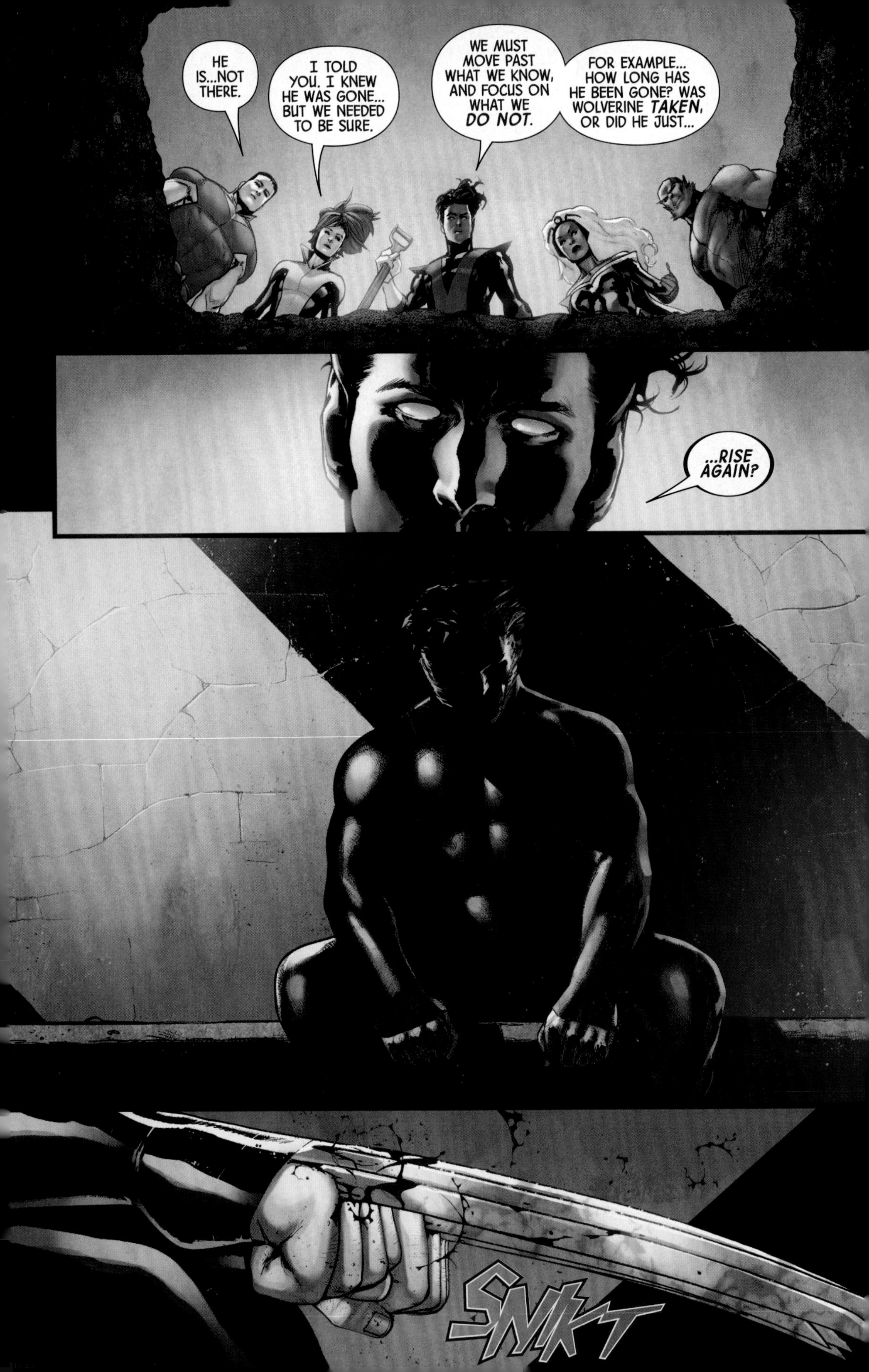
HE IS...NOT THERE.
I TOLD YOU. I KNEW HE WAS GONE... BUT WE NEEDED TO BE SURE.
WE MUST MOVE PAST WHAT WE KNOW, AND FOCUS ON WHAT WE DO NOT.
FOR EXAMPLE... HOW LONG HAS HE BEEN GONE? WAS WOLVERINE TAKEN, OR DID HE JUST...
...RISE AGAIN?
SNIKT

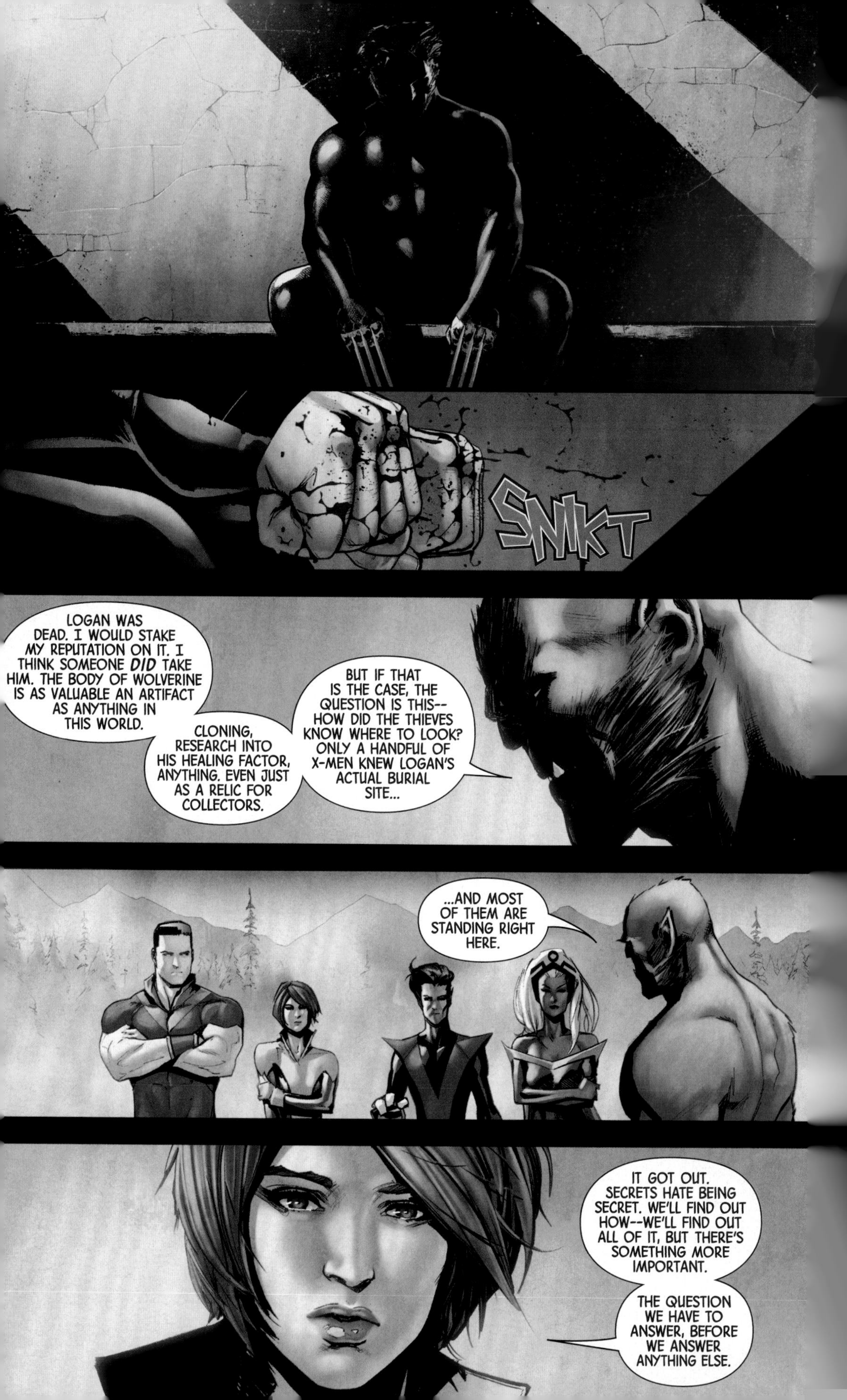
SNIKT
LOGAN WAS DEAD. I WOULD STAKE MY REPUTATION ON IT. I THINK SOMEONE *DID* TAKE HIM. THE BODY OF WOLVERINE IS AS VALUABLE AN ARTIFACT AS ANYTHING IN THIS WORLD.
CLONING, RESEARCH INTO HIS HEALING FACTOR, ANYTHING. EVEN JUST AS A RELIC FOR COLLECTORS.
BUT IF THAT IS THE CASE, THE QUESTION IS THIS--HOW DID THE THIEVES KNOW WHERE TO LOOK? ONLY A HANDFUL OF X-MEN KNEW LOGAN'S ACTUAL BURIAL SITE...
...AND MOST OF THEM ARE STANDING RIGHT HERE.
IT GOT OUT. SECRETS HATE BEING SECRET. WE'LL FIND OUT HOW--WE'LL FIND OUT ALL OF IT, BUT THERE'S SOMETHING MORE IMPORTANT.
THE QUESTION WE HAVE TO ANSWER, BEFORE WE ANSWER ANYTHING ELSE.

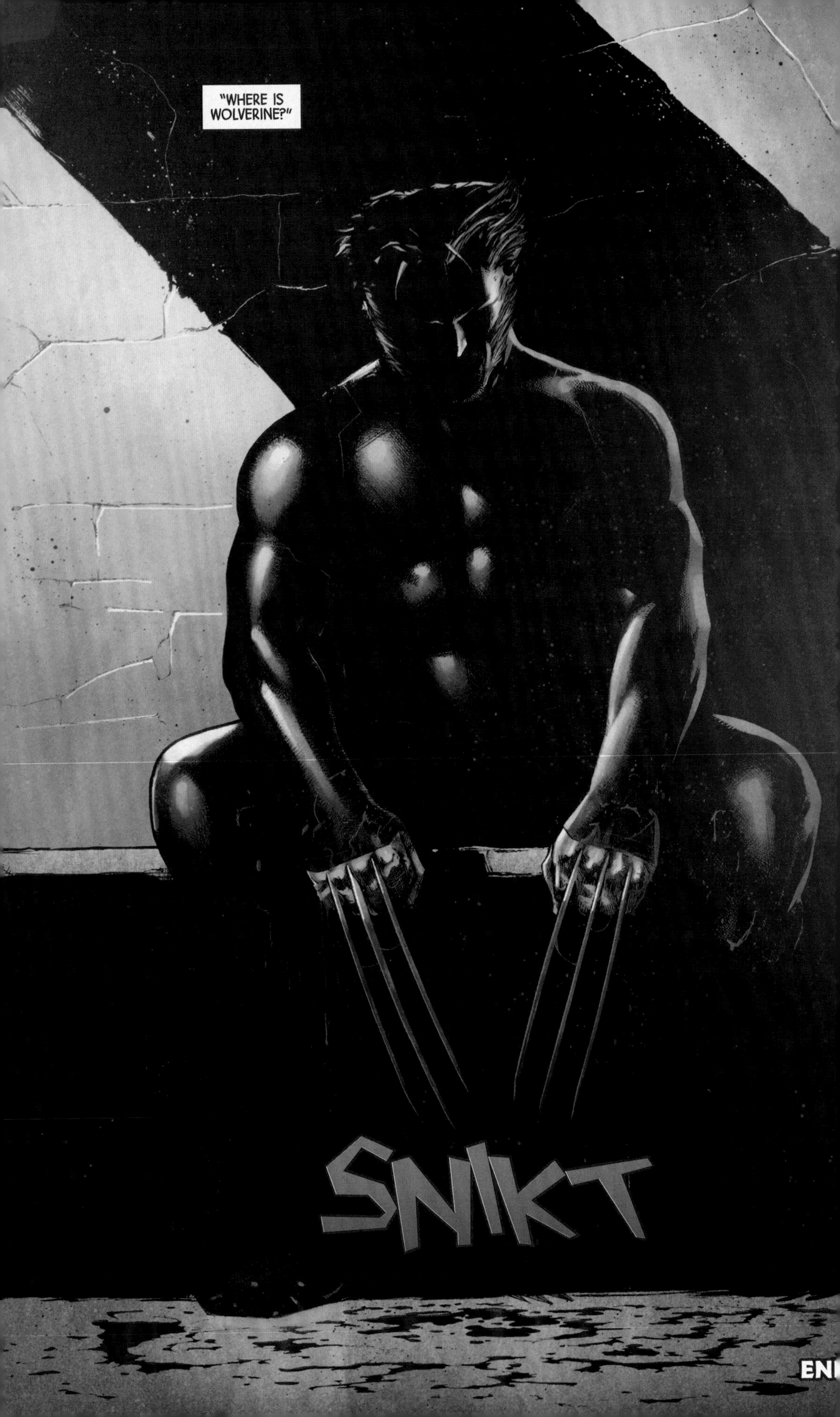
"WHERE IS WOLVERINE?"
SNIKT

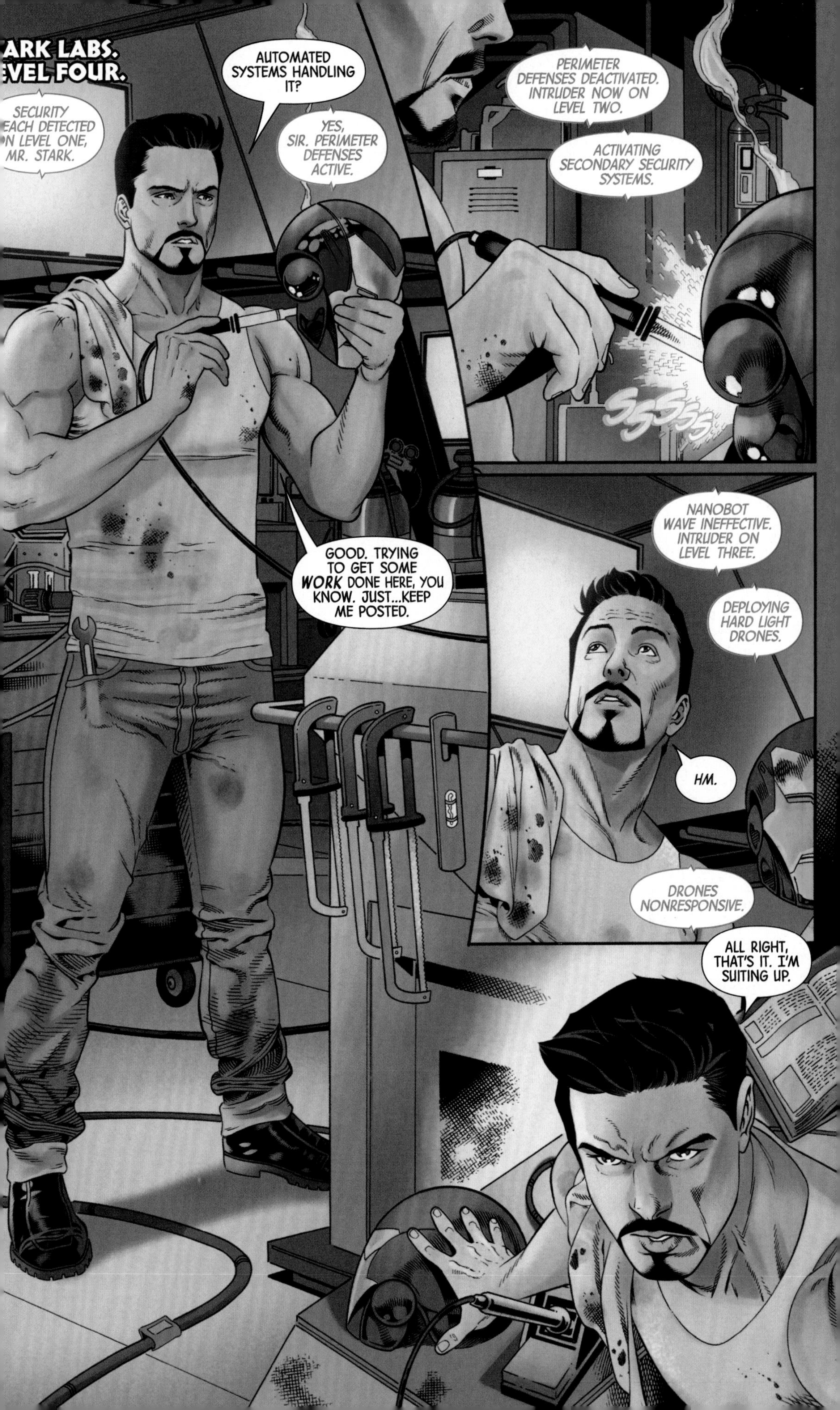

ARK LABS.
EVEL FOUR.
SECURITY
EACH DETECTED
N LEVEL ONE,
MR. STARK.
AUTOMATED SYSTEMS HANDLING IT?
YES, SIR. PERIMETER DEFENSES ACTIVE.
GOOD. TRYING TO GET SOME WORK DONE HERE, YOU KNOW. JUST...KEEP ME POSTED.
PERIMETER DEFENSES DEACTIVATED. INTRUDER NOW ON LEVEL TWO.
ACTIVATING SECONDARY SECURITY SYSTEMS.
SSSSS
NANOBOT WAVE INEFFECTIVE. INTRUDER ON LEVEL THREE.
DEPLOYING HARD LIGHT DRONES.
HM.
DRONES NONRESPONSIVE.
ALL RIGHT, THAT'S IT. I'M SUITING UP.

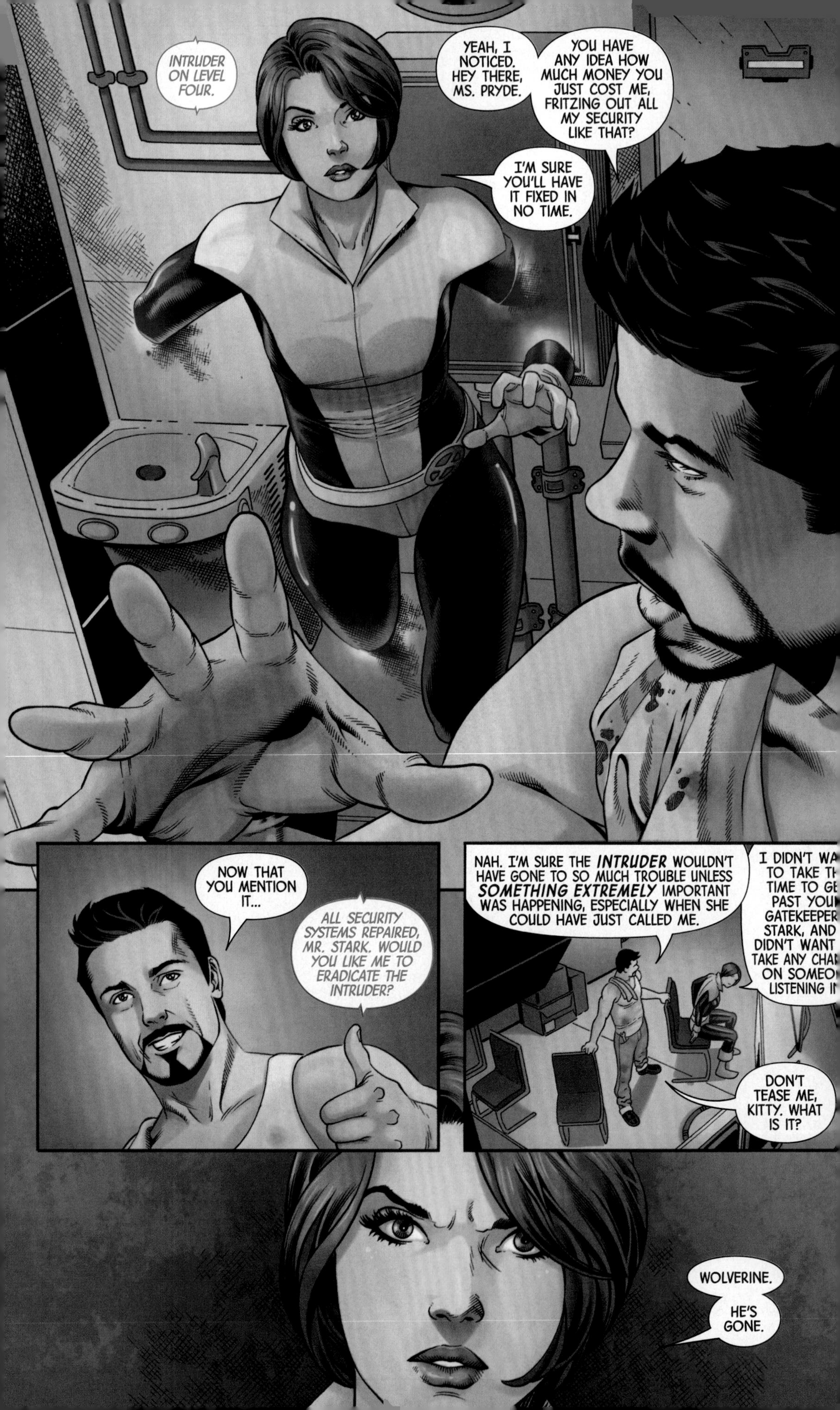
INTRUDER ON LEVEL FOUR.
YEAH, I NOTICED. HEY THERE, MS. PRYDE.
YOU HAVE ANY IDEA HOW MUCH MONEY YOU JUST COST ME, FRITZING OUT ALL MY SECURITY LIKE THAT?
I'M SURE YOU'LL HAVE IT FIXED IN NO TIME.
NOW THAT YOU MENTION IT...
ALL SECURITY SYSTEMS REPAIRED, MR. STARK. WOULD YOU LIKE ME TO ERADICATE THE INTRUDER?
NAH. I'M SURE THE INTRUDER WOULDN'T HAVE GONE TO SO MUCH TROUBLE UNLESS SOMETHING EXTREMELY IMPORTANT WAS HAPPENING, ESPECIALLY WHEN SHE COULD HAVE JUST CALLED ME.
DON'T TEASE ME, KITTY. WHAT IS IT?
WOLVERINE.
HE'S GONE.

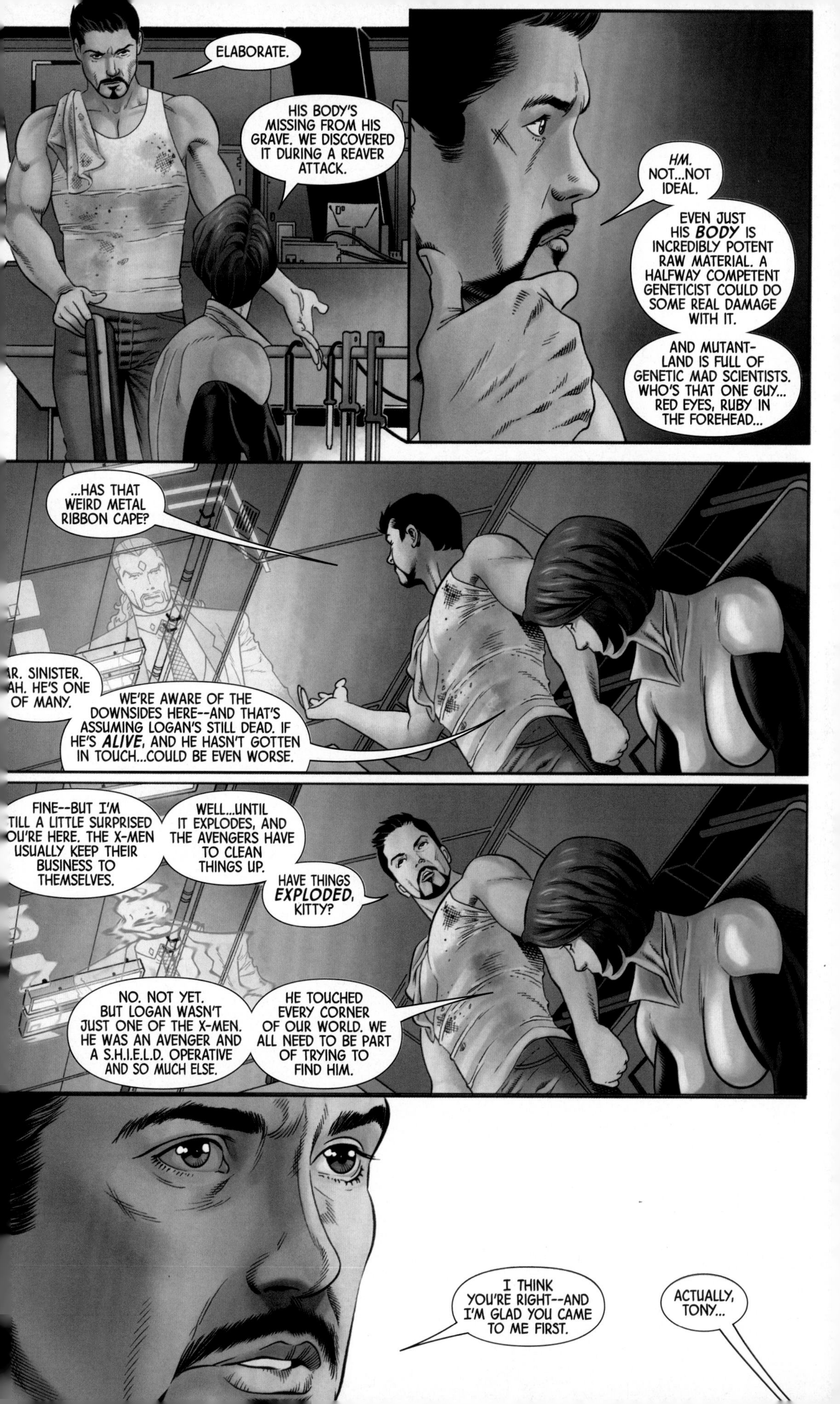

ELABORATE.
HIS BODY'S MISSING FROM HIS GRAVE. WE DISCOVERED IT DURING A REAVER ATTACK.
HM. NOT...NOT IDEAL.
EVEN JUST HIS BODY IS INCREDIBLY POTENT RAW MATERIAL. A HALFWAY COMPETENT GENETICIST COULD DO SOME REAL DAMAGE WITH IT.
AND MUTANT-LAND IS FULL OF GENETIC MAD SCIENTISTS. WHO'S THAT ONE GUY... RED EYES, RUBY IN THE FOREHEAD...
...HAS THAT WEIRD METAL RIBBON CAPE?
R. SINISTER. AH. HE'S ONE OF MANY.
WE'RE AWARE OF THE DOWNSIDES HERE--AND THAT'S ASSUMING LOGAN'S STILL DEAD. IF HE'S ALIVE, AND HE HASN'T GOTTEN IN TOUCH...COULD BE EVEN WORSE.
FINE--BUT I'M TILL A LITTLE SURPRISED OU'RE HERE. THE X-MEN USUALLY KEEP THEIR BUSINESS TO THEMSELVES.
WELL...UNTIL IT EXPLODES, AND THE AVENGERS HAVE TO CLEAN THINGS UP.
HAVE THINGS EXPLODED, KITTY?
NO. NOT YET. BUT LOGAN WASN'T JUST ONE OF THE X-MEN. HE WAS AN AVENGER AND A S.H.I.E.L.D. OPERATIVE AND SO MUCH ELSE.
HE TOUCHED EVERY CORNER OF OUR WORLD. WE ALL NEED TO BE PART OF TRYING TO FIND HIM.
I THINK YOU'RE RIGHT--AND I'M GLAD YOU CAME TO ME FIRST.
ACTUALLY, TONY...

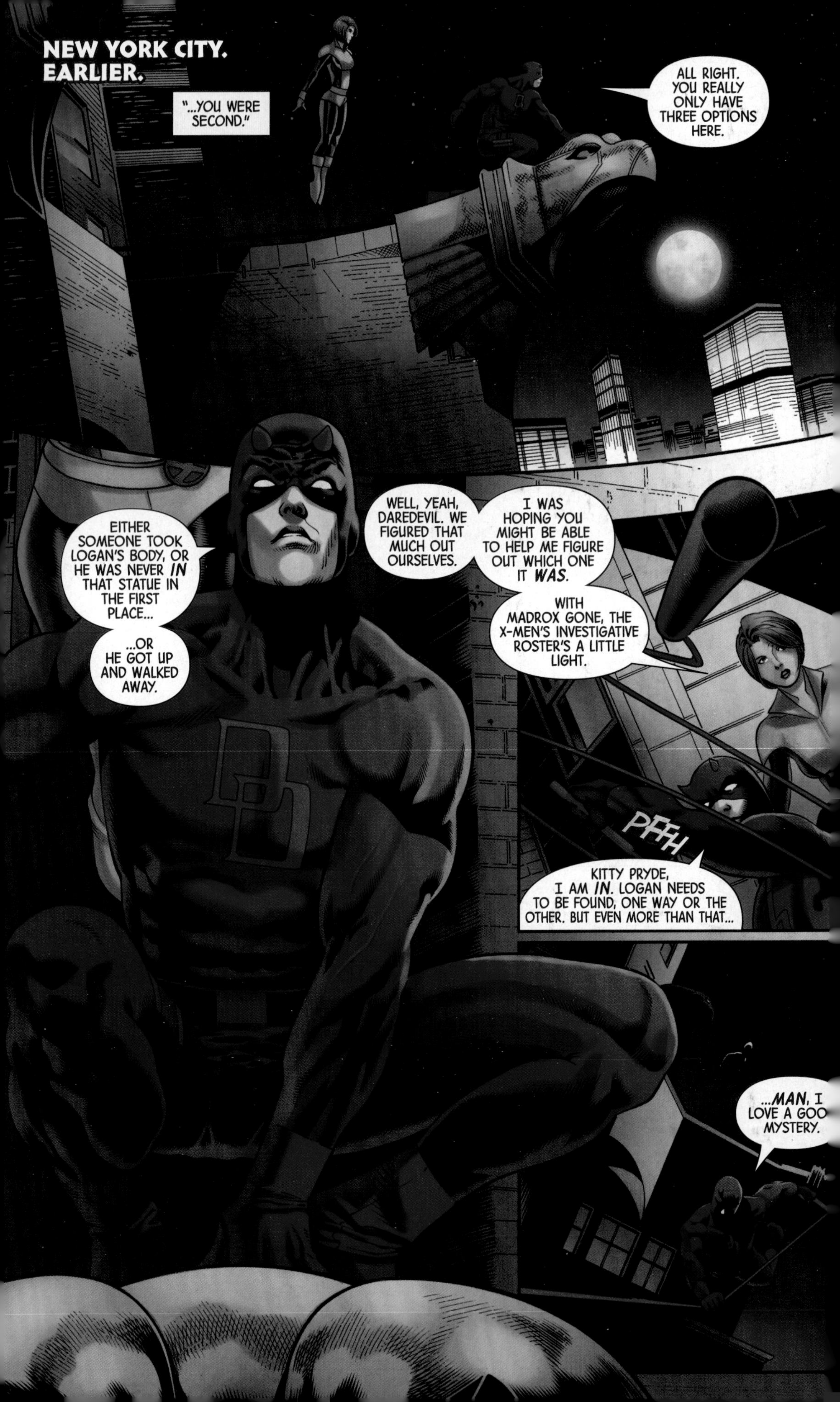
NEW YORK CITY. EARLIER.
"...YOU WERE SECOND."
ALL RIGHT. YOU REALLY ONLY HAVE THREE OPTIONS HERE.
EITHER SOMEONE TOOK LOGAN'S BODY, OR HE WAS NEVER IN THAT STATUE IN THE FIRST PLACE...
...OR HE GOT UP AND WALKED AWAY.
WELL, YEAH, DAREDEVIL. WE FIGURED THAT MUCH OUT OURSELVES.
I WAS HOPING YOU MIGHT BE ABLE TO HELP ME FIGURE OUT WHICH ONE IT WAS.
WITH MADROX GONE, THE X-MEN'S INVESTIGATIVE ROSTER'S A LITTLE LIGHT.
PFFH
KITTY PRYDE, I AM IN. LOGAN NEEDS TO BE FOUND, ONE WAY OR THE OTHER. BUT EVEN MORE THAN THAT...
...MAN, I LOVE A GOO MYSTERY.

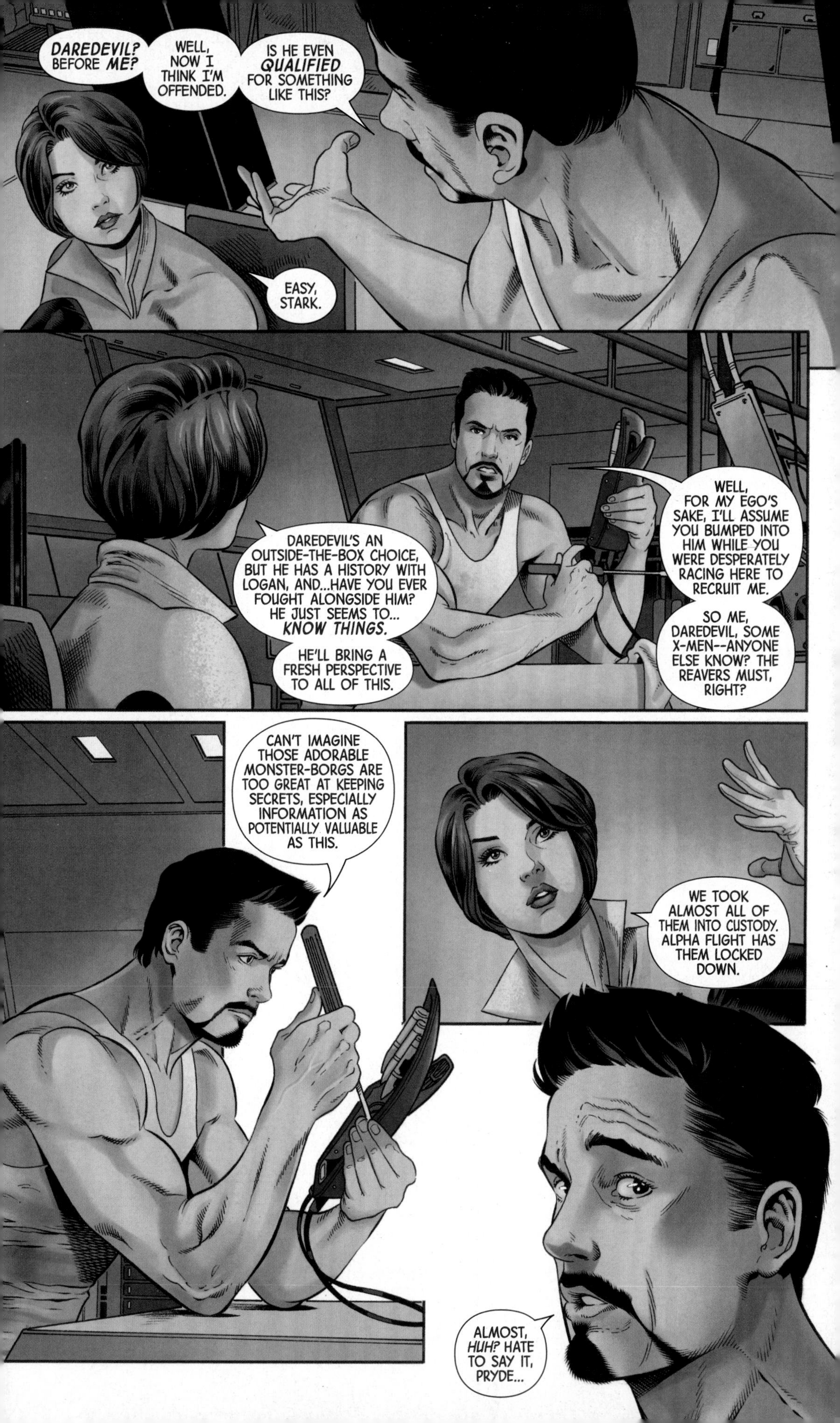

DAREDEVIL? BEFORE ME?
WELL, NOW I THINK I'M OFFENDED.
IS HE EVEN QUALIFIED FOR SOMETHING LIKE THIS?
EASY, STARK.
DAREDEVIL'S AN OUTSIDE-THE-BOX CHOICE, BUT HE HAS A HISTORY WITH LOGAN, AND...HAVE YOU EVER FOUGHT ALONGSIDE HIM? HE JUST SEEMS TO... KNOW THINGS.
HE'LL BRING A FRESH PERSPECTIVE TO ALL OF THIS.
WELL, FOR MY EGO'S SAKE, I'LL ASSUME YOU BUMPED INTO HIM WHILE YOU WERE DESPERATELY RACING HERE TO RECRUIT ME.
SO ME, DAREDEVIL, SOME X-MEN--ANYONE ELSE KNOW? THE REAVERS MUST, RIGHT?
CAN'T IMAGINE THOSE ADORABLE MONSTER-BORGS ARE TOO GREAT AT KEEPING SECRETS, ESPECIALLY INFORMATION AS POTENTIALLY VALUABLE AS THIS.
WE TOOK ALMOST ALL OF THEM INTO CUSTODY. ALPHA FLIGHT HAS THEM LOCKED DOWN.
ALMOST, HUH? HATE TO SAY IT, PRYDE...

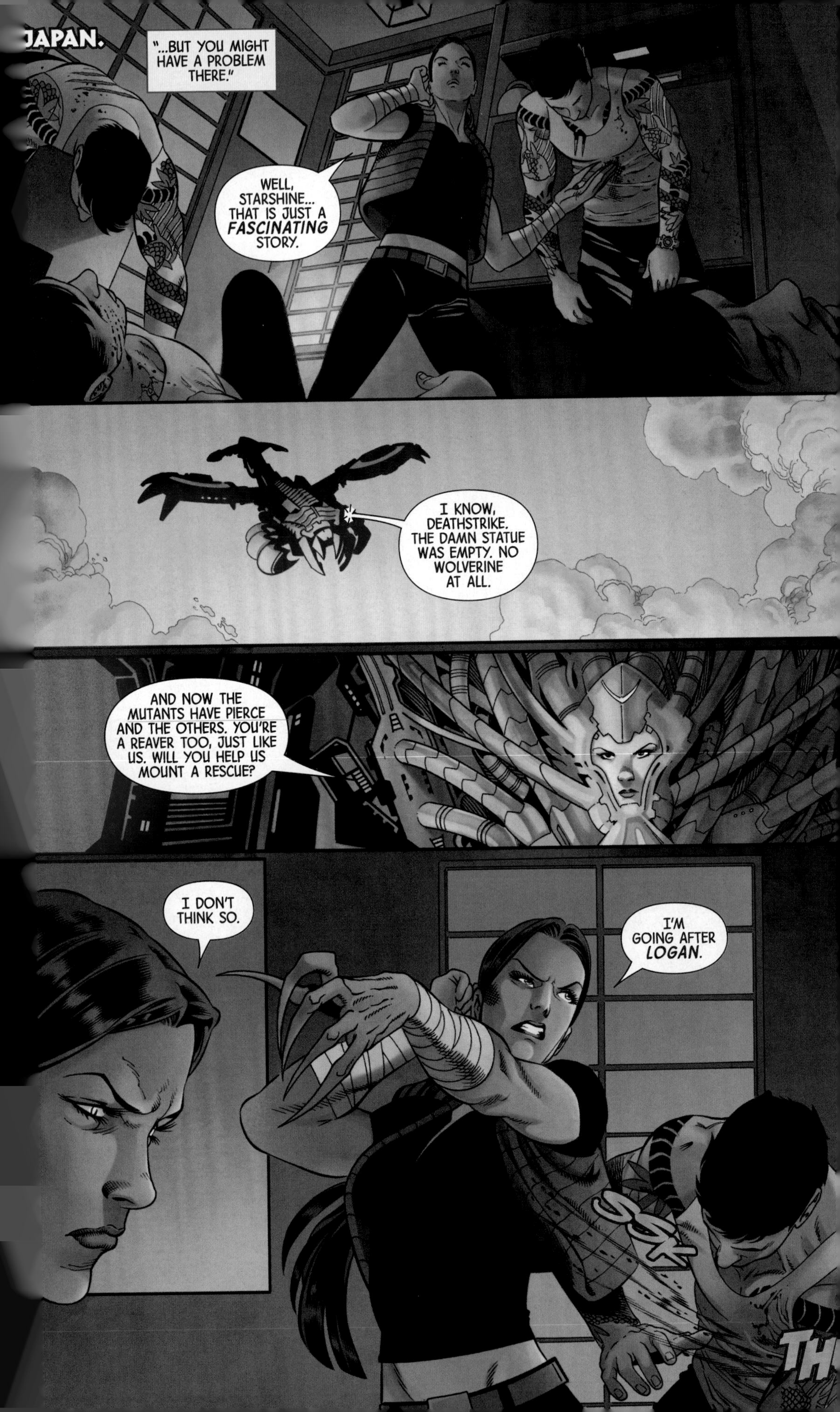
JAPAN.
"...BUT YOU MIGHT HAVE A PROBLEM THERE."
WELL, STARSHINE... THAT IS JUST A FASCINATING STORY.
I KNOW, DEATHSTRIKE. THE DAMN STATUE WAS EMPTY. NO WOLVERINE AT ALL.
AND NOW THE MUTANTS HAVE PIERCE AND THE OTHERS. YOU'RE A REAVER TOO, JUST LIKE US. WILL YOU HELP US MOUNT A RESCUE?
I DON'T THINK SO.
I'M GOING AFTER LOGAN.
SSK
TH

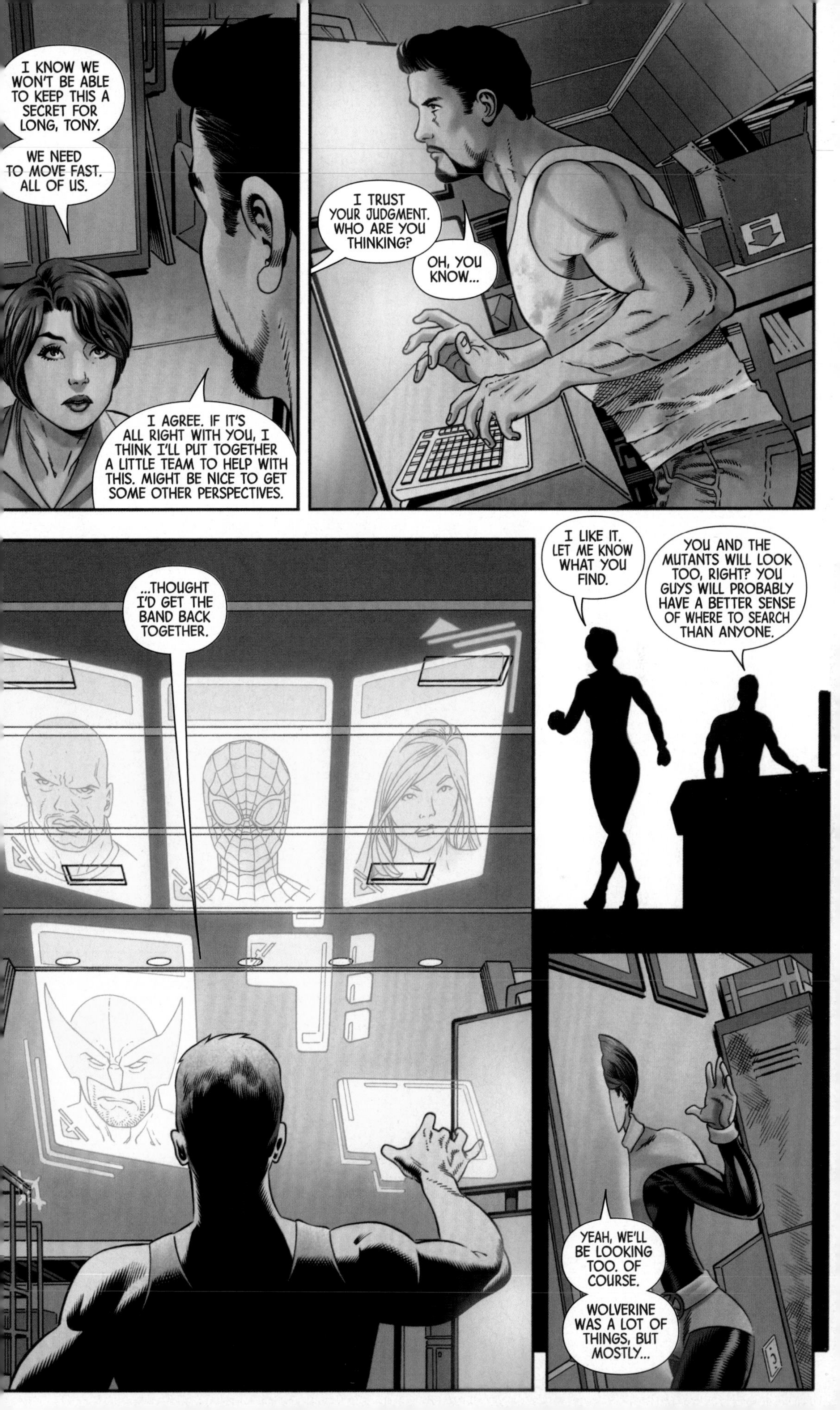

I KNOW WE WON'T BE ABLE TO KEEP THIS A SECRET FOR LONG, TONY.
WE NEED TO MOVE FAST. ALL OF US.
I AGREE. IF IT'S ALL RIGHT WITH YOU, I THINK I'LL PUT TOGETHER A LITTLE TEAM TO HELP WITH THIS. MIGHT BE NICE TO GET SOME OTHER PERSPECTIVES.
I TRUST YOUR JUDGMENT. WHO ARE YOU THINKING?
OH, YOU KNOW...
...THOUGHT I'D GET THE BAND BACK TOGETHER.
I LIKE IT. LET ME KNOW WHAT YOU FIND.
YOU AND THE MUTANTS WILL LOOK TOO, RIGHT? YOU GUYS WILL PROBABLY HAVE A BETTER SENSE OF WHERE TO SEARCH THAN ANYONE.
YEAH, WE'LL BE LOOKING TOO. OF COURSE.
WOLVERINE WAS A LOT OF THINGS, BUT MOSTLY...

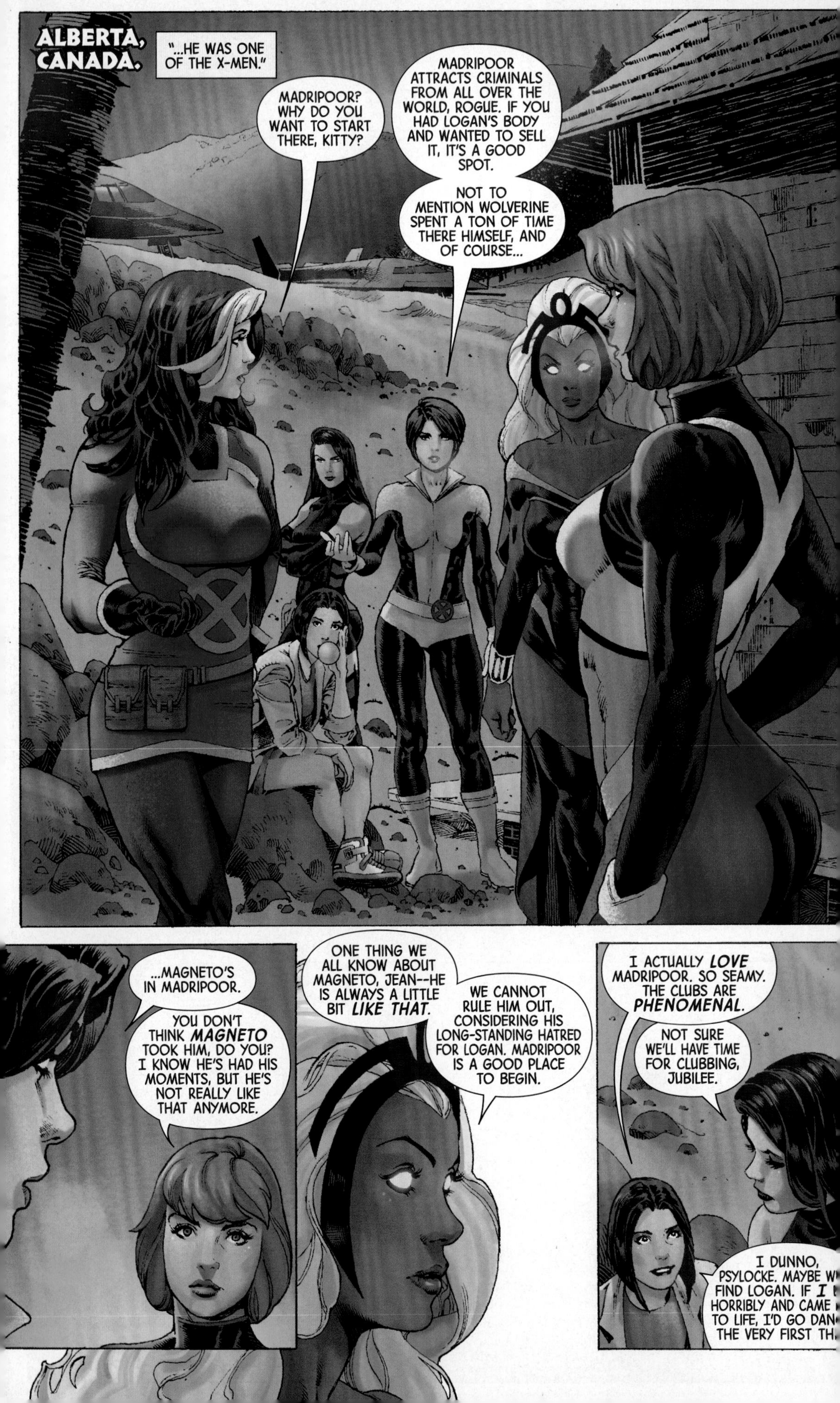

ALBERTA, CANADA.
"...HE WAS ONE OF THE X-MEN."
MADRIPOOR? WHY DO YOU WANT TO START THERE, KITTY?
MADRIPOOR ATTRACTS CRIMINALS FROM ALL OVER THE WORLD, ROGUE. IF YOU HAD LOGAN'S BODY AND WANTED TO SELL IT, IT'S A GOOD SPOT.
NOT TO MENTION WOLVERINE SPENT A TON OF TIME THERE HIMSELF, AND OF COURSE...
...MAGNETO'S IN MADRIPOOR.
YOU DON'T THINK MAGNETO TOOK HIM, DO YOU? I KNOW HE'S HAD HIS MOMENTS, BUT HE'S NOT REALLY LIKE THAT ANYMORE.
ONE THING WE ALL KNOW ABOUT MAGNETO, JEAN--HE IS ALWAYS A LITTLE BIT LIKE THAT.
WE CANNOT RULE HIM OUT, CONSIDERING HIS LONG-STANDING HATRED FOR LOGAN. MADRIPOOR IS A GOOD PLACE TO BEGIN.
I ACTUALLY LOVE MADRIPOOR. SO SEAMY. THE CLUBS ARE PHENOMENAL.
NOT SURE WE'LL HAVE TIME FOR CLUBBING, JUBILEE.
I DUNNO, PSYLOCKE. MAYBE W
FIND LOGAN. IF I
HORRIBLY AND CAME
TO LIFE, I'D GO DAN
THE VERY FIRST TH

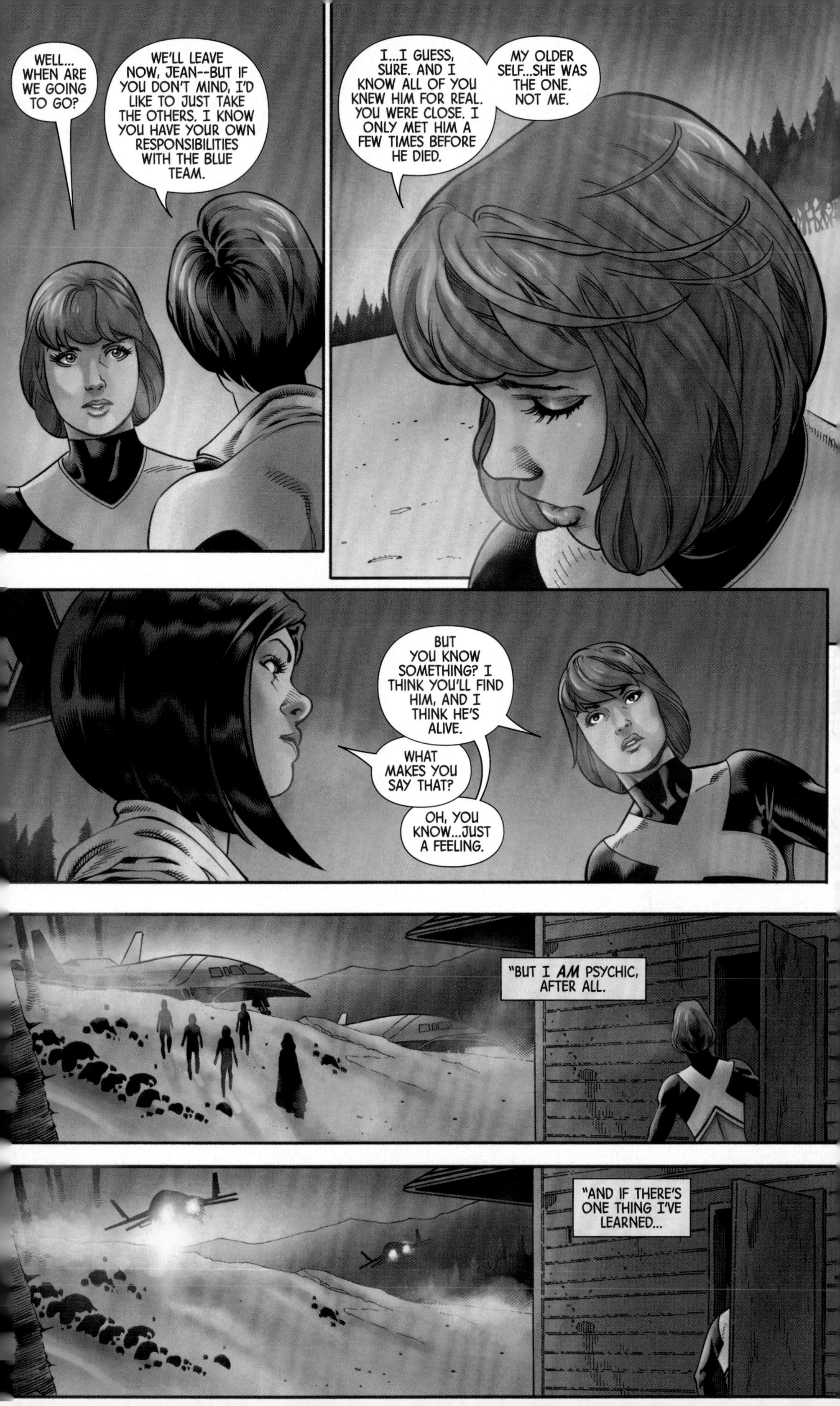
WELL... WHEN ARE WE GOING TO GO?
WE'LL LEAVE NOW, JEAN--BUT IF YOU DON'T MIND, I'D LIKE TO JUST TAKE THE OTHERS. I KNOW YOU HAVE YOUR OWN RESPONSIBILITIES WITH THE BLUE TEAM.
I...I GUESS, SURE. AND I KNOW ALL OF YOU KNEW HIM FOR REAL. YOU WERE CLOSE. I ONLY MET HIM A FEW TIMES BEFORE HE DIED.
MY OLDER SELF...SHE WAS THE ONE. NOT ME.
BUT YOU KNOW SOMETHING? I THINK YOU'LL FIND HIM, AND I THINK HE'S ALIVE.
WHAT MAKES YOU SAY THAT?
OH, YOU KNOW...JUST A FEELING.
"BUT I *AM* PSYCHIC, AFTER ALL.
"AND IF THERE'S ONE THING I'VE LEARNED...

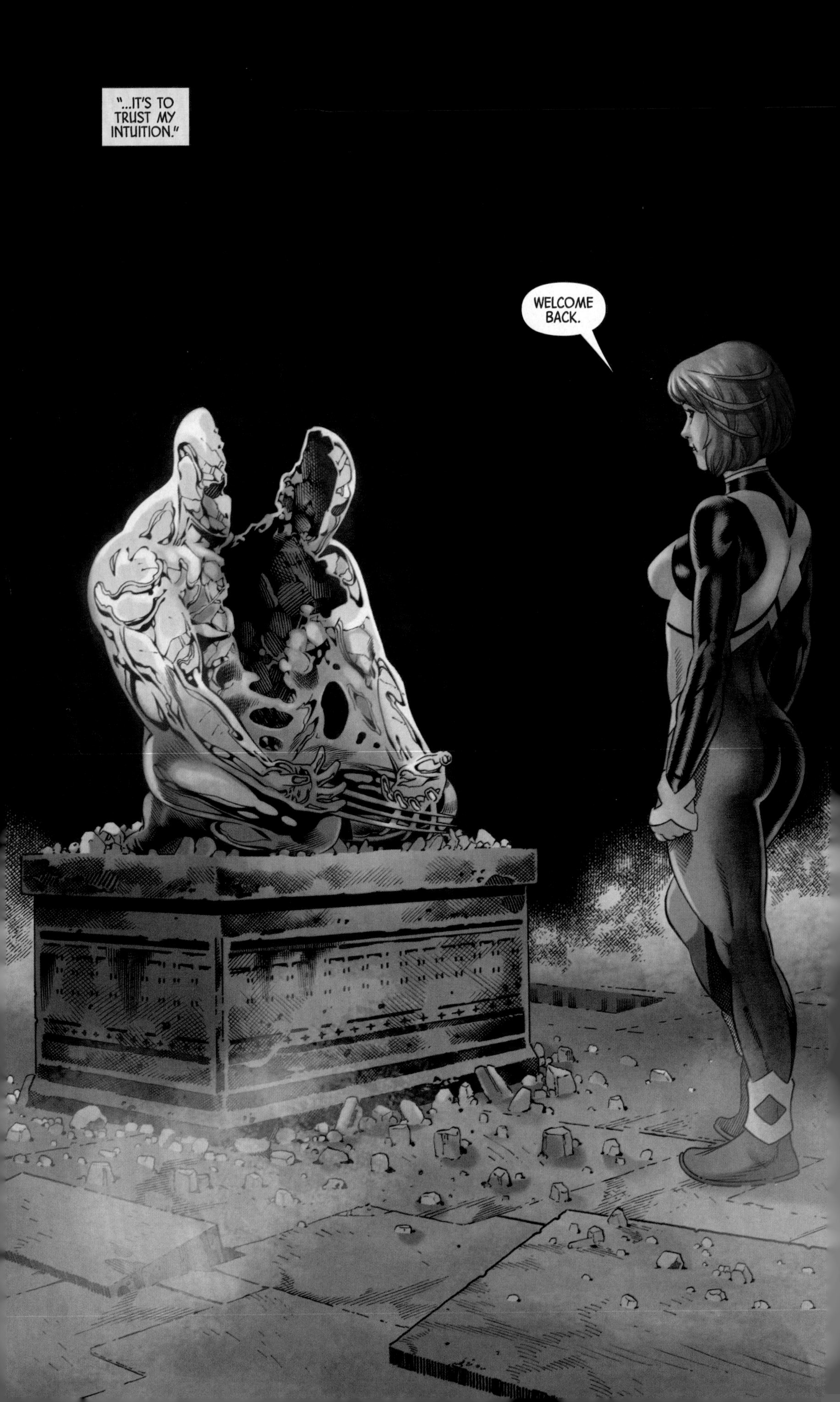
"...IT'S TO TRUST MY INTUITION."
WELCOME BACK.

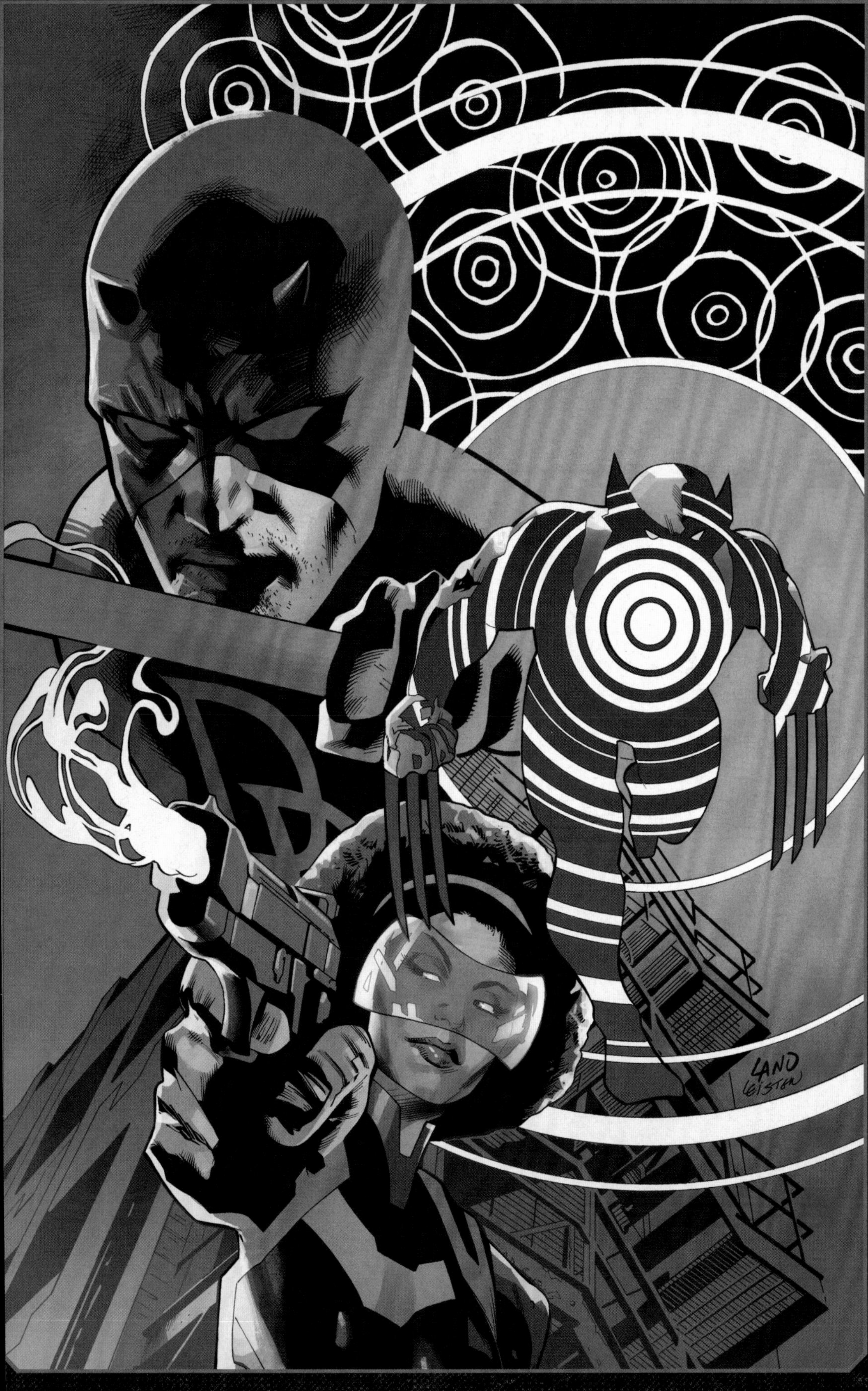

WEAPON LOST 1

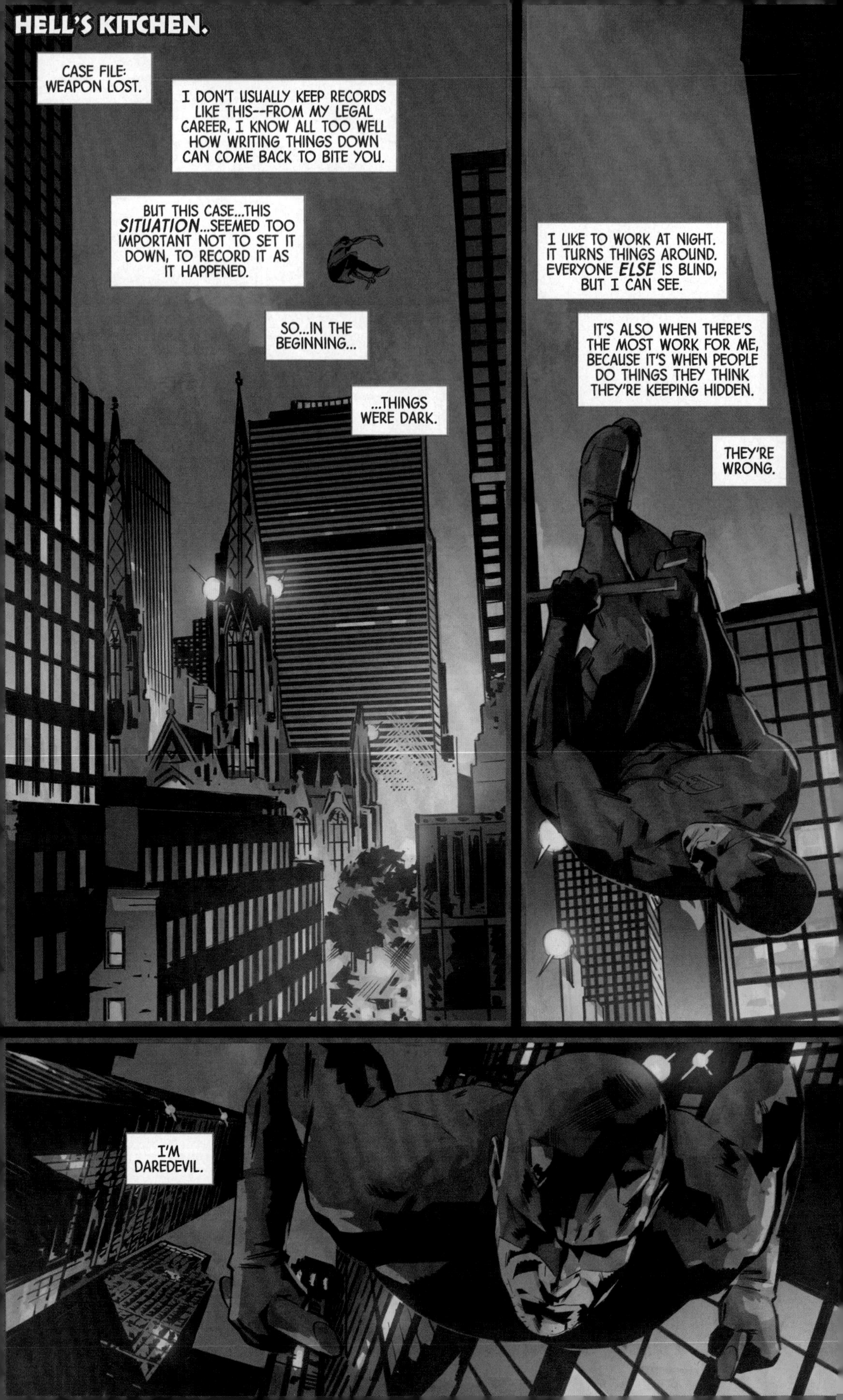
HELL'S KITCHEN.
CASE FILE: WEAPON LOST.
I DON'T USUALLY KEEP RECORDS LIKE THIS--FROM MY LEGAL CAREER, I KNOW ALL TOO WELL HOW WRITING THINGS DOWN CAN COME BACK TO BITE YOU.
BUT THIS CASE...THIS *SITUATION*...SEEMED TOO IMPORTANT NOT TO SET IT DOWN, TO RECORD IT AS IT HAPPENED.
SO...IN THE BEGINNING...
...THINGS WERE DARK.
I LIKE TO WORK AT NIGHT. IT TURNS THINGS AROUND. EVERYONE *ELSE* IS BLIND, BUT I CAN SEE.
IT'S ALSO WHEN THERE'S THE MOST WORK FOR ME, BECAUSE IT'S WHEN PEOPLE DO THINGS THEY THINK THEY'RE KEEPING HIDDEN.
THEY'RE WRONG.
I'M DAREDEVIL.

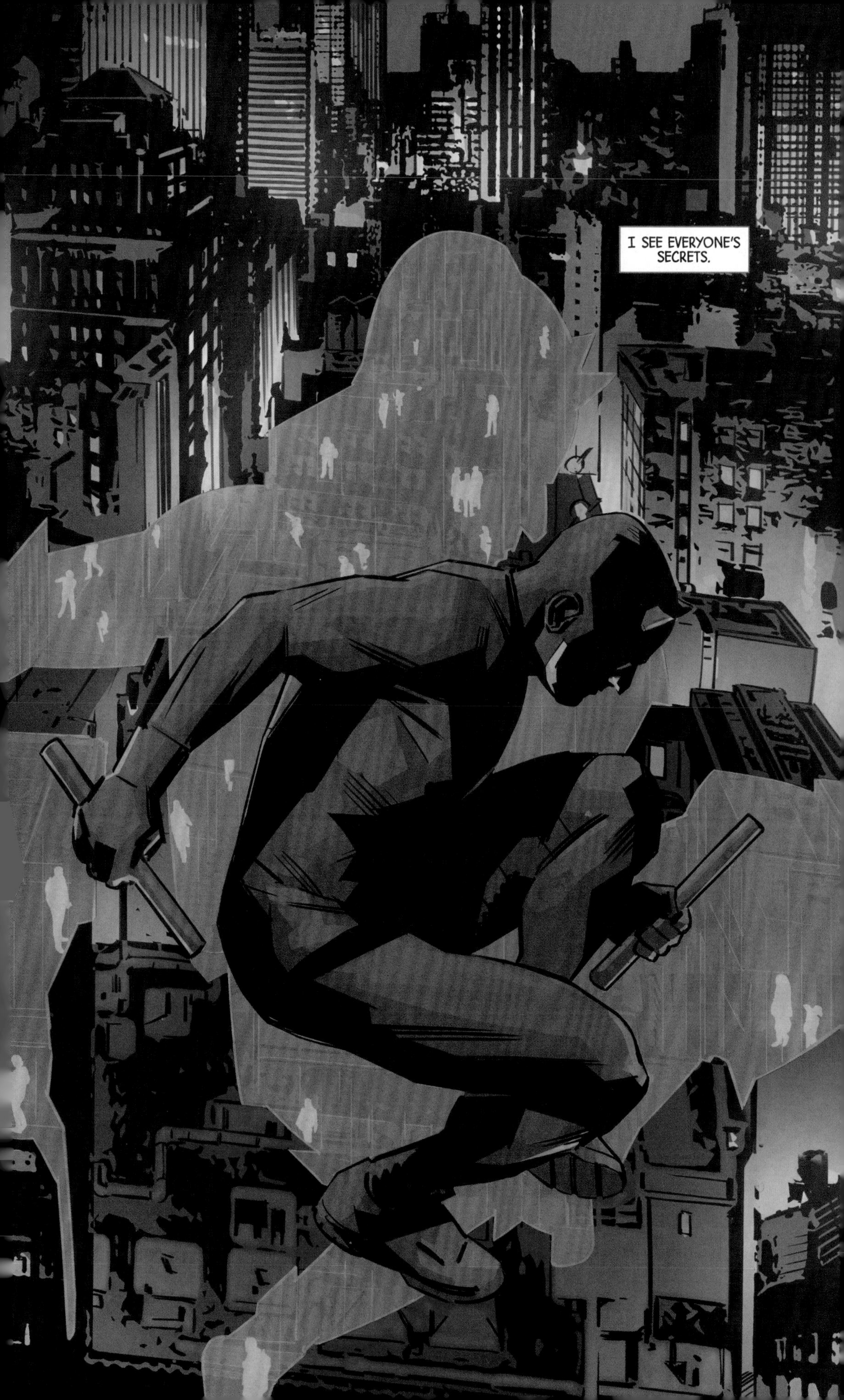
I SEE EVERYONE'S SECRETS.

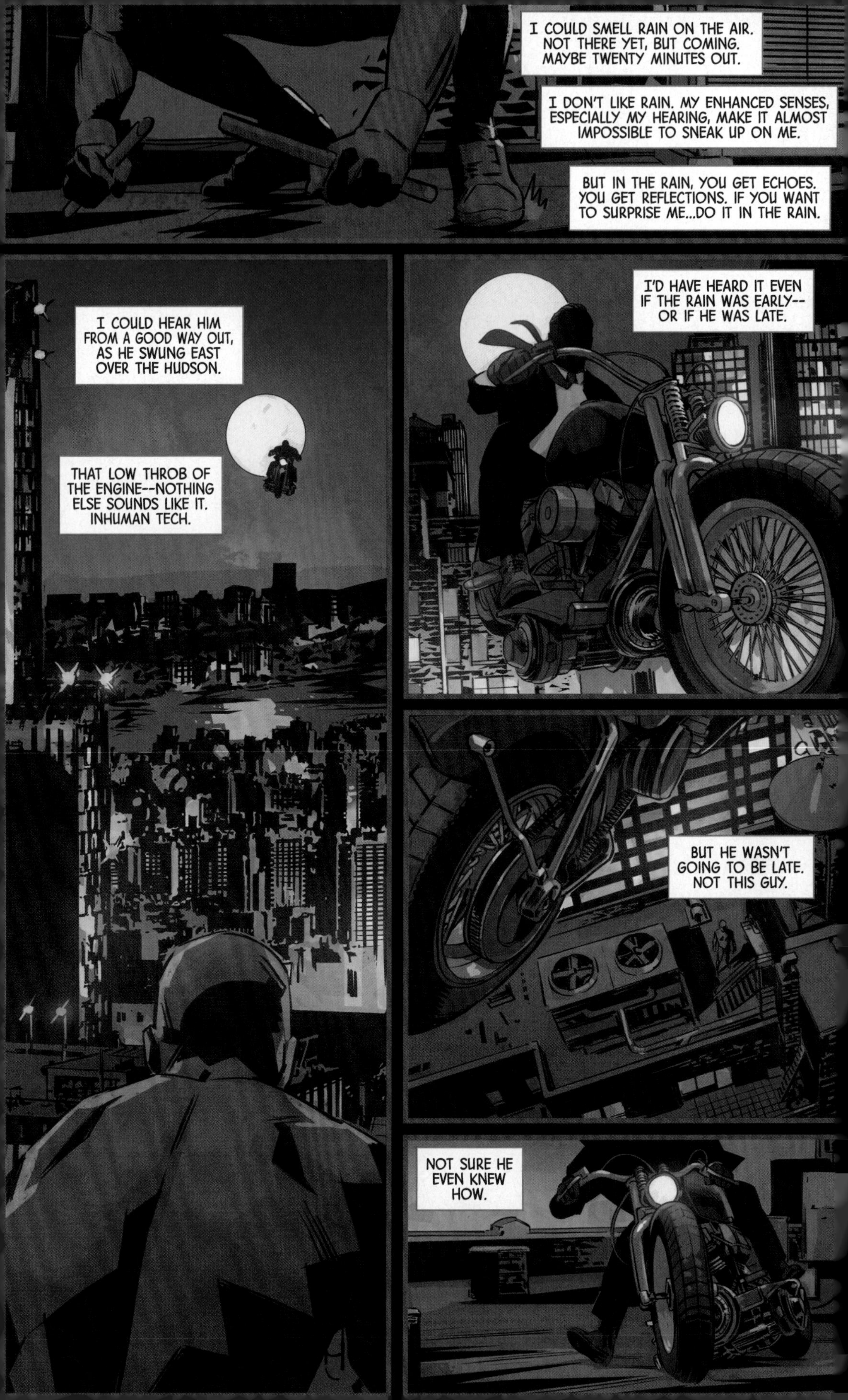
I COULD SMELL RAIN ON THE AIR. NOT THERE YET, BUT COMING. MAYBE TWENTY MINUTES OUT.
I DON'T LIKE RAIN. MY ENHANCED SENSES, ESPECIALLY MY HEARING, MAKE IT ALMOST IMPOSSIBLE TO SNEAK UP ON ME.
BUT IN THE RAIN, YOU GET ECHOES. YOU GET REFLECTIONS. IF YOU WANT TO SURPRISE ME...DO IT IN THE RAIN.
I COULD HEAR HIM FROM A GOOD WAY OUT, AS HE SWUNG EAST OVER THE HUDSON.
THAT LOW THROB OF THE ENGINE--NOTHING ELSE SOUNDS LIKE IT. INHUMAN TECH.
I'D HAVE HEARD IT EVEN IF THE RAIN WAS EARLY-- OR IF HE WAS LATE.
BUT HE WASN'T GOING TO BE LATE. NOT THIS GUY.
NOT SURE HE EVEN KNEW HOW.

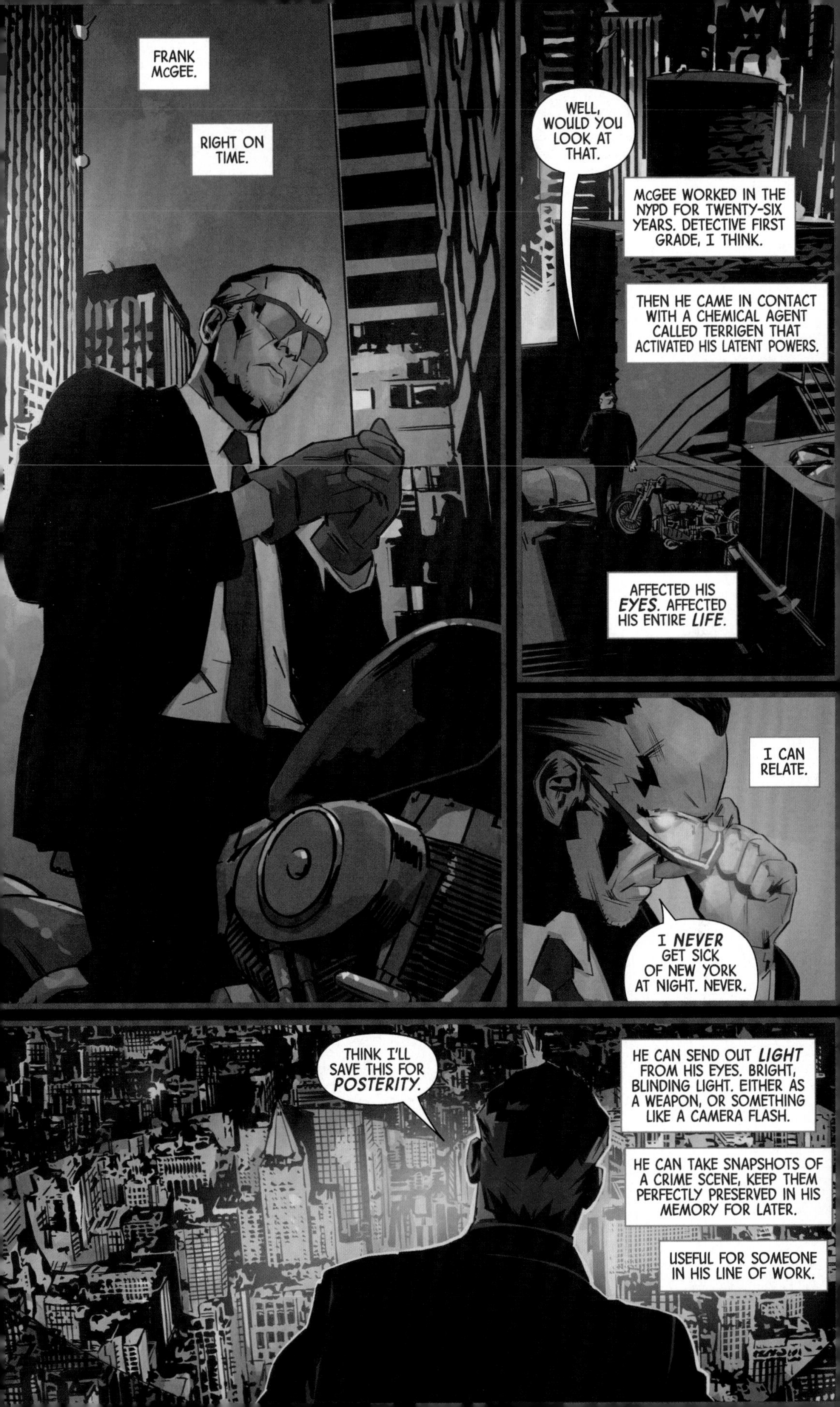
FRANK McGEE.
RIGHT ON TIME.
WELL, WOULD YOU LOOK AT THAT.
McGEE WORKED IN THE NYPD FOR TWENTY-SIX YEARS. DETECTIVE FIRST GRADE, I THINK.
THEN HE CAME IN CONTACT WITH A CHEMICAL AGENT CALLED TERRIGEN THAT ACTIVATED HIS LATENT POWERS.
AFFECTED HIS *EYES*. AFFECTED HIS ENTIRE *LIFE*.
I CAN RELATE.
I *NEVER* GET SICK OF NEW YORK AT NIGHT. NEVER.
THINK I'LL SAVE THIS FOR *POSTERITY*.
HE CAN SEND OUT *LIGHT* FROM HIS EYES. BRIGHT, BLINDING LIGHT. EITHER AS A WEAPON, OR SOMETHING LIKE A CAMERA FLASH.
HE CAN TAKE SNAPSHOTS OF A CRIME SCENE, KEEP THEM PERFECTLY PRESERVED IN HIS MEMORY FOR LATER.
USEFUL FOR SOMEONE IN HIS LINE OF WORK.

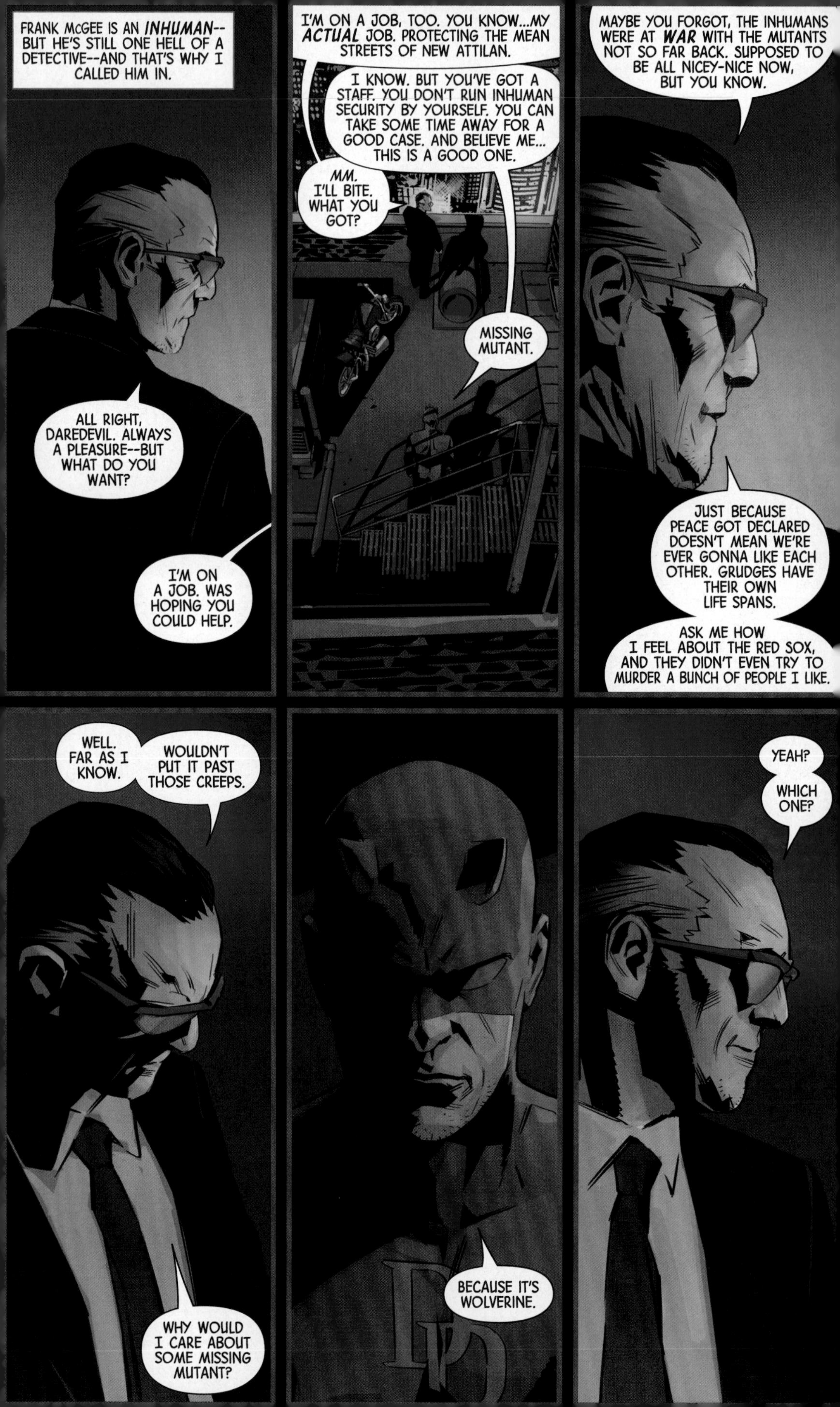
FRANK McGEE IS AN INHUMAN--BUT HE'S STILL ONE HELL OF A DETECTIVE--AND THAT'S WHY I CALLED HIM IN.
ALL RIGHT, DAREDEVIL. ALWAYS A PLEASURE--BUT WHAT DO YOU WANT?
I'M ON A JOB. WAS HOPING YOU COULD HELP.
I'M ON A JOB, TOO. YOU KNOW...MY ACTUAL JOB. PROTECTING THE MEAN STREETS OF NEW ATTILAN.
I KNOW. BUT YOU'VE GOT A STAFF. YOU DON'T RUN INHUMAN SECURITY BY YOURSELF. YOU CAN TAKE SOME TIME AWAY FOR A GOOD CASE. AND BELIEVE ME... THIS IS A GOOD ONE.
MM. I'LL BITE. WHAT YOU GOT?
MISSING MUTANT.
MAYBE YOU FORGOT, THE INHUMANS WERE AT WAR WITH THE MUTANTS NOT SO FAR BACK. SUPPOSED TO BE ALL NICEY-NICE NOW, BUT YOU KNOW.
JUST BECAUSE PEACE GOT DECLARED DOESN'T MEAN WE'RE EVER GONNA LIKE EACH OTHER. GRUDGES HAVE THEIR OWN LIFE SPANS.
ASK ME HOW I FEEL ABOUT THE RED SOX, AND THEY DIDN'T EVEN TRY TO MURDER A BUNCH OF PEOPLE I LIKE.
WELL. FAR AS I KNOW.
WOULDN'T PUT IT PAST THOSE CREEPS.
WHY WOULD I CARE ABOUT SOME MISSING MUTANT?
BECAUSE IT'S WOLVERINE.
YEAH?
WHICH ONE?

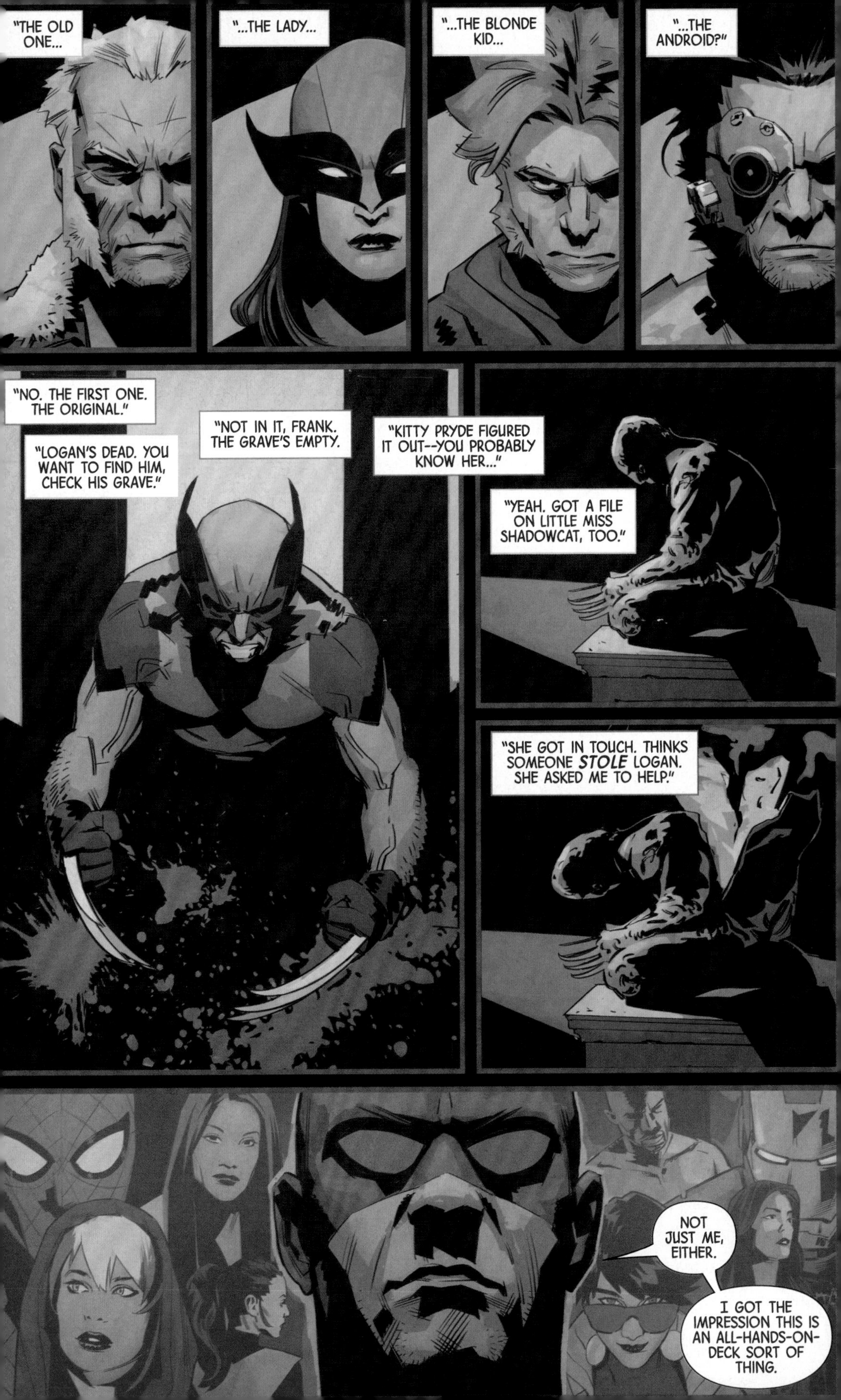

"THE OLD ONE...
"...THE LADY...
"...THE BLONDE KID...
"...THE ANDROID?"
"NO. THE FIRST ONE. THE ORIGINAL."
"LOGAN'S DEAD. YOU WANT TO FIND HIM, CHECK HIS GRAVE."
"NOT IN IT, FRANK. THE GRAVE'S EMPTY.
"KITTY PRYDE FIGURED IT OUT--YOU PROBABLY KNOW HER..."
"YEAH. GOT A FILE ON LITTLE MISS SHADOWCAT, TOO."
"SHE GOT IN TOUCH. THINKS SOMEONE STOLE LOGAN. SHE ASKED ME TO HELP."
NOT JUST ME, EITHER.
I GOT THE IMPRESSION THIS IS AN ALL-HANDS-ON-DECK SORT OF THING.

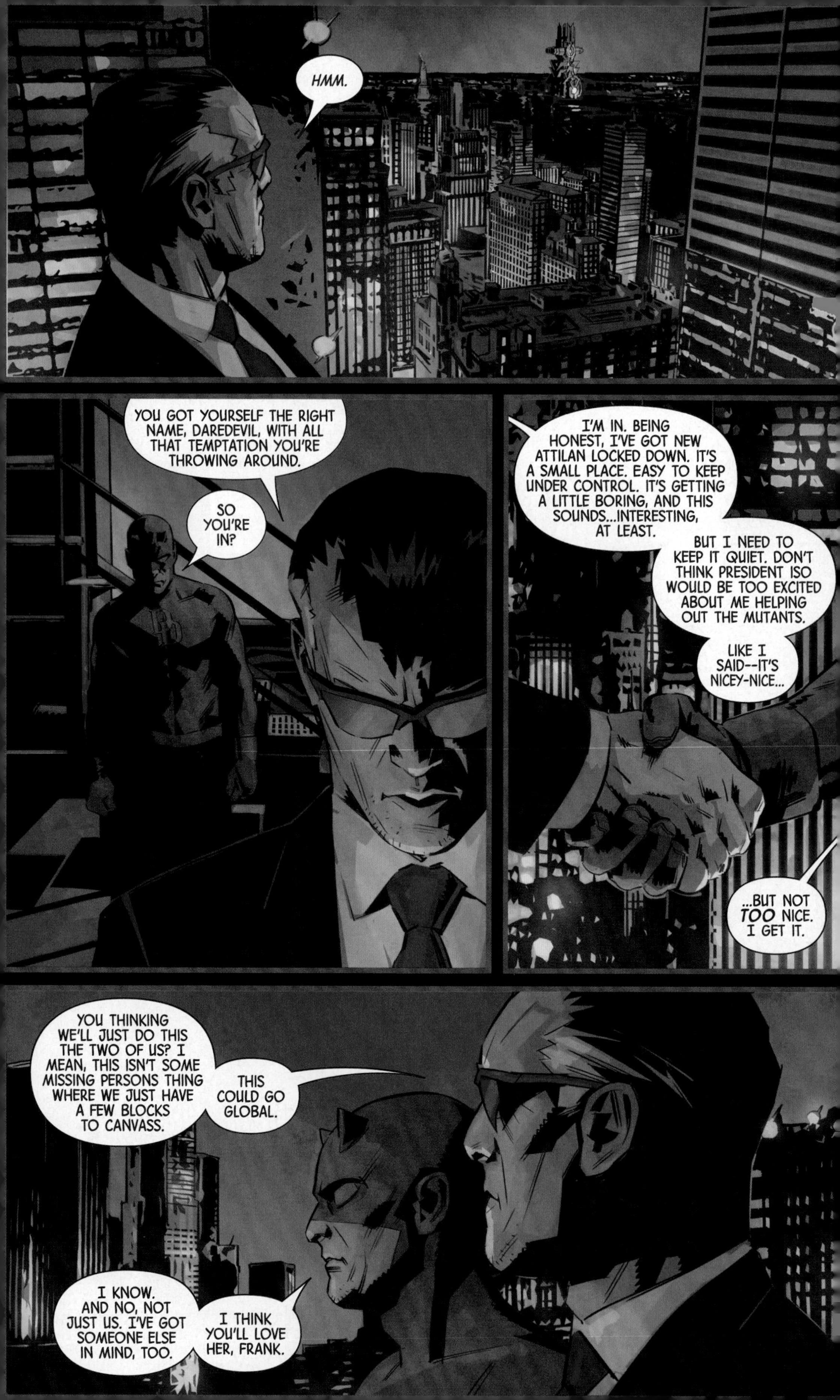
HMM.
YOU GOT YOURSELF THE RIGHT NAME, DAREDEVIL, WITH ALL THAT TEMPTATION YOU'RE THROWING AROUND.
SO YOU'RE IN?
I'M IN. BEING HONEST, I'VE GOT NEW ATTILAN LOCKED DOWN. IT'S A SMALL PLACE. EASY TO KEEP UNDER CONTROL. IT'S GETTING A LITTLE BORING, AND THIS SOUNDS...INTERESTING, AT LEAST.
BUT I NEED TO KEEP IT QUIET. DON'T THINK PRESIDENT ISO WOULD BE TOO EXCITED ABOUT ME HELPING OUT THE MUTANTS.
LIKE I SAID--IT'S NICEY-NICE...
...BUT NOT *TOO* NICE. I GET IT.
YOU THINKING WE'LL JUST DO THIS THE TWO OF US? I MEAN, THIS ISN'T SOME MISSING PERSONS THING WHERE WE JUST HAVE A FEW BLOCKS TO CANVASS.
THIS COULD GO GLOBAL.
I KNOW. AND NO, NOT JUST US. I'VE GOT SOMEONE ELSE IN MIND, TOO.
I THINK YOU'LL LOVE HER, FRANK.

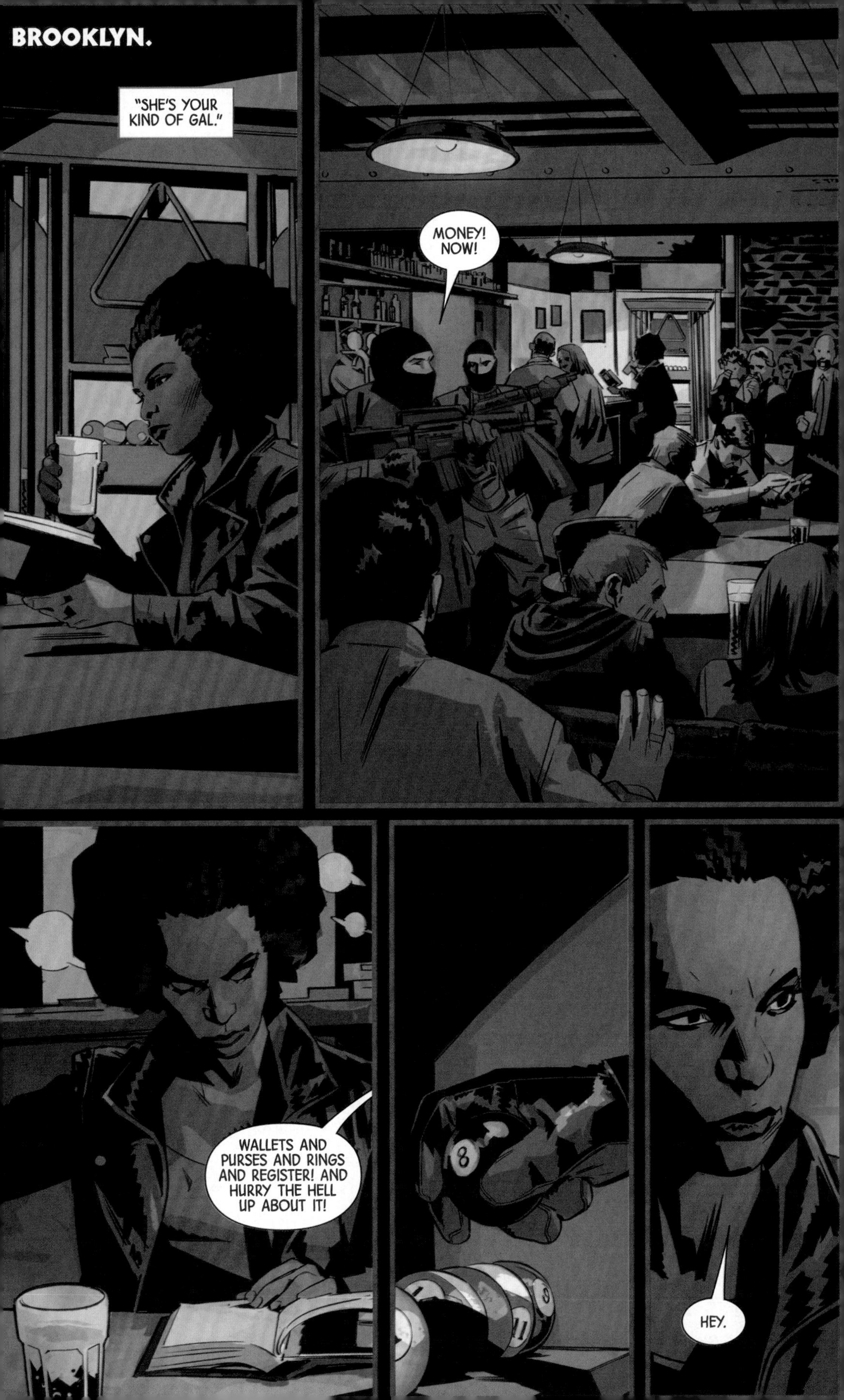
BROOKLYN.
"SHE'S YOUR KIND OF GAL."
MONEY! NOW!
WALLETS AND PURSES AND RINGS AND REGISTER! AND HURRY THE HELL UP ABOUT IT!
HEY.

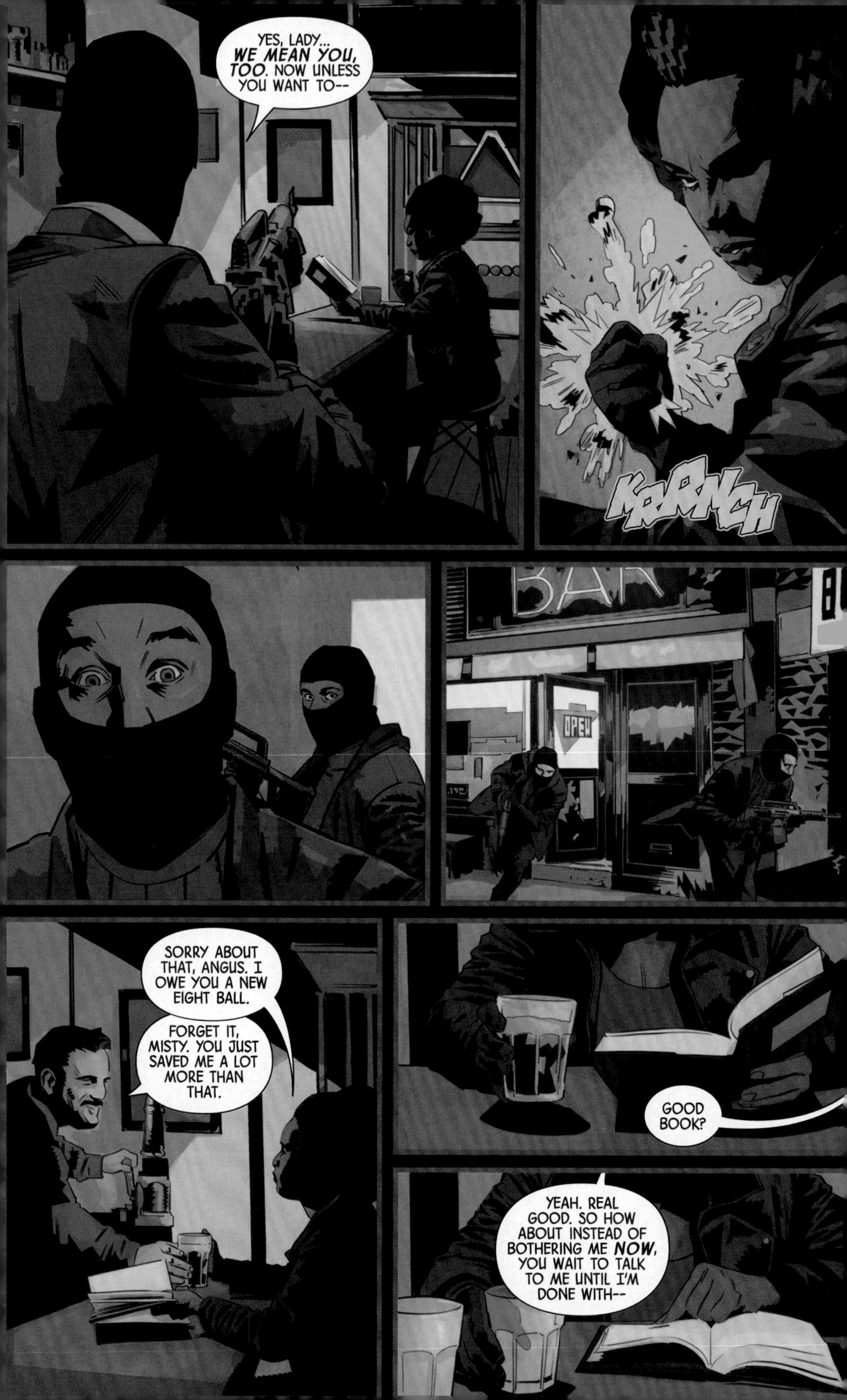
YES, LADY... *WE MEAN YOU, TOO*. NOW UNLESS YOU WANT TO--
KRUNCH
BAR
OPEN
SORRY ABOUT THAT, ANGUS. I OWE YOU A NEW EIGHT BALL.
FORGET IT, MISTY. YOU JUST SAVED ME A LOT MORE THAN THAT.
GOOD BOOK?
YEAH. REAL GOOD. SO HOW ABOUT INSTEAD OF BOTHERING ME *NOW*, YOU WAIT TO TALK TO ME UNTIL I'M DONE WITH--

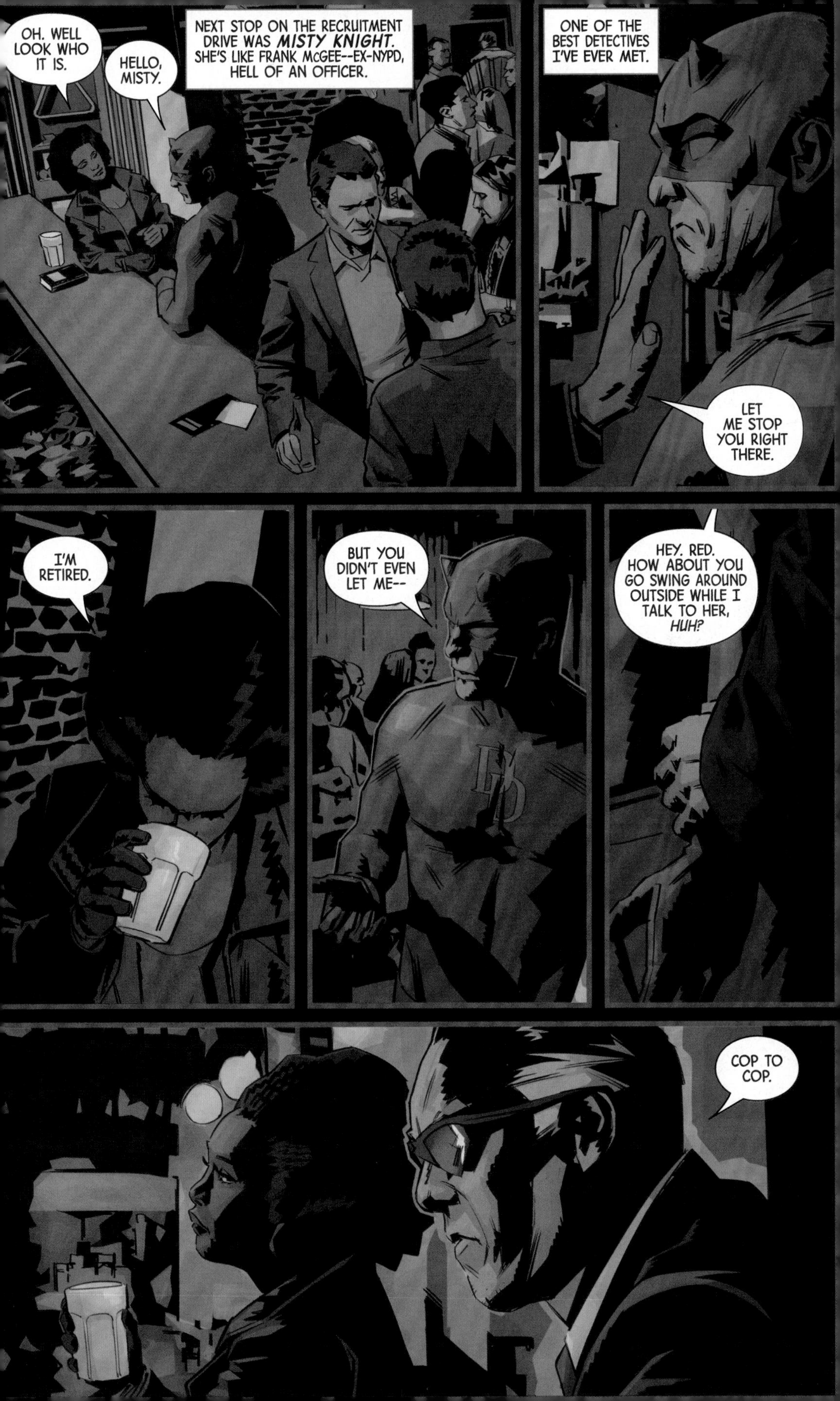
OH. WELL LOOK WHO IT IS.
HELLO, MISTY.
NEXT STOP ON THE RECRUITMENT DRIVE WAS MISTY KNIGHT. SHE'S LIKE FRANK McGEE--EX-NYPD, HELL OF AN OFFICER.
ONE OF THE BEST DETECTIVES I'VE EVER MET.
LET ME STOP YOU RIGHT THERE.
I'M RETIRED.
BUT YOU DIDN'T EVEN LET ME--
HEY. RED. HOW ABOUT YOU GO SWING AROUND OUTSIDE WHILE I TALK TO HER, HUH?
COP TO COP.

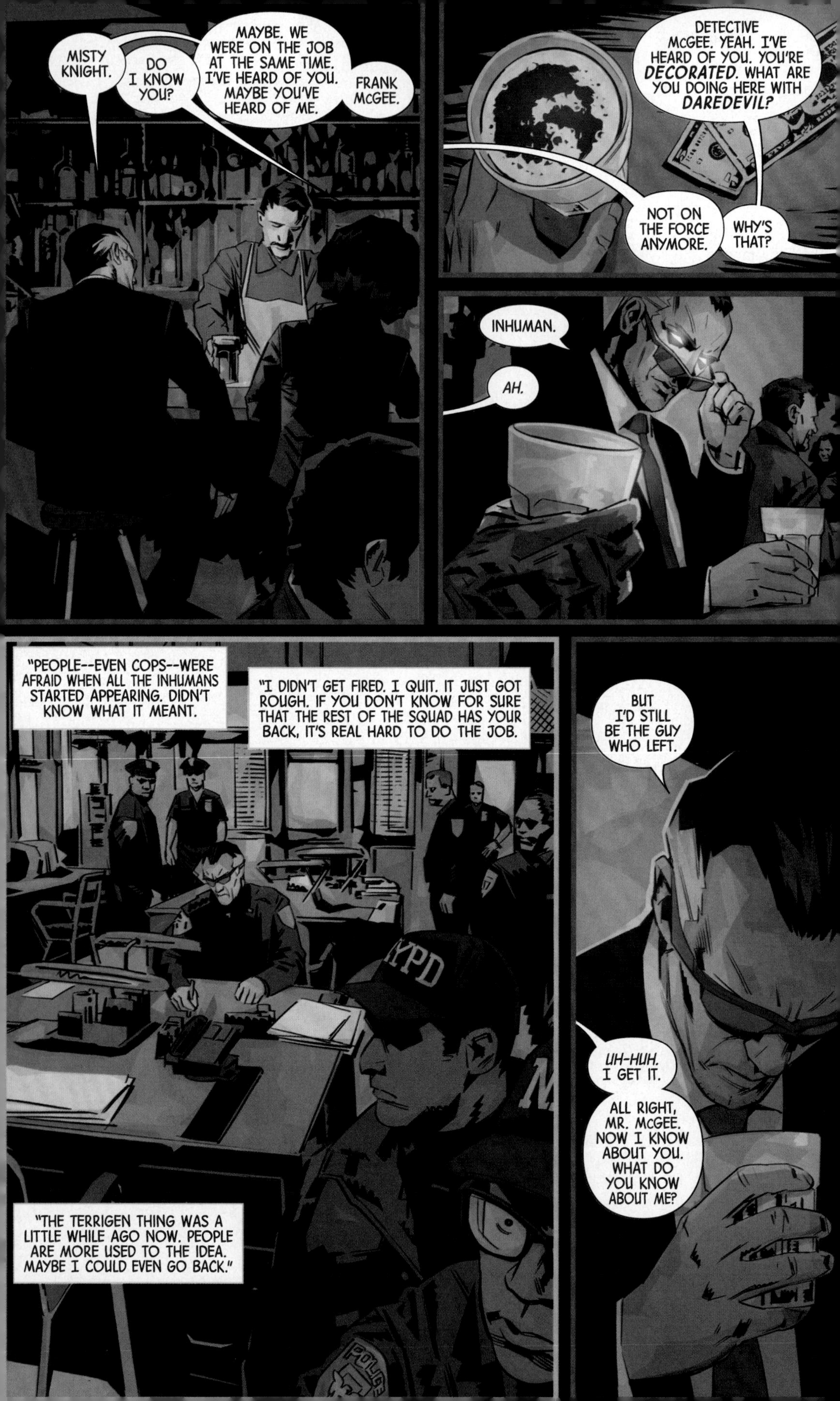
MISTY KNIGHT.
DO I KNOW YOU?
MAYBE. WE WERE ON THE JOB AT THE SAME TIME. I'VE HEARD OF YOU. MAYBE YOU'VE HEARD OF ME.
FRANK McGEE.
DETECTIVE McGEE. YEAH. I'VE HEARD OF YOU. YOU'RE DECORATED. WHAT ARE YOU DOING HERE WITH DAREDEVIL?
NOT ON THE FORCE ANYMORE.
WHY'S THAT?
INHUMAN.
AH.
"PEOPLE--EVEN COPS--WERE AFRAID WHEN ALL THE INHUMANS STARTED APPEARING. DIDN'T KNOW WHAT IT MEANT.
"I DIDN'T GET FIRED. I QUIT. IT JUST GOT ROUGH. IF YOU DON'T KNOW FOR SURE THAT THE REST OF THE SQUAD HAS YOUR BACK, IT'S REAL HARD TO DO THE JOB.
"THE TERRIGEN THING WAS A LITTLE WHILE AGO NOW. PEOPLE ARE MORE USED TO THE IDEA. MAYBE I COULD EVEN GO BACK."
BUT I'D STILL BE THE GUY WHO LEFT.
UH-HUH. I GET IT.
ALL RIGHT, MR. McGEE. NOW I KNOW ABOUT YOU. WHAT DO YOU KNOW ABOUT ME?

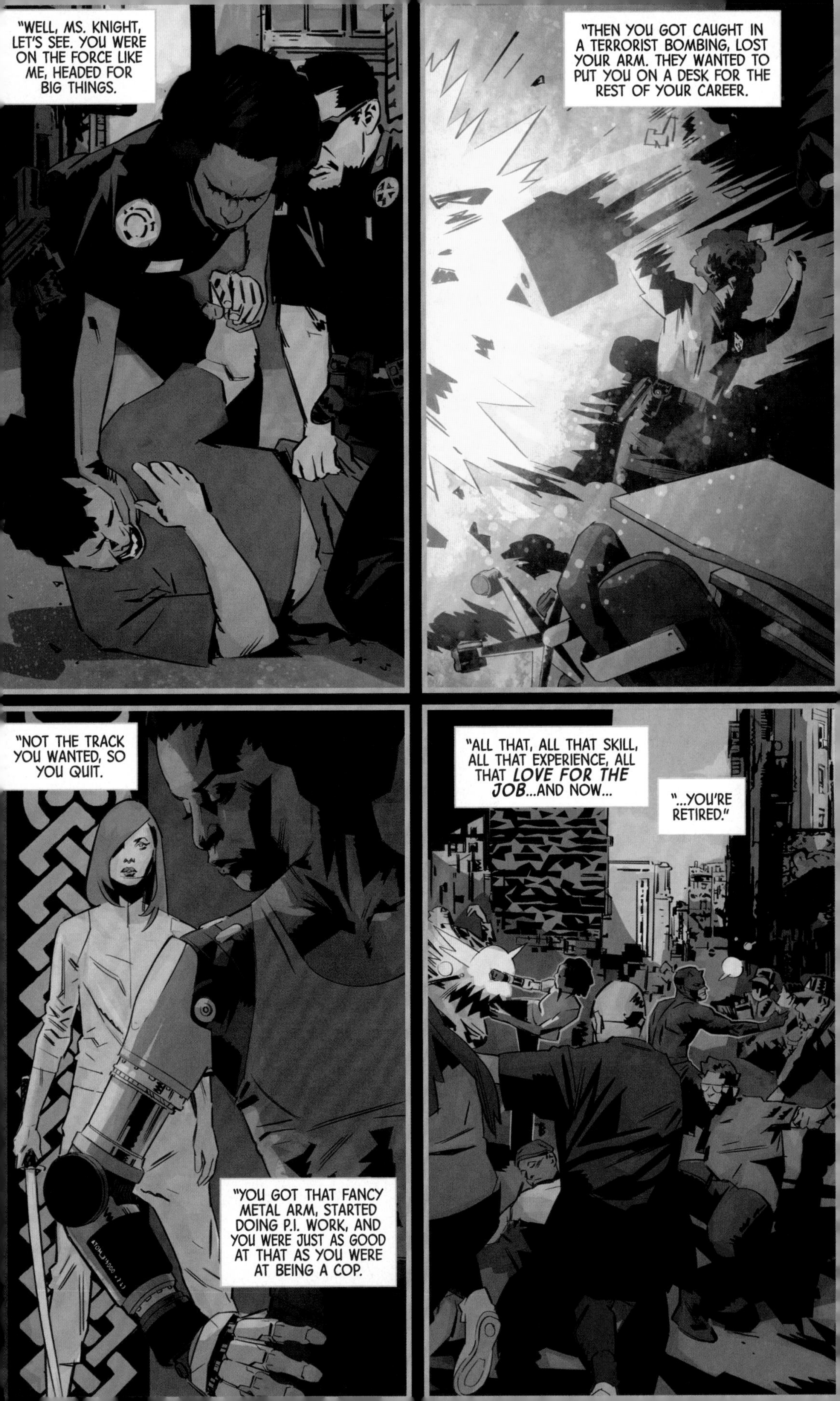
"WELL, MS. KNIGHT, LET'S SEE. YOU WERE ON THE FORCE LIKE ME, HEADED FOR BIG THINGS.
"THEN YOU GOT CAUGHT IN A TERRORIST BOMBING, LOST YOUR ARM. THEY WANTED TO PUT YOU ON A DESK FOR THE REST OF YOUR CAREER.
"NOT THE TRACK YOU WANTED, SO YOU QUIT.
"YOU GOT THAT FANCY METAL ARM, STARTED DOING P.I. WORK, AND YOU WERE JUST AS GOOD AT THAT AS YOU WERE AT BEING A COP.
"ALL THAT, ALL THAT SKILL, ALL THAT EXPERIENCE, ALL THAT *LOVE FOR THE JOB*...AND NOW...
"...YOU'RE RETIRED."

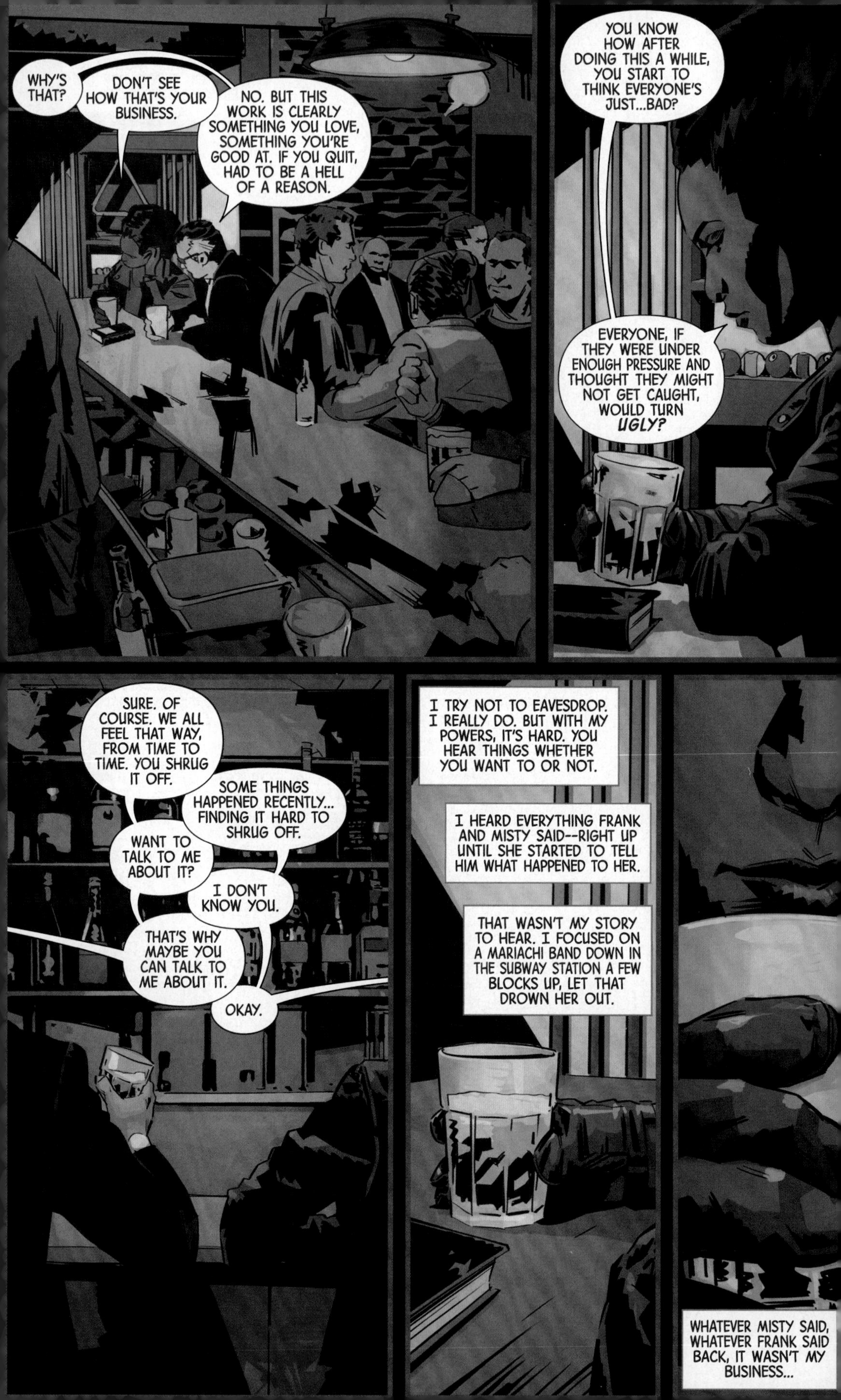
WHY'S THAT?
DON'T SEE HOW THAT'S YOUR BUSINESS.
NO. BUT THIS WORK IS CLEARLY SOMETHING YOU LOVE, SOMETHING YOU'RE GOOD AT. IF YOU QUIT, HAD TO BE A HELL OF A REASON.
YOU KNOW HOW AFTER DOING THIS A WHILE, YOU START TO THINK EVERYONE'S JUST...BAD?
EVERYONE, IF THEY WERE UNDER ENOUGH PRESSURE AND THOUGHT THEY MIGHT NOT GET CAUGHT, WOULD TURN *UGLY?*
SURE. OF COURSE. WE ALL FEEL THAT WAY, FROM TIME TO TIME. YOU SHRUG IT OFF.
SOME THINGS HAPPENED RECENTLY... FINDING IT HARD TO SHRUG OFF.
WANT TO TALK TO ME ABOUT IT?
I DON'T KNOW YOU.
THAT'S WHY MAYBE YOU CAN TALK TO ME ABOUT IT.
OKAY.
I TRY NOT TO EAVESDROP. I REALLY DO. BUT WITH MY POWERS, IT'S HARD. YOU HEAR THINGS WHETHER YOU WANT TO OR NOT.
I HEARD EVERYTHING FRANK AND MISTY SAID--RIGHT UP UNTIL SHE STARTED TO TELL HIM WHAT HAPPENED TO HER.
THAT WASN'T MY STORY TO HEAR. I FOCUSED ON A MARIACHI BAND DOWN IN THE SUBWAY STATION A FEW BLOCKS UP, LET THAT DROWN HER OUT.
WHATEVER MISTY SAID, WHATEVER FRANK SAID BACK, IT WASN'T MY BUSINESS...

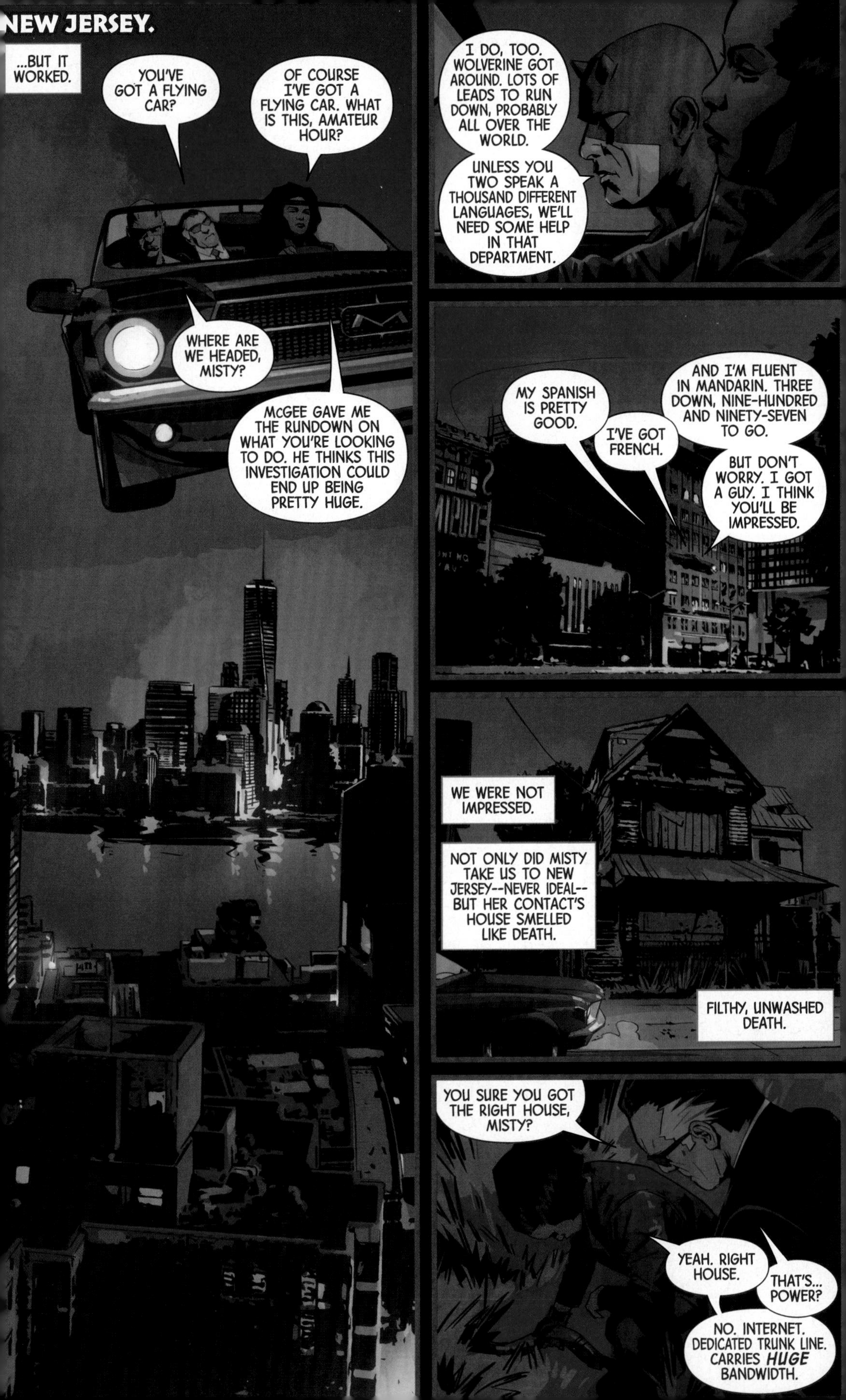
NEW JERSEY.
...BUT IT WORKED.
YOU'VE GOT A FLYING CAR?
OF COURSE I'VE GOT A FLYING CAR. WHAT IS THIS, AMATEUR HOUR?
WHERE ARE WE HEADED, MISTY?
McGEE GAVE ME THE RUNDOWN ON WHAT YOU'RE LOOKING TO DO. HE THINKS THIS INVESTIGATION COULD END UP BEING PRETTY HUGE.
I DO, TOO. WOLVERINE GOT AROUND. LOTS OF LEADS TO RUN DOWN, PROBABLY ALL OVER THE WORLD.
UNLESS YOU TWO SPEAK A THOUSAND DIFFERENT LANGUAGES, WE'LL NEED SOME HELP IN THAT DEPARTMENT.
MY SPANISH IS PRETTY GOOD.
I'VE GOT FRENCH.
AND I'M FLUENT IN MANDARIN. THREE DOWN, NINE-HUNDRED AND NINETY-SEVEN TO GO.
BUT DON'T WORRY. I GOT A GUY. I THINK YOU'LL BE IMPRESSED.
WE WERE NOT IMPRESSED.
NOT ONLY DID MISTY TAKE US TO NEW JERSEY--NEVER IDEAL--BUT HER CONTACT'S HOUSE SMELLED LIKE DEATH.
FILTHY, UNWASHED DEATH.
YOU SURE YOU GOT THE RIGHT HOUSE, MISTY?
YEAH. RIGHT HOUSE.
THAT'S... POWER?
NO. INTERNET. DEDICATED TRUNK LINE. CARRIES ***HUGE*** BANDWIDTH.

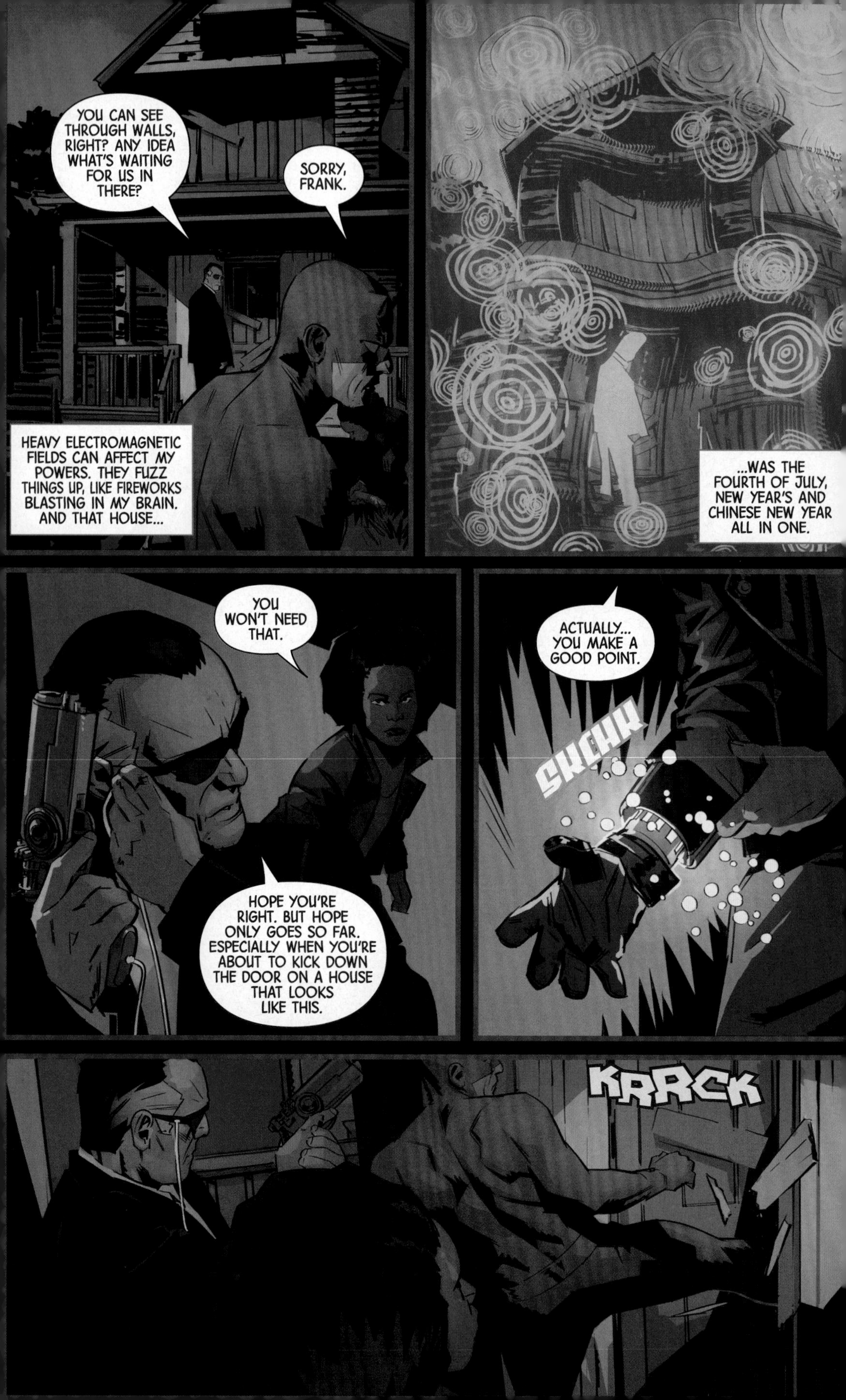
YOU CAN SEE THROUGH WALLS, RIGHT? ANY IDEA WHAT'S WAITING FOR US IN THERE?
SORRY, FRANK.
HEAVY ELECTROMAGNETIC FIELDS CAN AFFECT MY POWERS. THEY FUZZ THINGS UP, LIKE FIREWORKS BLASTING IN MY BRAIN. AND THAT HOUSE...
...WAS THE FOURTH OF JULY, NEW YEAR'S AND CHINESE NEW YEAR ALL IN ONE.
YOU WON'T NEED THAT.
HOPE YOU'RE RIGHT. BUT HOPE ONLY GOES SO FAR. ESPECIALLY WHEN YOU'RE ABOUT TO KICK DOWN THE DOOR ON A HOUSE THAT LOOKS LIKE THIS.
ACTUALLY... YOU MAKE A GOOD POINT.
SKCHK
KRRCK

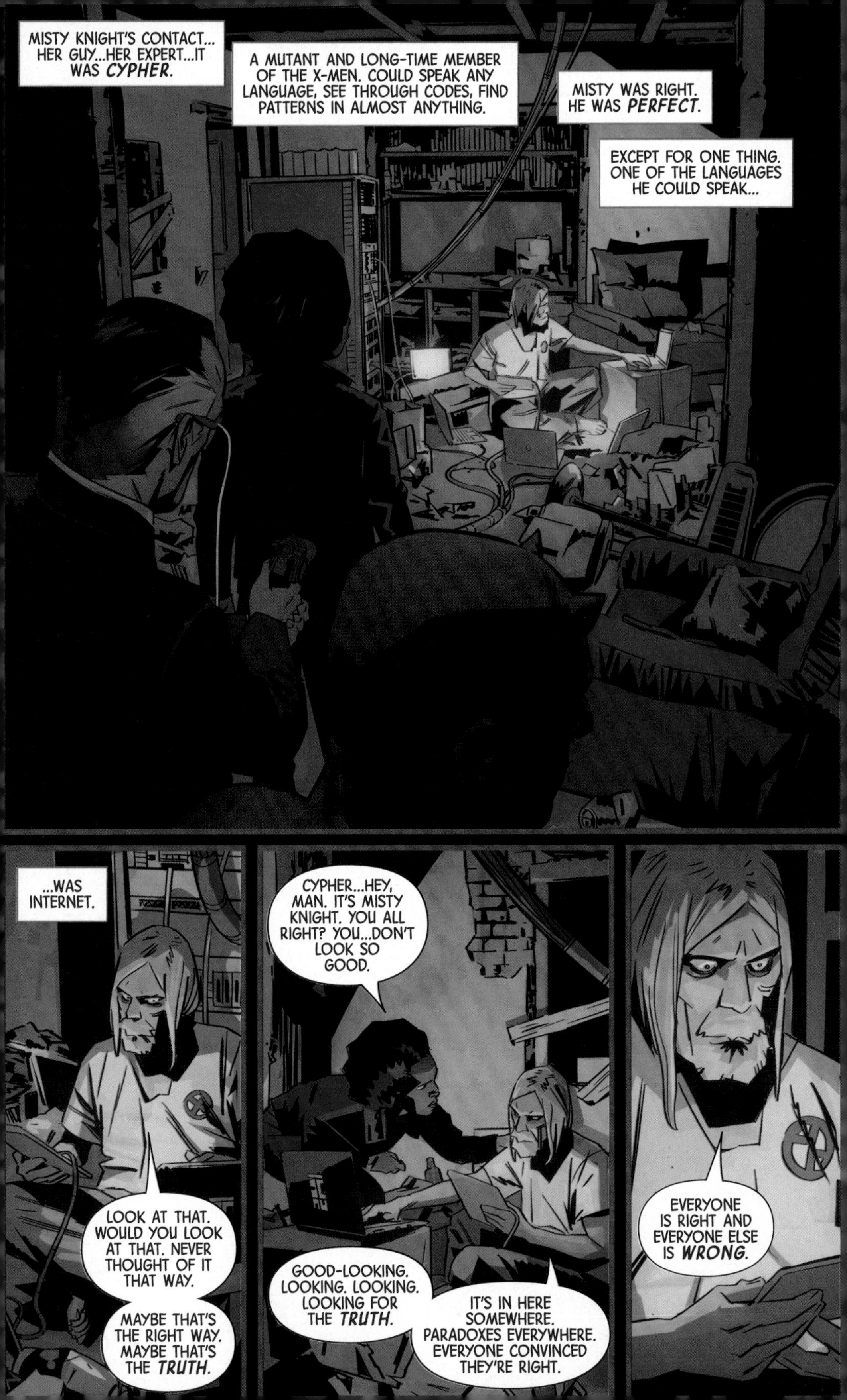
MISTY KNIGHT'S CONTACT... HER GUY...HER EXPERT...IT WAS *CYPHER*.
A MUTANT AND LONG-TIME MEMBER OF THE X-MEN. COULD SPEAK ANY LANGUAGE, SEE THROUGH CODES, FIND PATTERNS IN ALMOST ANYTHING.
MISTY WAS RIGHT. HE WAS *PERFECT*.
EXCEPT FOR ONE THING. ONE OF THE LANGUAGES HE COULD SPEAK...
...WAS INTERNET.
LOOK AT THAT. WOULD YOU LOOK AT THAT. NEVER THOUGHT OF IT THAT WAY.
MAYBE THAT'S THE RIGHT WAY. MAYBE THAT'S THE *TRUTH*.
CYPHER...HEY, MAN. IT'S MISTY KNIGHT. YOU ALL RIGHT? YOU...DON'T LOOK SO GOOD.
GOOD-LOOKING. LOOKING. LOOKING. LOOKING FOR THE *TRUTH*.
IT'S IN HERE SOMEWHERE. PARADOXES EVERYWHERE. EVERYONE CONVINCED THEY'RE RIGHT.
EVERYONE IS RIGHT AND EVERYONE ELSE IS *WRONG*.

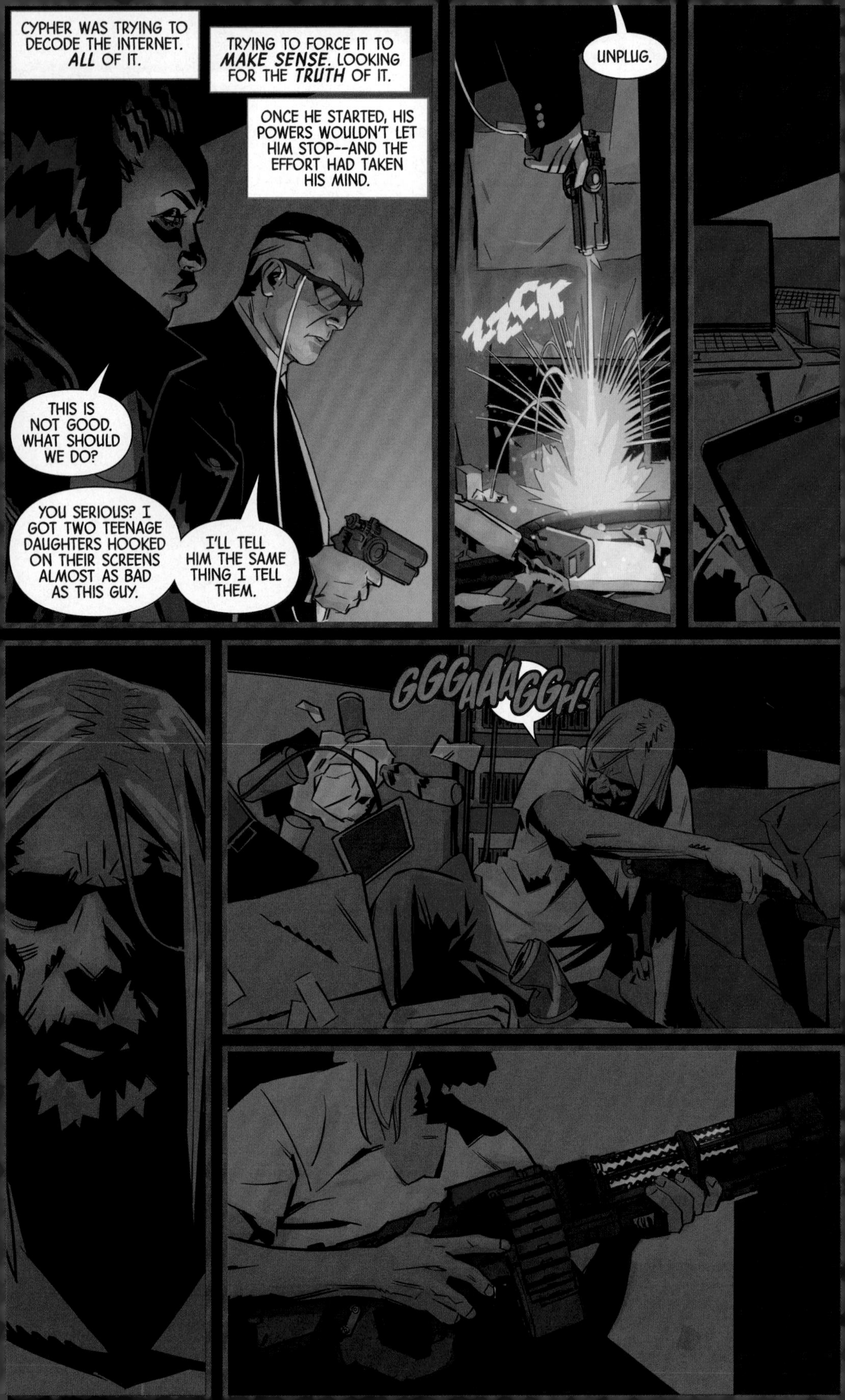

CYPHER WAS TRYING TO DECODE THE INTERNET. ALL OF IT.
TRYING TO FORCE IT TO MAKE SENSE. LOOKING FOR THE TRUTH OF IT.
ONCE HE STARTED, HIS POWERS WOULDN'T LET HIM STOP--AND THE EFFORT HAD TAKEN HIS MIND.
THIS IS NOT GOOD. WHAT SHOULD WE DO?
YOU SERIOUS? I GOT TWO TEENAGE DAUGHTERS HOOKED ON THEIR SCREENS ALMOST AS BAD AS THIS GUY.
I'LL TELL HIM THE SAME THING I TELL THEM.
UNPLUG.
ZZCK
GGGAAAGGH!

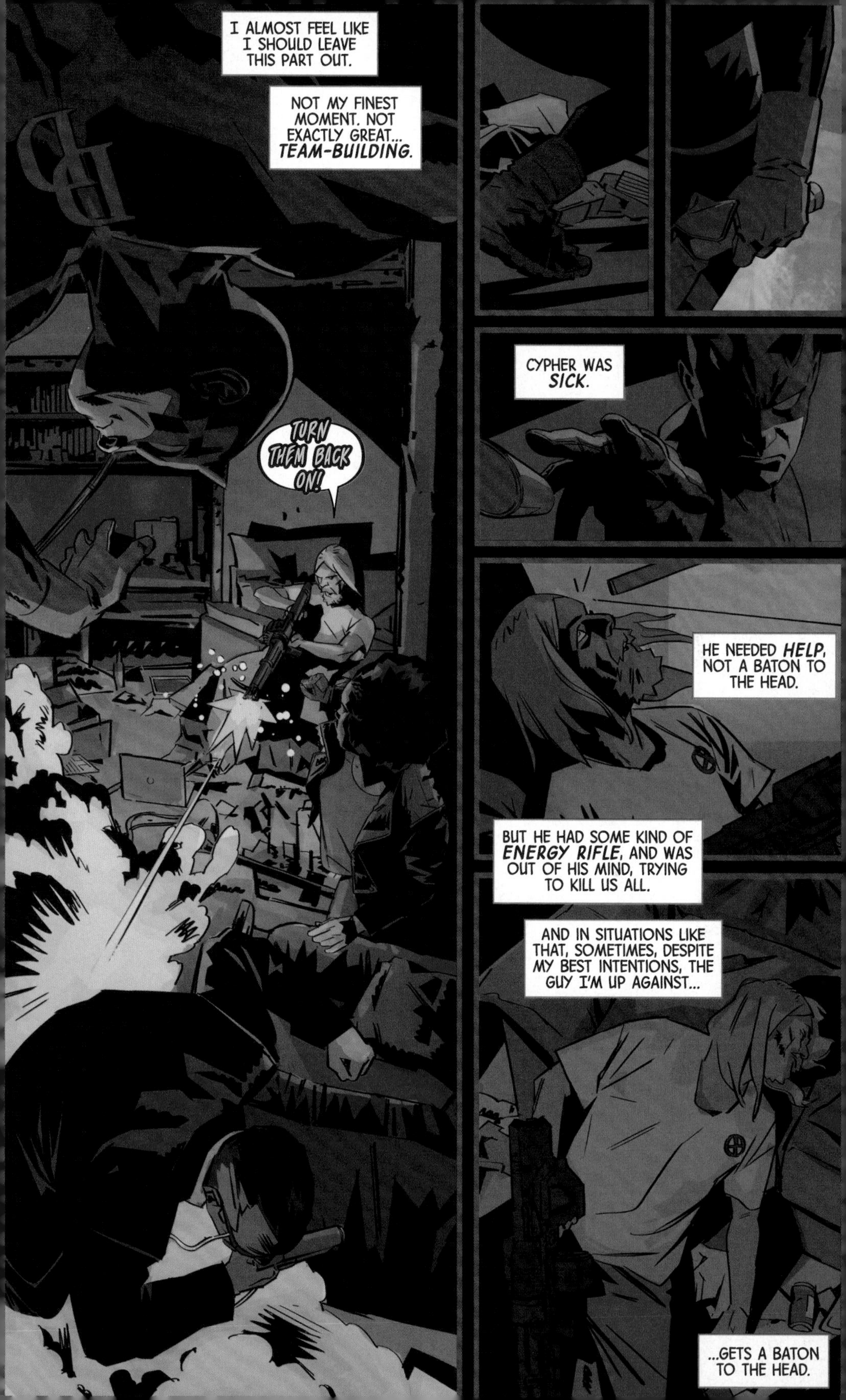
I ALMOST FEEL LIKE I SHOULD LEAVE THIS PART OUT.
NOT MY FINEST MOMENT. NOT EXACTLY GREAT... TEAM-BUILDING.
TURN THEM BACK ON!
CYPHER WAS SICK.
HE NEEDED HELP, NOT A BATON TO THE HEAD.
BUT HE HAD SOME KIND OF ENERGY RIFLE, AND WAS OUT OF HIS MIND, TRYING TO KILL US ALL.
AND IN SITUATIONS LIKE THAT, SOMETIMES, DESPITE MY BEST INTENTIONS, THE GUY I'M UP AGAINST...
...GETS A BATON TO THE HEAD.

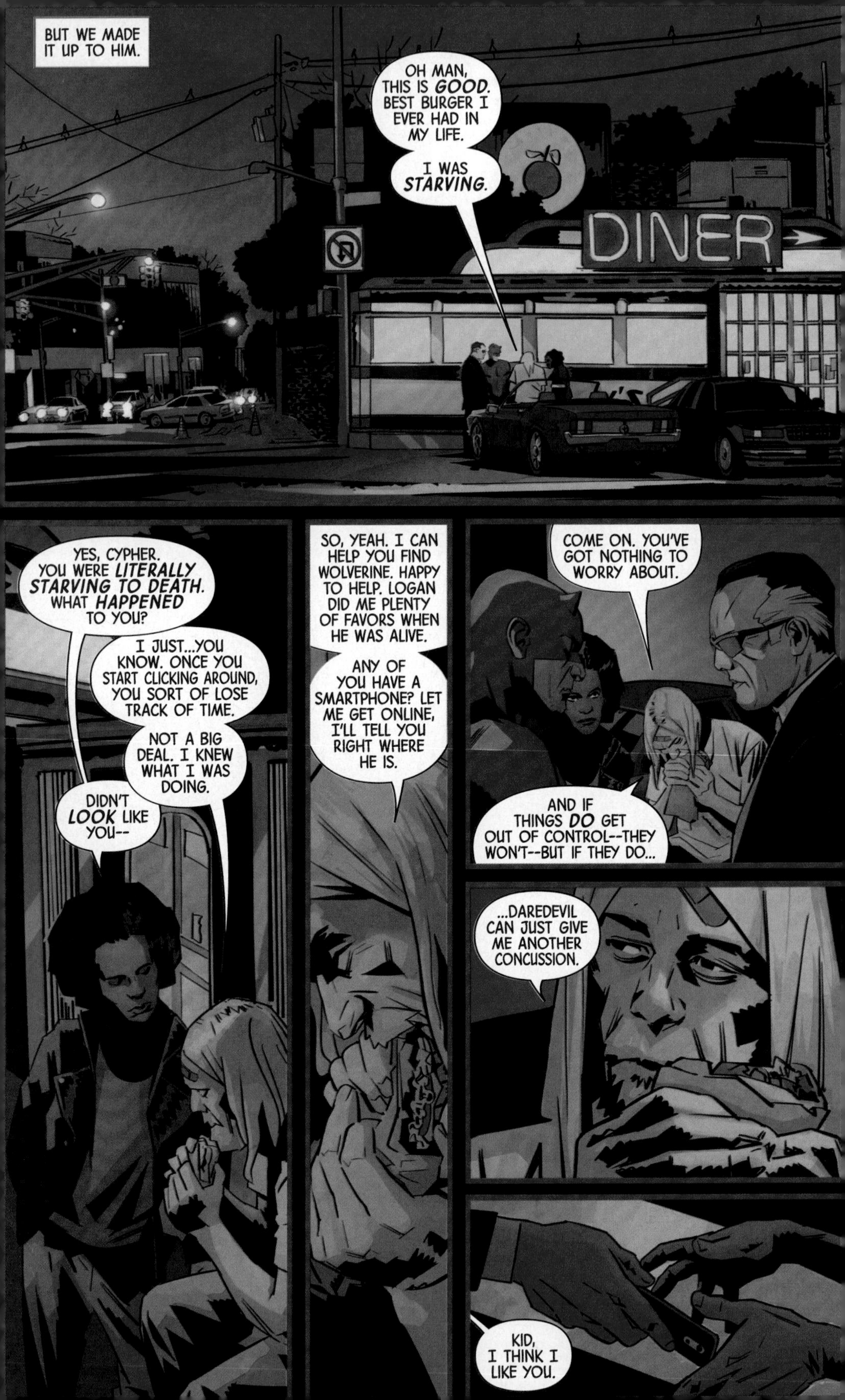
BUT WE MADE IT UP TO HIM.
OH MAN, THIS IS GOOD. BEST BURGER I EVER HAD IN MY LIFE.
I WAS STARVING.
DINER
YES, CYPHER. YOU WERE LITERALLY STARVING TO DEATH. WHAT HAPPENED TO YOU?
I JUST...YOU KNOW. ONCE YOU START CLICKING AROUND, YOU SORT OF LOSE TRACK OF TIME.
NOT A BIG DEAL. I KNEW WHAT I WAS DOING.
DIDN'T LOOK LIKE YOU--
SO, YEAH. I CAN HELP YOU FIND WOLVERINE. HAPPY TO HELP. LOGAN DID ME PLENTY OF FAVORS WHEN HE WAS ALIVE.
ANY OF YOU HAVE A SMARTPHONE? LET ME GET ONLINE, I'LL TELL YOU RIGHT WHERE HE IS.
COME ON. YOU'VE GOT NOTHING TO WORRY ABOUT.
AND IF THINGS DO GET OUT OF CONTROL--THEY WON'T--BUT IF THEY DO...
...DAREDEVIL CAN JUST GIVE ME ANOTHER CONCUSSION.
KID, I THINK I LIKE YOU.

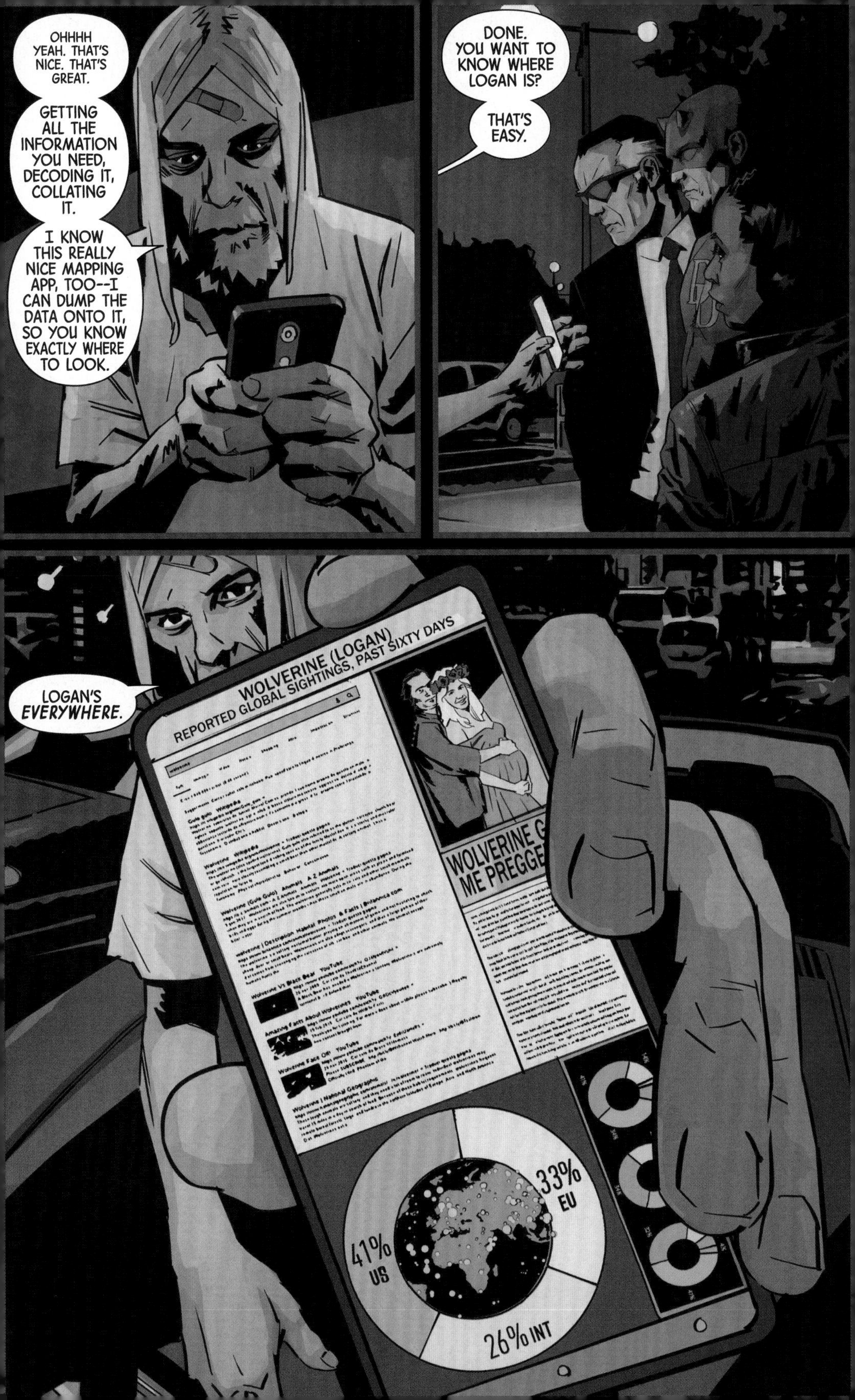
OHHHH YEAH. THAT'S NICE. THAT'S GREAT.
GETTING ALL THE INFORMATION YOU NEED, DECODING IT, COLLATING IT.
I KNOW THIS REALLY NICE MAPPING APP, TOO--I CAN DUMP THE DATA ONTO IT, SO YOU KNOW EXACTLY WHERE TO LOOK.
DONE. YOU WANT TO KNOW WHERE LOGAN IS?
THAT'S EASY.
LOGAN'S *EVERYWHERE.*
WOLVERINE (LOGAN)
REPORTED GLOBAL SIGHTINGS, PAST SIXTY DAYS
41% US
33% EU
26% INT

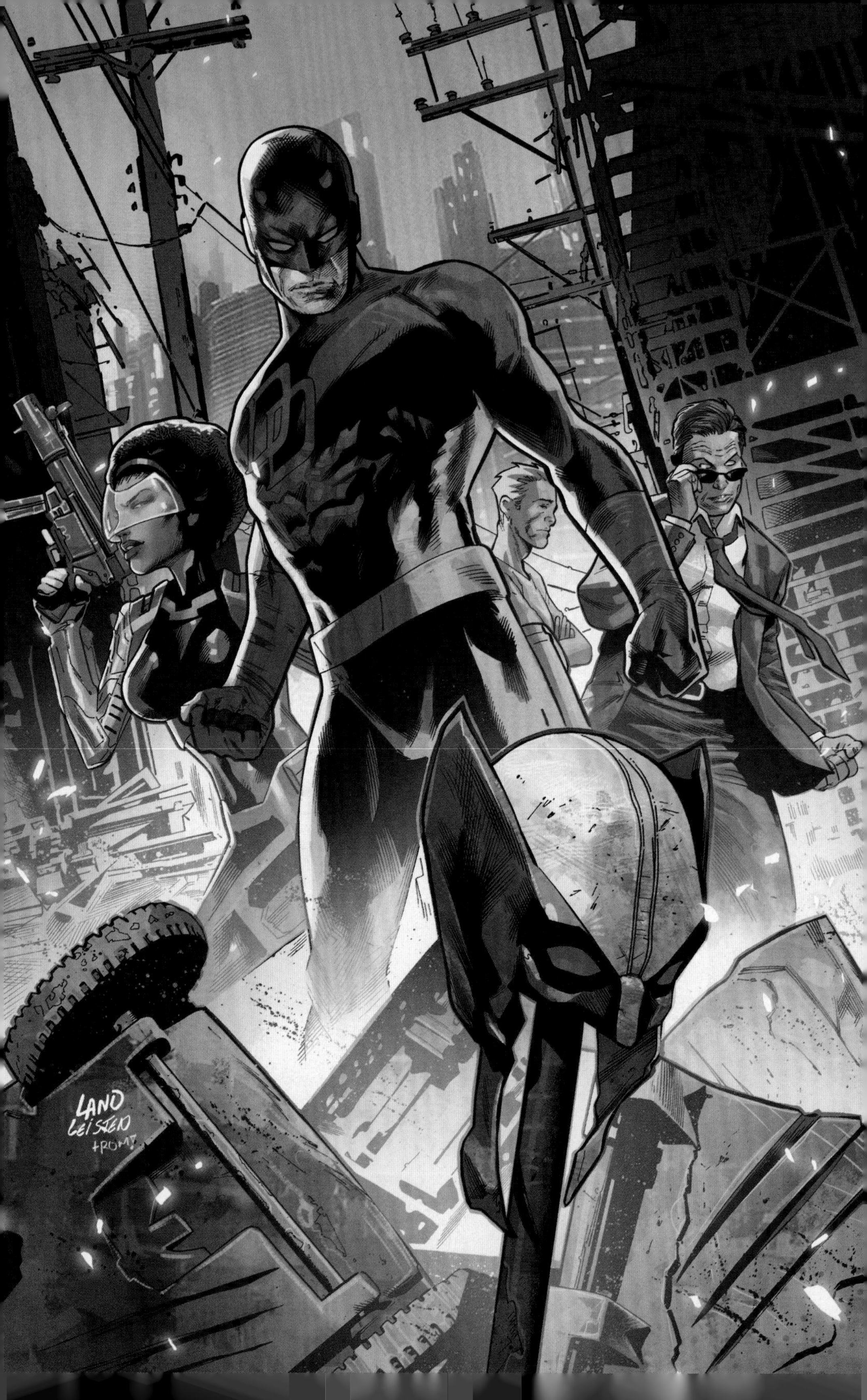
LANO
LEISTEN

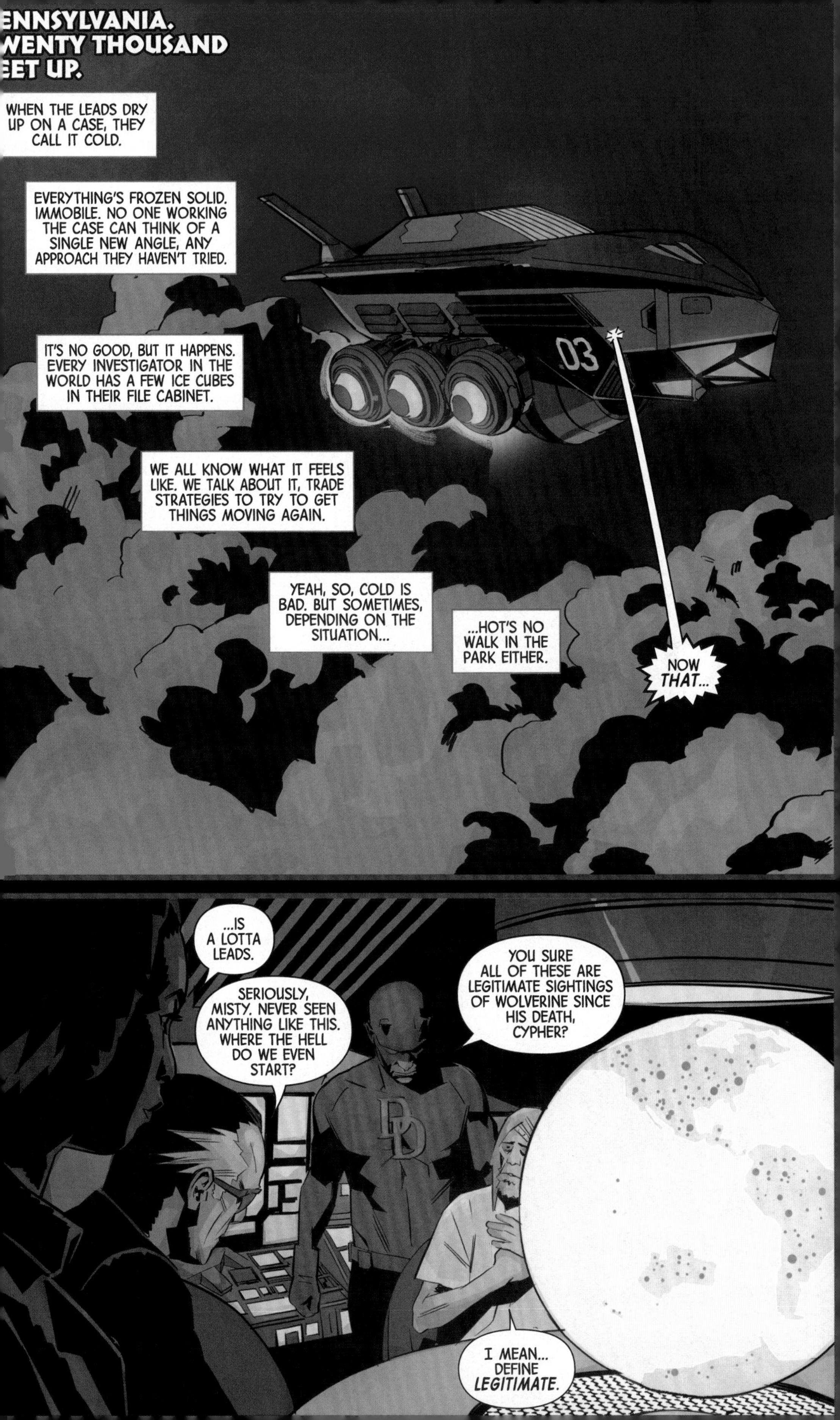
ENNSYLVANIA.
WENTY THOUSAND
EET UP.
WHEN THE LEADS DRY UP ON A CASE, THEY CALL IT COLD.
EVERYTHING'S FROZEN SOLID. IMMOBILE. NO ONE WORKING THE CASE CAN THINK OF A SINGLE NEW ANGLE, ANY APPROACH THEY HAVEN'T TRIED.
IT'S NO GOOD, BUT IT HAPPENS. EVERY INVESTIGATOR IN THE WORLD HAS A FEW ICE CUBES IN THEIR FILE CABINET.
03
WE ALL KNOW WHAT IT FEELS LIKE. WE TALK ABOUT IT, TRADE STRATEGIES TO TRY TO GET THINGS MOVING AGAIN.
YEAH, SO, COLD IS BAD. BUT SOMETIMES, DEPENDING ON THE SITUATION...
...HOT'S NO WALK IN THE PARK EITHER.
NOW THAT...
...IS A LOTTA LEADS.
SERIOUSLY, MISTY. NEVER SEEN ANYTHING LIKE THIS. WHERE THE HELL DO WE EVEN START?
YOU SURE ALL OF THESE ARE LEGITIMATE SIGHTINGS OF WOLVERINE SINCE HIS DEATH, CYPHER?
I MEAN... DEFINE LEGITIMATE.

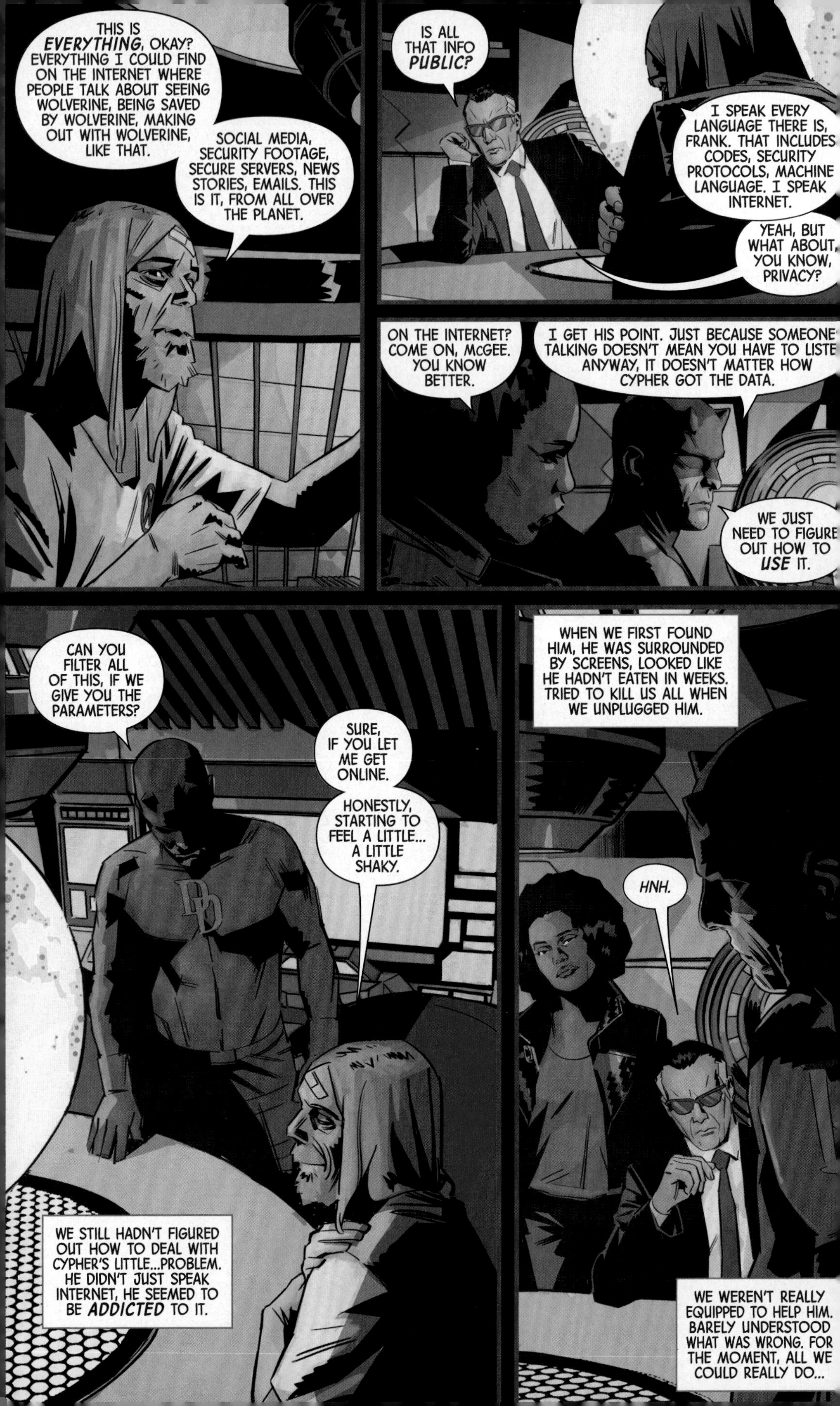

THIS IS EVERYTHING, OKAY? EVERYTHING I COULD FIND ON THE INTERNET WHERE PEOPLE TALK ABOUT SEEING WOLVERINE, BEING SAVED BY WOLVERINE, MAKING OUT WITH WOLVERINE, LIKE THAT.
SOCIAL MEDIA, SECURITY FOOTAGE, SECURE SERVERS, NEWS STORIES, EMAILS. THIS IS IT, FROM ALL OVER THE PLANET.
IS ALL THAT INFO PUBLIC?
I SPEAK EVERY LANGUAGE THERE IS, FRANK. THAT INCLUDES CODES, SECURITY PROTOCOLS, MACHINE LANGUAGE. I SPEAK INTERNET.
YEAH, BUT WHAT ABOUT, YOU KNOW, PRIVACY?
ON THE INTERNET? COME ON, McGEE. YOU KNOW BETTER.
I GET HIS POINT. JUST BECAUSE SOMEONE TALKING DOESN'T MEAN YOU HAVE TO LISTE ANYWAY, IT DOESN'T MATTER HOW CYPHER GOT THE DATA.
WE JUST NEED TO FIGURE OUT HOW TO USE IT.
CAN YOU FILTER ALL OF THIS, IF WE GIVE YOU THE PARAMETERS?
SURE, IF YOU LET ME GET ONLINE.
HONESTLY, STARTING TO FEEL A LITTLE... A LITTLE SHAKY.
WE STILL HADN'T FIGURED OUT HOW TO DEAL WITH CYPHER'S LITTLE...PROBLEM. HE DIDN'T JUST SPEAK INTERNET, HE SEEMED TO BE ADDICTED TO IT.
WHEN WE FIRST FOUND HIM, HE WAS SURROUNDED BY SCREENS, LOOKED LIKE HE HADN'T EATEN IN WEEKS. TRIED TO KILL US ALL WHEN WE UNPLUGGED HIM.
HNH.
WE WEREN'T REALLY EQUIPPED TO HELP HIM. BARELY UNDERSTOOD WHAT WAS WRONG. FOR THE MOMENT, ALL WE COULD REALLY DO...

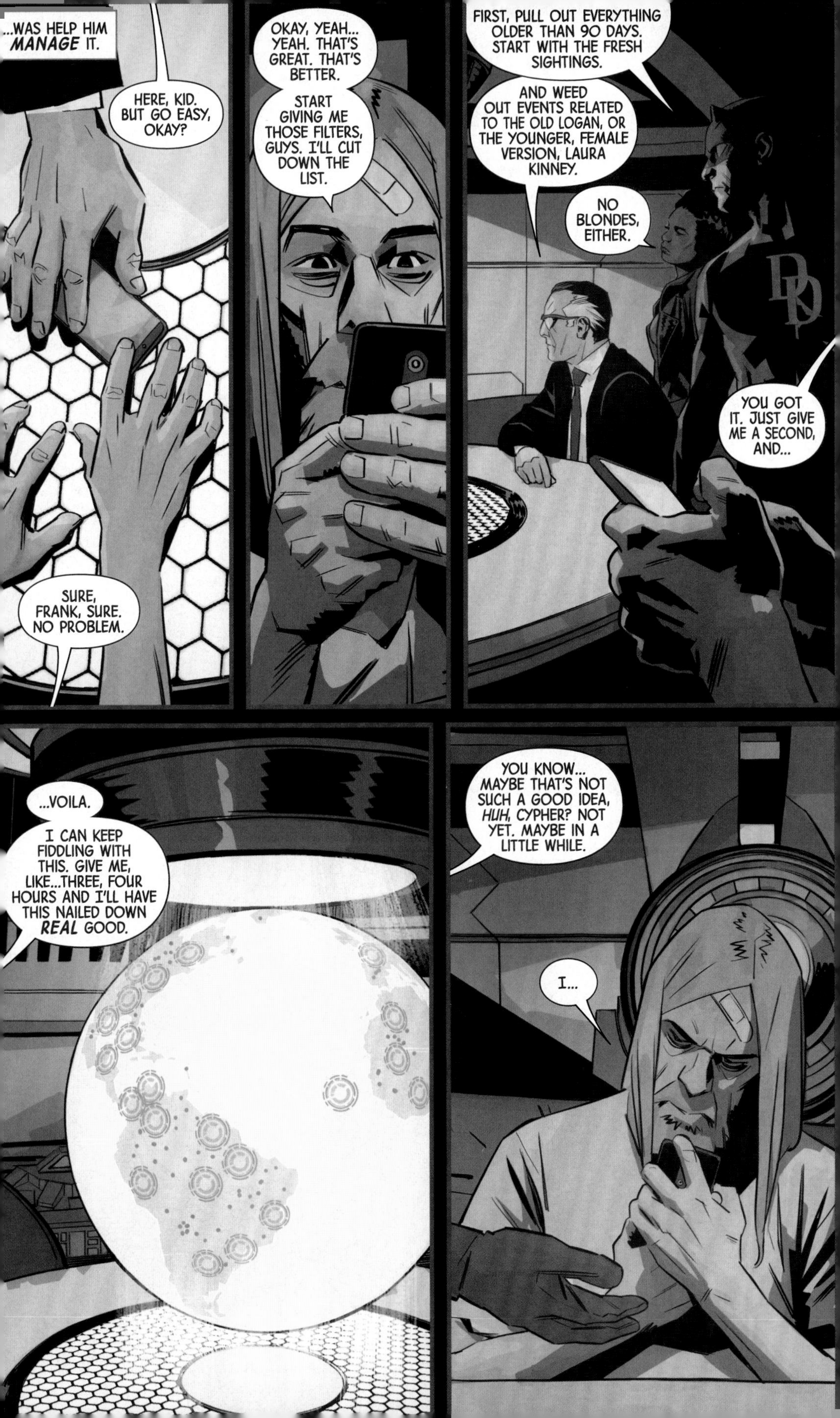
...WAS HELP HIM *MANAGE* IT.
HERE, KID. BUT GO EASY, OKAY?
SURE, FRANK, SURE. NO PROBLEM.
OKAY, YEAH... YEAH. THAT'S GREAT. THAT'S BETTER.
START GIVING ME THOSE FILTERS, GUYS. I'LL CUT DOWN THE LIST.
FIRST, PULL OUT EVERYTHING OLDER THAN 90 DAYS. START WITH THE FRESH SIGHTINGS.
AND WEED OUT EVENTS RELATED TO THE OLD LOGAN, OR THE YOUNGER, FEMALE VERSION, LAURA KINNEY.
NO BLONDES, EITHER.
YOU GOT IT. JUST GIVE ME A SECOND, AND...
...VOILA.
I CAN KEEP FIDDLING WITH THIS. GIVE ME, LIKE...THREE, FOUR HOURS AND I'LL HAVE THIS NAILED DOWN *REAL* GOOD.
YOU KNOW... MAYBE THAT'S NOT SUCH A GOOD IDEA, *HUH*, CYPHER? NOT YET. MAYBE IN A LITTLE WHILE.
I...

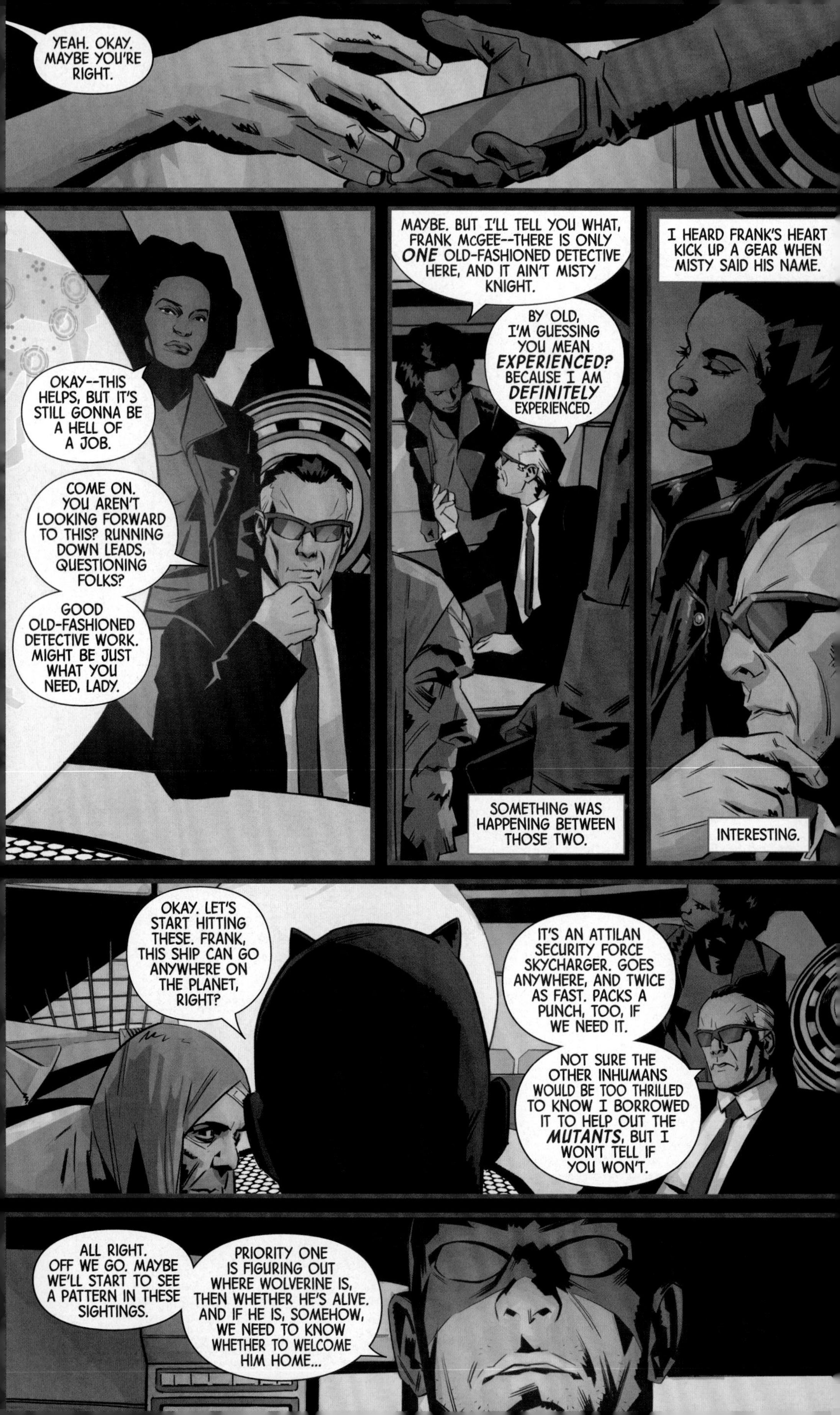
YEAH. OKAY. MAYBE YOU'RE RIGHT.
OKAY--THIS HELPS, BUT IT'S STILL GONNA BE A HELL OF A JOB.
COME ON. YOU AREN'T LOOKING FORWARD TO THIS? RUNNING DOWN LEADS, QUESTIONING FOLKS?
GOOD OLD-FASHIONED DETECTIVE WORK. MIGHT BE JUST WHAT YOU NEED, LADY.
MAYBE. BUT I'LL TELL YOU WHAT, FRANK McGEE--THERE IS ONLY ONE OLD-FASHIONED DETECTIVE HERE, AND IT AIN'T MISTY KNIGHT.
BY OLD, I'M GUESSING YOU MEAN EXPERIENCED? BECAUSE I AM DEFINITELY EXPERIENCED.
SOMETHING WAS HAPPENING BETWEEN THOSE TWO.
I HEARD FRANK'S HEART KICK UP A GEAR WHEN MISTY SAID HIS NAME.
INTERESTING.
OKAY. LET'S START HITTING THESE. FRANK, THIS SHIP CAN GO ANYWHERE ON THE PLANET, RIGHT?
IT'S AN ATTILAN SECURITY FORCE SKYCHARGER. GOES ANYWHERE, AND TWICE AS FAST. PACKS A PUNCH, TOO, IF WE NEED IT.
NOT SURE THE OTHER INHUMANS WOULD BE TOO THRILLED TO KNOW I BORROWED IT TO HELP OUT THE MUTANTS, BUT I WON'T TELL IF YOU WON'T.
ALL RIGHT. OFF WE GO. MAYBE WE'LL START TO SEE A PATTERN IN THESE SIGHTINGS.
PRIORITY ONE IS FIGURING OUT WHERE WOLVERINE IS, THEN WHETHER HE'S ALIVE. AND IF HE IS, SOMEHOW, WE NEED TO KNOW WHETHER TO WELCOME HIM HOME...

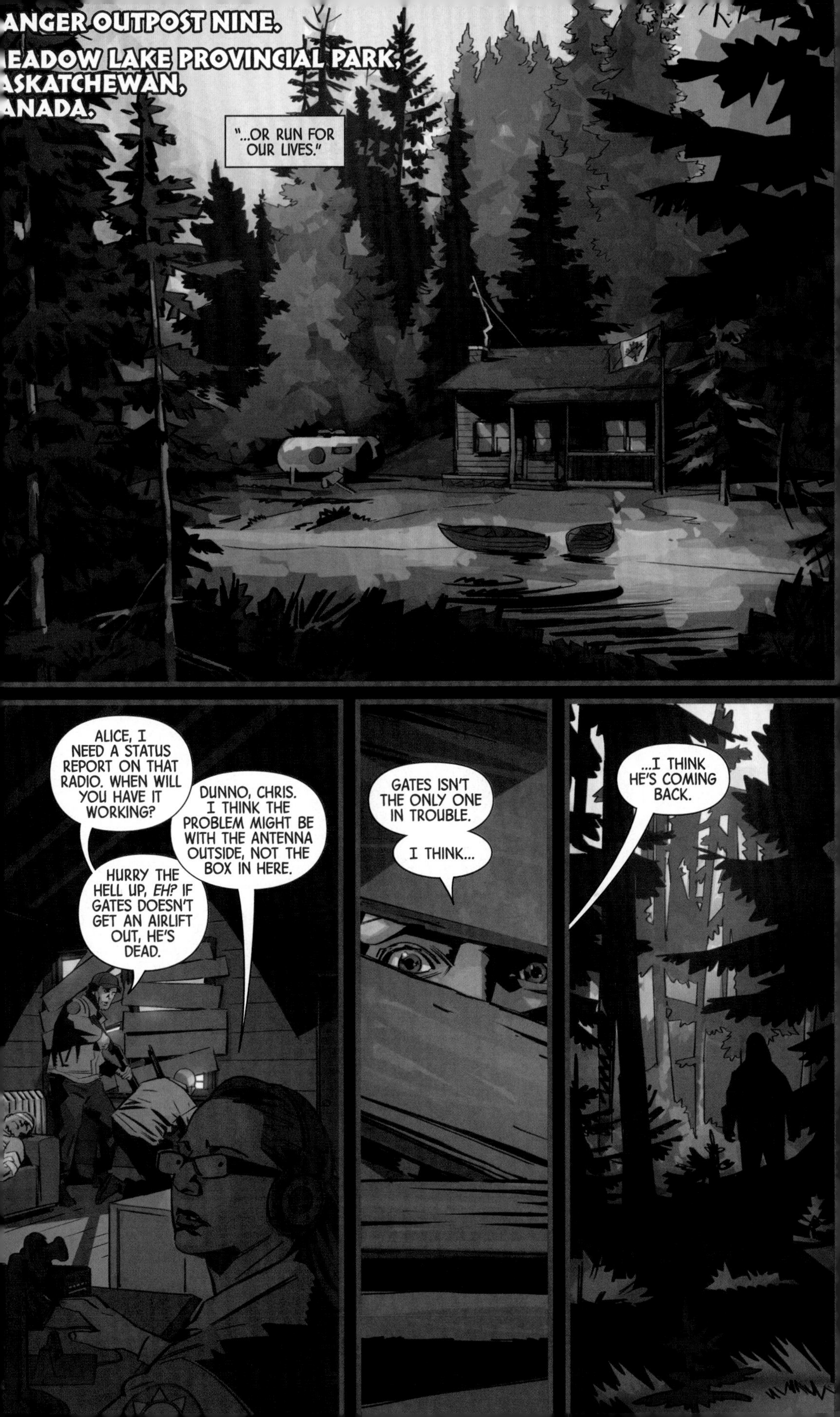
ANGER OUTPOST NINE.
EADOW LAKE PROVINCIAL PARK, ASKATCHEWAN, ANADA.
"...OR RUN FOR OUR LIVES."
ALICE, I NEED A STATUS REPORT ON THAT RADIO. WHEN WILL YOU HAVE IT WORKING?
HURRY THE HELL UP, *EH?* IF GATES DOESN'T GET AN AIRLIFT OUT, HE'S DEAD.
DUNNO, CHRIS. I THINK THE PROBLEM MIGHT BE WITH THE ANTENNA OUTSIDE, NOT THE BOX IN HERE.
GATES ISN'T THE ONLY ONE IN TROUBLE.
I THINK...
...I THINK HE'S COMING BACK.

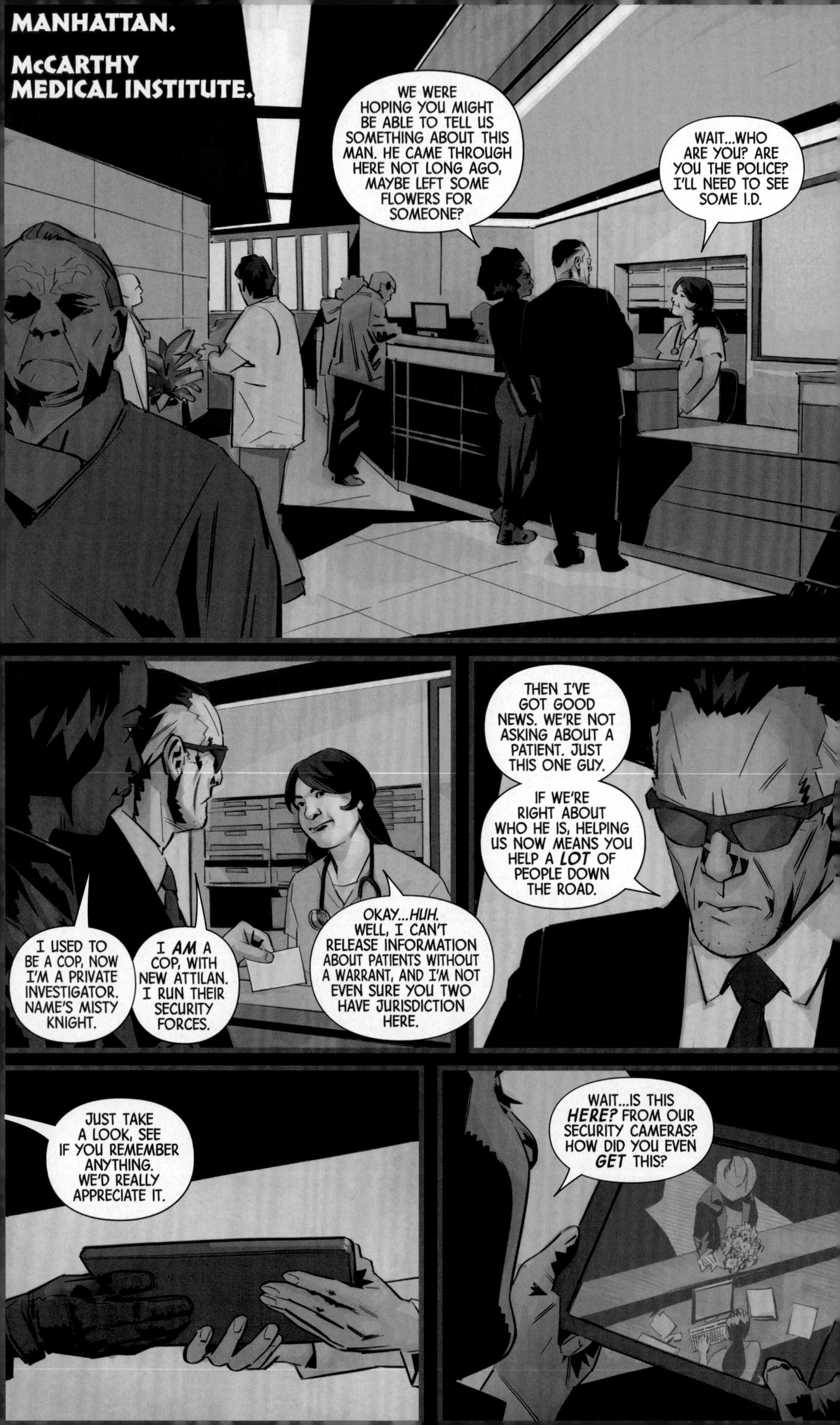
MANHATTAN.
McCARTHY MEDICAL INSTITUTE.
WE WERE HOPING YOU MIGHT BE ABLE TO TELL US SOMETHING ABOUT THIS MAN. HE CAME THROUGH HERE NOT LONG AGO, MAYBE LEFT SOME FLOWERS FOR SOMEONE?
WAIT...WHO ARE YOU? ARE YOU THE POLICE? I'LL NEED TO SEE SOME I.D.
I USED TO BE A COP, NOW I'M A PRIVATE INVESTIGATOR. NAME'S MISTY KNIGHT.
I *AM* A COP, WITH NEW ATTILAN. I RUN THEIR SECURITY FORCES.
OKAY...*HUH.* WELL, I CAN'T RELEASE INFORMATION ABOUT PATIENTS WITHOUT A WARRANT, AND I'M NOT EVEN SURE YOU TWO HAVE JURISDICTION HERE.
THEN I'VE GOT GOOD NEWS. WE'RE NOT ASKING ABOUT A PATIENT. JUST THIS ONE GUY.
IF WE'RE RIGHT ABOUT WHO HE IS, HELPING US NOW MEANS YOU HELP A *LOT* OF PEOPLE DOWN THE ROAD.
JUST TAKE A LOOK, SEE IF YOU REMEMBER ANYTHING. WE'D REALLY APPRECIATE IT.
WAIT...IS THIS *HERE?* FROM OUR SECURITY CAMERAS? HOW DID YOU EVEN *GET* THIS?

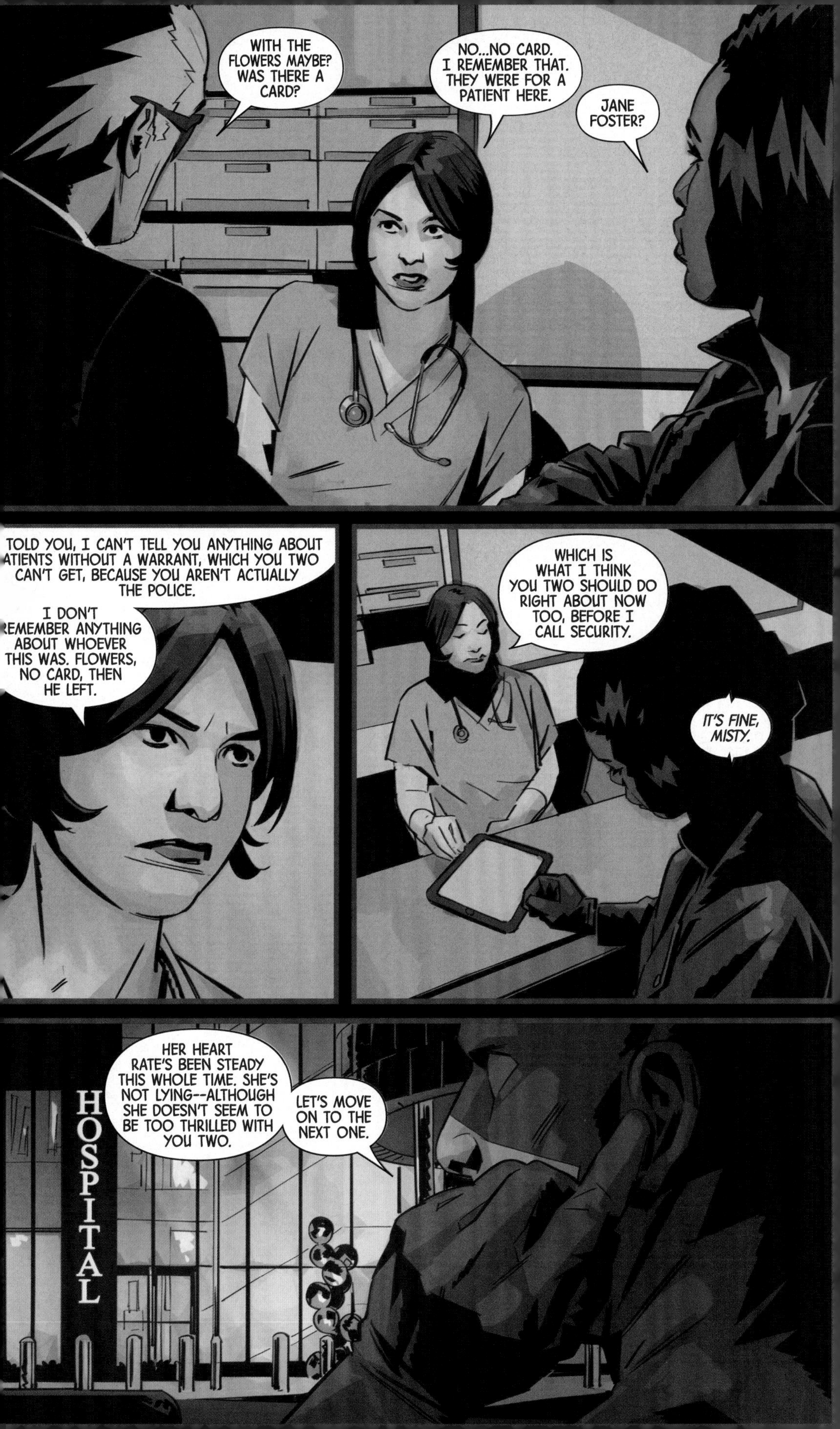

WITH THE FLOWERS MAYBE? WAS THERE A CARD?
NO...NO CARD. I REMEMBER THAT. THEY WERE FOR A PATIENT HERE.
JANE FOSTER?
TOLD YOU, I CAN'T TELL YOU ANYTHING ABOUT ATIENTS WITHOUT A WARRANT, WHICH YOU TWO CAN'T GET, BECAUSE YOU AREN'T ACTUALLY THE POLICE.
I DON'T REMEMBER ANYTHING ABOUT WHOEVER THIS WAS. FLOWERS, NO CARD, THEN HE LEFT.
WHICH IS WHAT I THINK YOU TWO SHOULD DO RIGHT ABOUT NOW TOO, BEFORE I CALL SECURITY.
IT'S FINE, MISTY.
HOSPITAL
HER HEART RATE'S BEEN STEADY THIS WHOLE TIME. SHE'S NOT LYING--ALTHOUGH SHE DOESN'T SEEM TO BE TOO THRILLED WITH YOU TWO.
LET'S MOVE ON TO THE NEXT ONE.

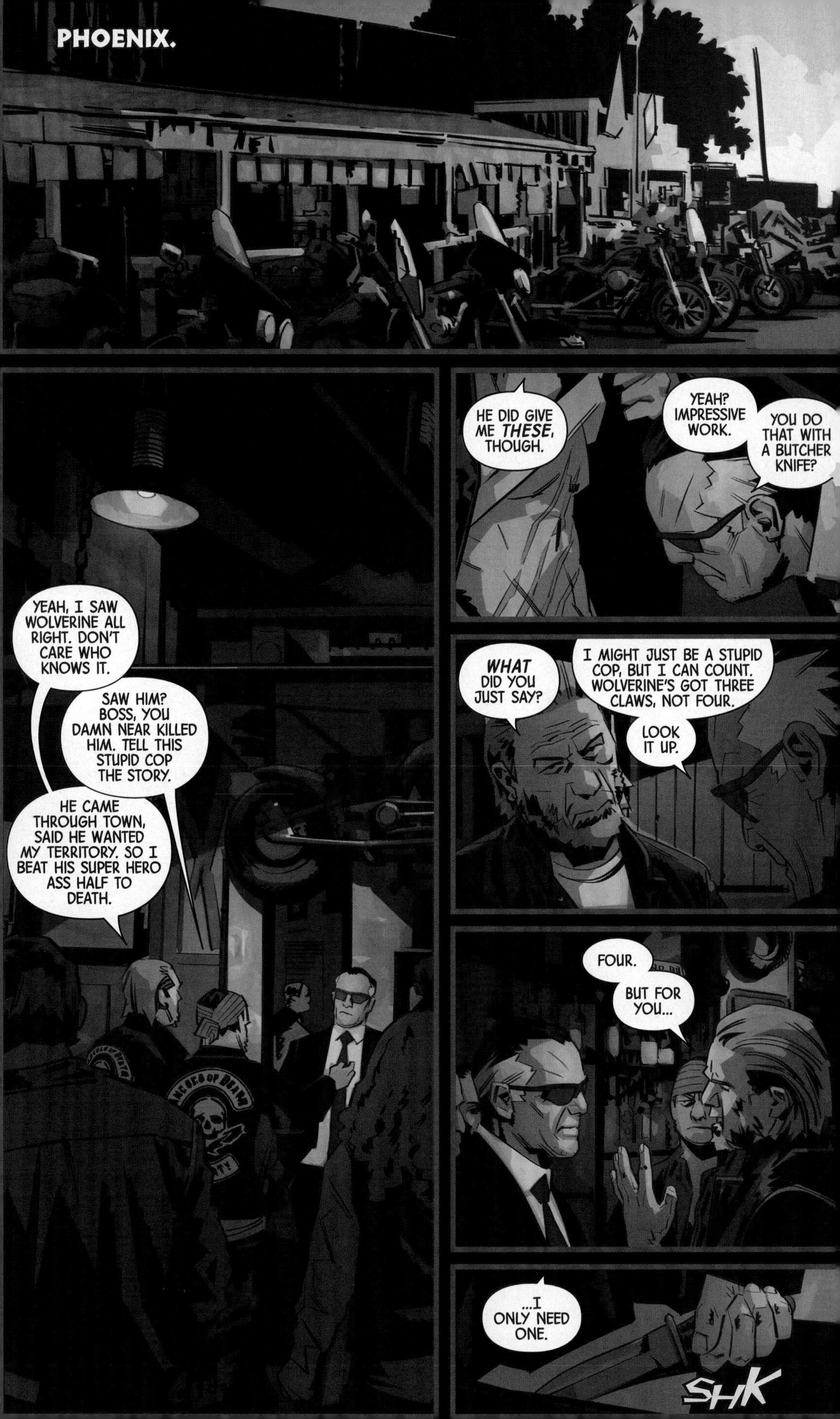
PHOENIX.
YEAH, I SAW WOLVERINE ALL RIGHT. DON'T CARE WHO KNOWS IT.
SAW HIM? BOSS, YOU DAMN NEAR KILLED HIM. TELL THIS STUPID COP THE STORY.
HE CAME THROUGH TOWN, SAID HE WANTED MY TERRITORY. SO I BEAT HIS SUPER HERO ASS HALF TO DEATH.
HE DID GIVE ME THESE, THOUGH.
YEAH? IMPRESSIVE WORK.
YOU DO THAT WITH A BUTCHER KNIFE?
WHAT DID YOU JUST SAY?
I MIGHT JUST BE A STUPID COP, BUT I CAN COUNT. WOLVERINE'S GOT THREE CLAWS, NOT FOUR.
LOOK IT UP.
FOUR.
BUT FOR YOU...
...I ONLY NEED ONE.
SHK

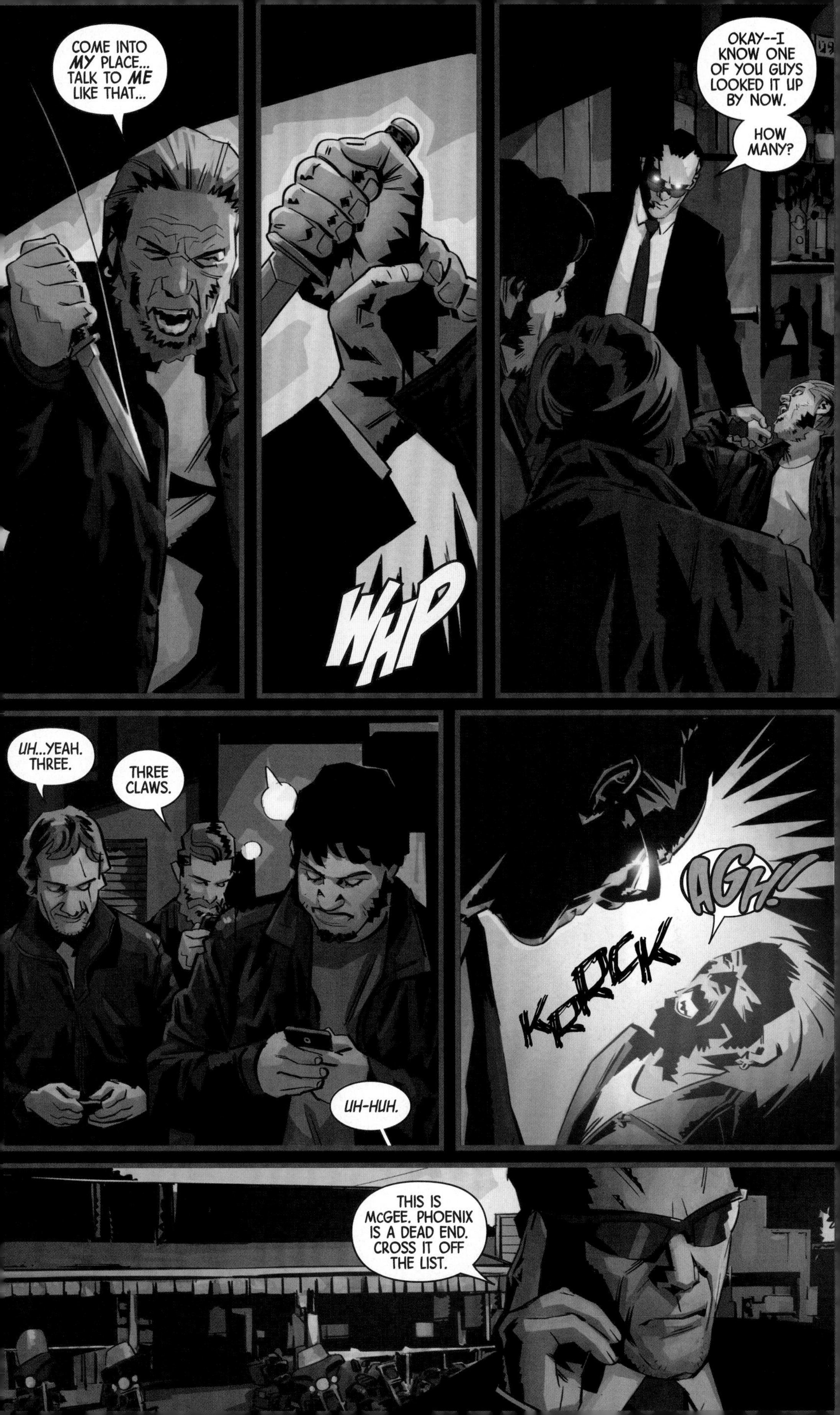
COME INTO *MY* PLACE... TALK TO *ME* LIKE THAT...
WHIP
OKAY--I KNOW ONE OF YOU GUYS LOOKED IT UP BY NOW.
HOW MANY?
UH...YEAH. THREE.
THREE CLAWS.
UH-HUH.
KRRCK
AGH!
THIS IS McGEE. PHOENIX IS A DEAD END. CROSS IT OFF THE LIST.

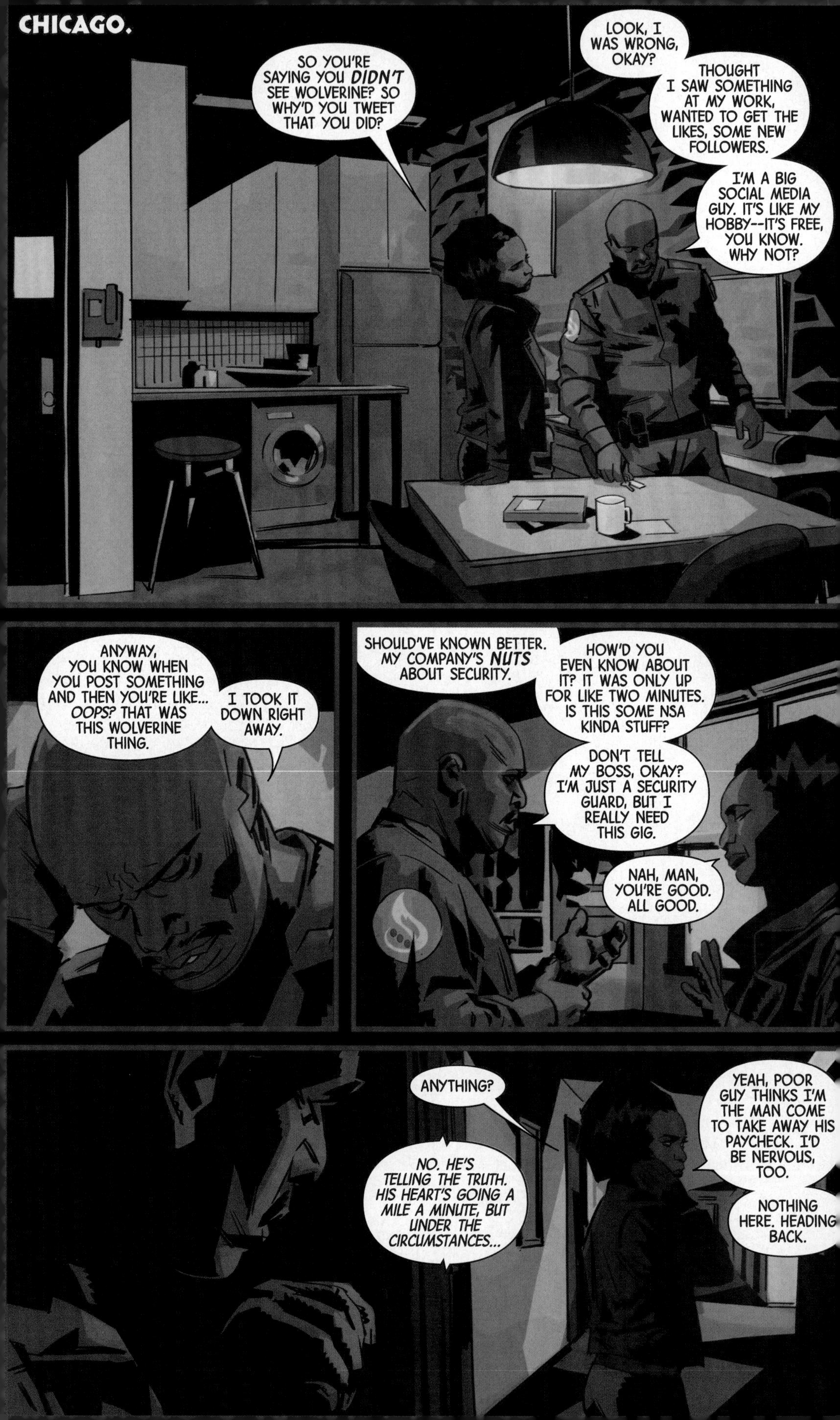
CHICAGO.
SO YOU'RE SAYING YOU DIDN'T SEE WOLVERINE? SO WHY'D YOU TWEET THAT YOU DID?
LOOK, I WAS WRONG, OKAY?
THOUGHT I SAW SOMETHING AT MY WORK, WANTED TO GET THE LIKES, SOME NEW FOLLOWERS.
I'M A BIG SOCIAL MEDIA GUY. IT'S LIKE MY HOBBY--IT'S FREE, YOU KNOW. WHY NOT?
ANYWAY, YOU KNOW WHEN YOU POST SOMETHING AND THEN YOU'RE LIKE... OOPS? THAT WAS THIS WOLVERINE THING.
I TOOK IT DOWN RIGHT AWAY.
SHOULD'VE KNOWN BETTER. MY COMPANY'S NUTS ABOUT SECURITY.
HOW'D YOU EVEN KNOW ABOUT IT? IT WAS ONLY UP FOR LIKE TWO MINUTES. IS THIS SOME NSA KINDA STUFF?
DON'T TELL MY BOSS, OKAY? I'M JUST A SECURITY GUARD, BUT I REALLY NEED THIS GIG.
NAH, MAN, YOU'RE GOOD. ALL GOOD.
ANYTHING?
NO. HE'S TELLING THE TRUTH. HIS HEART'S GOING A MILE A MINUTE, BUT UNDER THE CIRCUMSTANCES...
YEAH, POOR GUY THINKS I'M THE MAN COME TO TAKE AWAY HIS PAYCHECK. I'D BE NERVOUS, TOO.
NOTHING HERE. HEADING BACK.

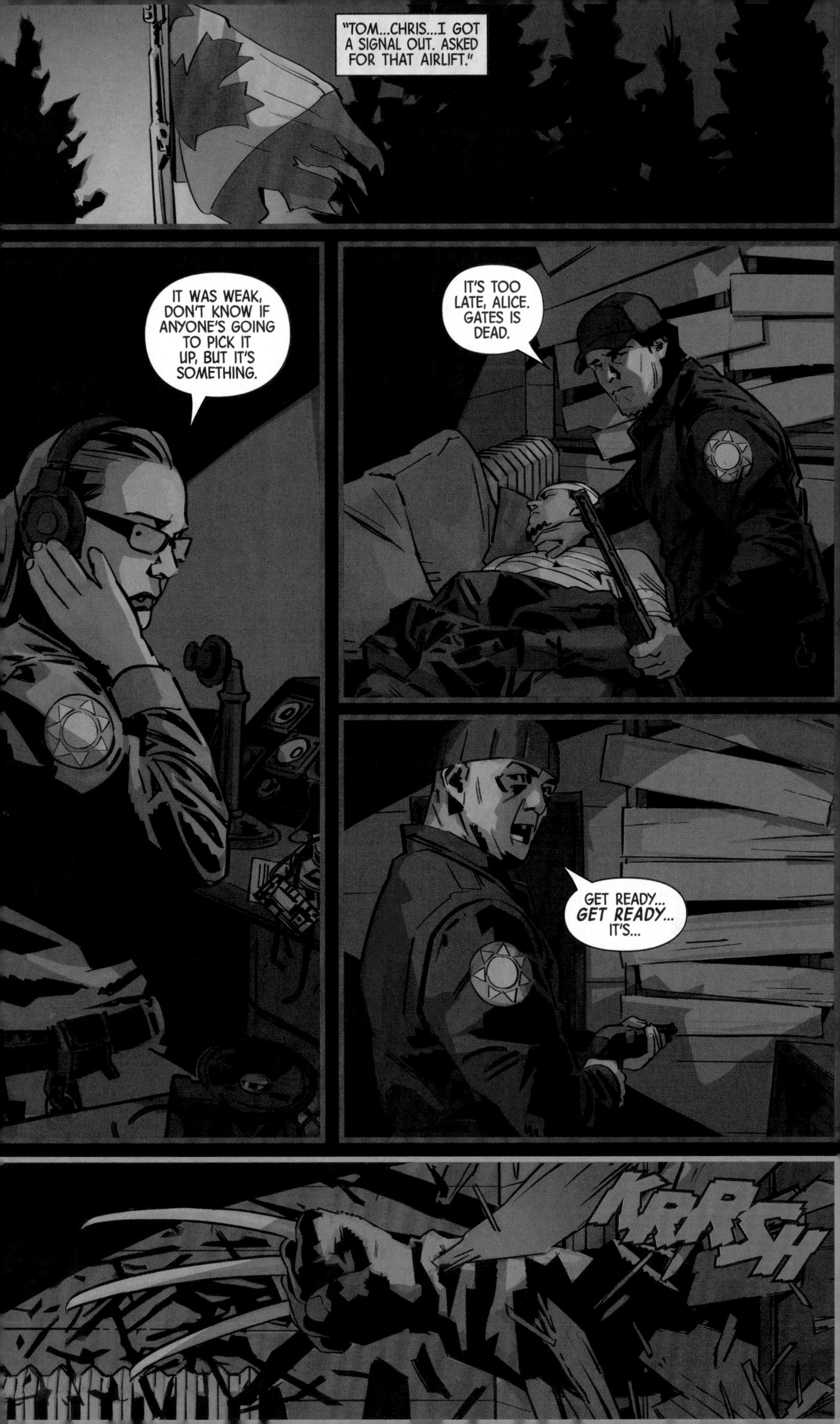
"TOM...CHRIS...I GOT A SIGNAL OUT. ASKED FOR THAT AIRLIFT."
IT WAS WEAK, DON'T KNOW IF ANYONE'S GOING TO PICK IT UP, BUT IT'S SOMETHING.
IT'S TOO LATE, ALICE. GATES IS DEAD.
GET READY... GET READY... IT'S...

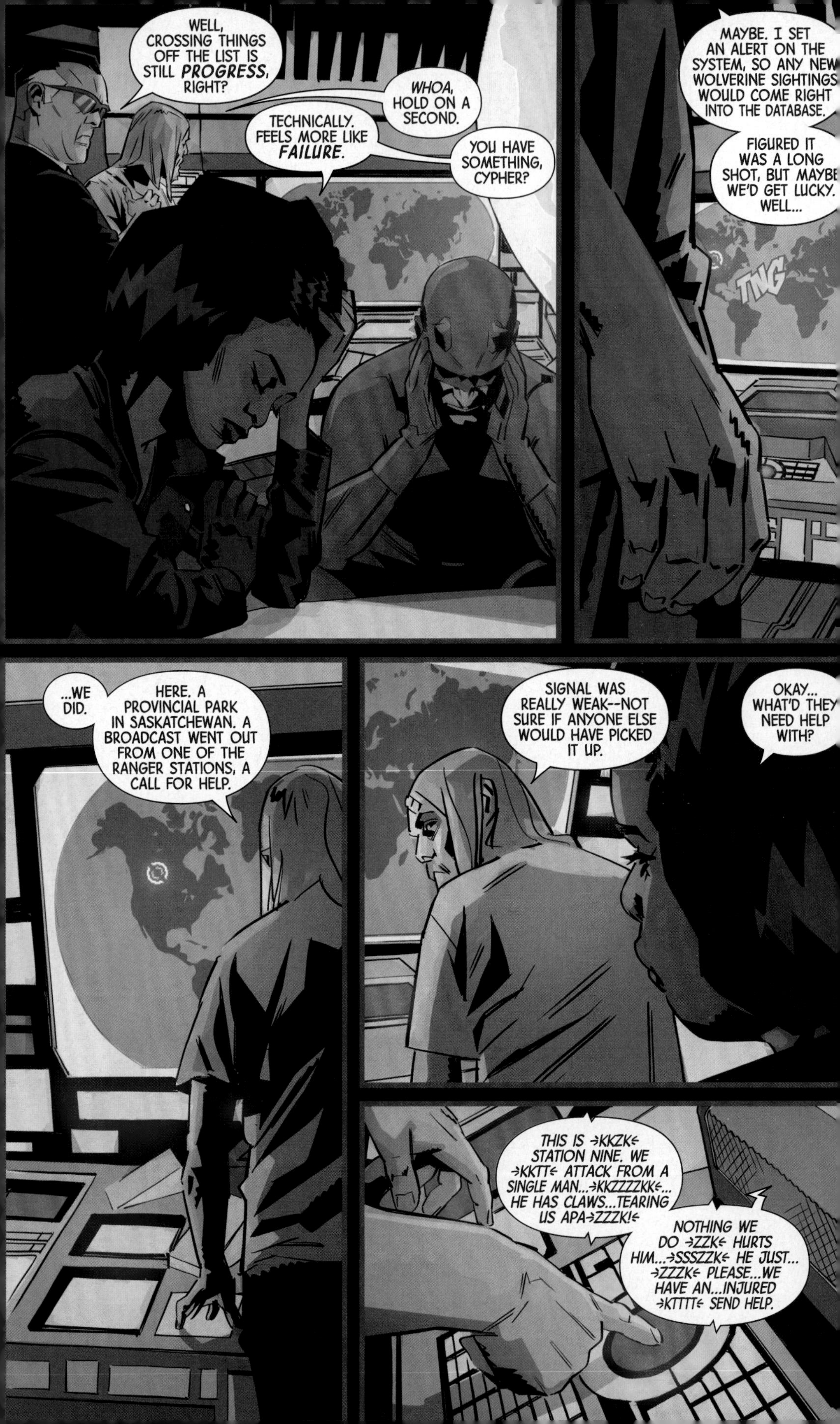
WELL, CROSSING THINGS OFF THE LIST IS STILL PROGRESS, RIGHT?
TECHNICALLY. FEELS MORE LIKE FAILURE.
WHOA, HOLD ON A SECOND.
YOU HAVE SOMETHING, CYPHER?
MAYBE. I SET AN ALERT ON THE SYSTEM, SO ANY NEW WOLVERINE SIGHTINGS WOULD COME RIGHT INTO THE DATABASE.
FIGURED IT WAS A LONG SHOT, BUT MAYBE WE'D GET LUCKY. WELL...
TNG
...WE DID.
HERE. A PROVINCIAL PARK IN SASKATCHEWAN. A BROADCAST WENT OUT FROM ONE OF THE RANGER STATIONS, A CALL FOR HELP.
SIGNAL WAS REALLY WEAK--NOT SURE IF ANYONE ELSE WOULD HAVE PICKED IT UP.
OKAY... WHAT'D THEY NEED HELP WITH?
THIS IS →KKZK← STATION NINE. WE →KKTT← ATTACK FROM A SINGLE MAN...→KKZZZZKK←... HE HAS CLAWS...TEARING US APA→ZZZK!←
NOTHING WE DO →ZZK← HURTS HIM...→SSSZZK← HE JUST... →ZZZK← PLEASE...WE HAVE AN...INJURED →KTTTT← SEND HELP.

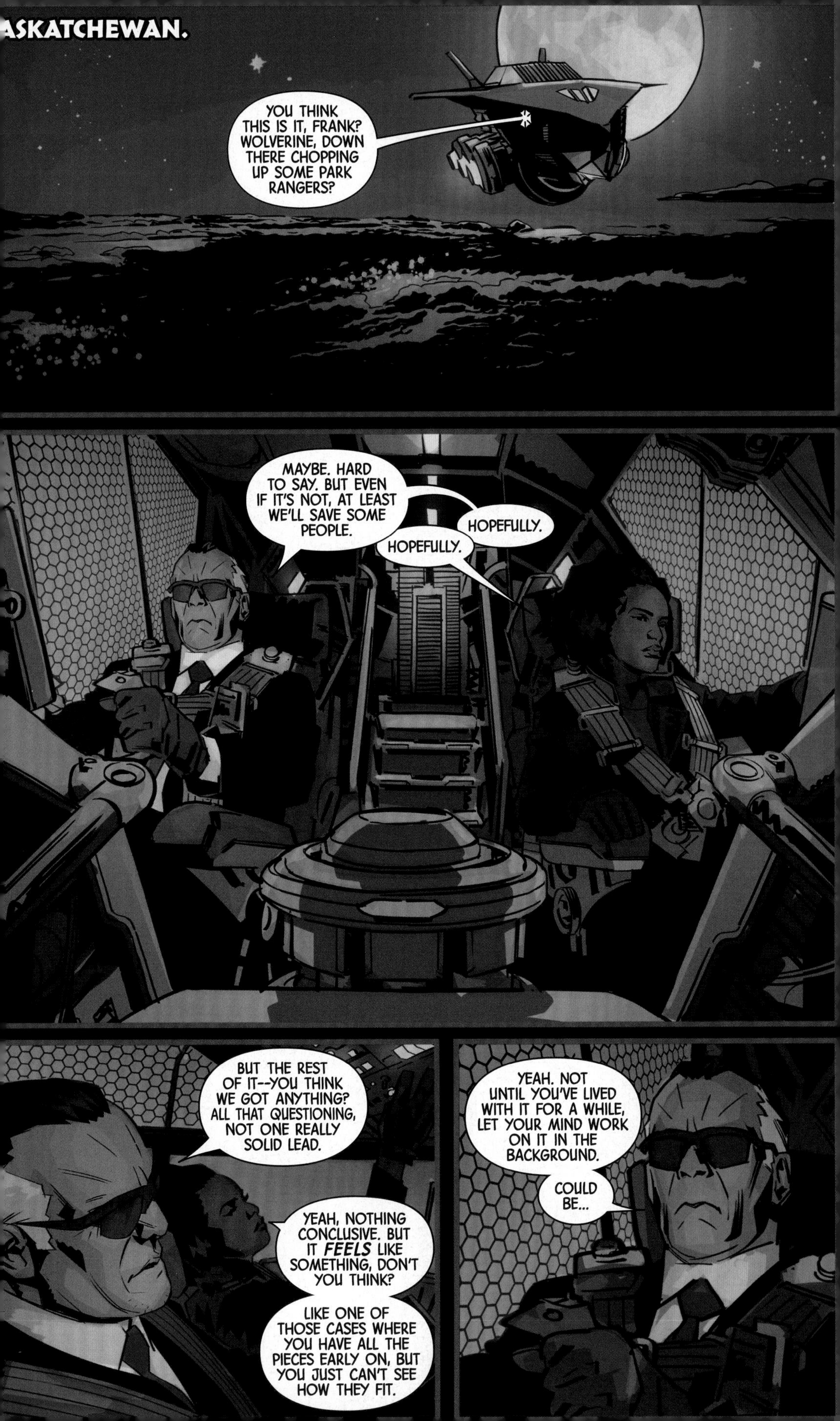
ASKATCHEWAN.
YOU THINK THIS IS IT, FRANK? WOLVERINE, DOWN THERE CHOPPING UP SOME PARK RANGERS?
MAYBE. HARD TO SAY. BUT EVEN IF IT'S NOT, AT LEAST WE'LL SAVE SOME PEOPLE.
HOPEFULLY.
HOPEFULLY.
BUT THE REST OF IT--YOU THINK WE GOT ANYTHING? ALL THAT QUESTIONING, NOT ONE REALLY SOLID LEAD.
YEAH, NOTHING CONCLUSIVE. BUT IT FEELS LIKE SOMETHING, DON'T YOU THINK?
LIKE ONE OF THOSE CASES WHERE YOU HAVE ALL THE PIECES EARLY ON, BUT YOU JUST CAN'T SEE HOW THEY FIT.
YEAH. NOT UNTIL YOU'VE LIVED WITH IT FOR A WHILE, LET YOUR MIND WORK ON IT IN THE BACKGROUND.
COULD BE...

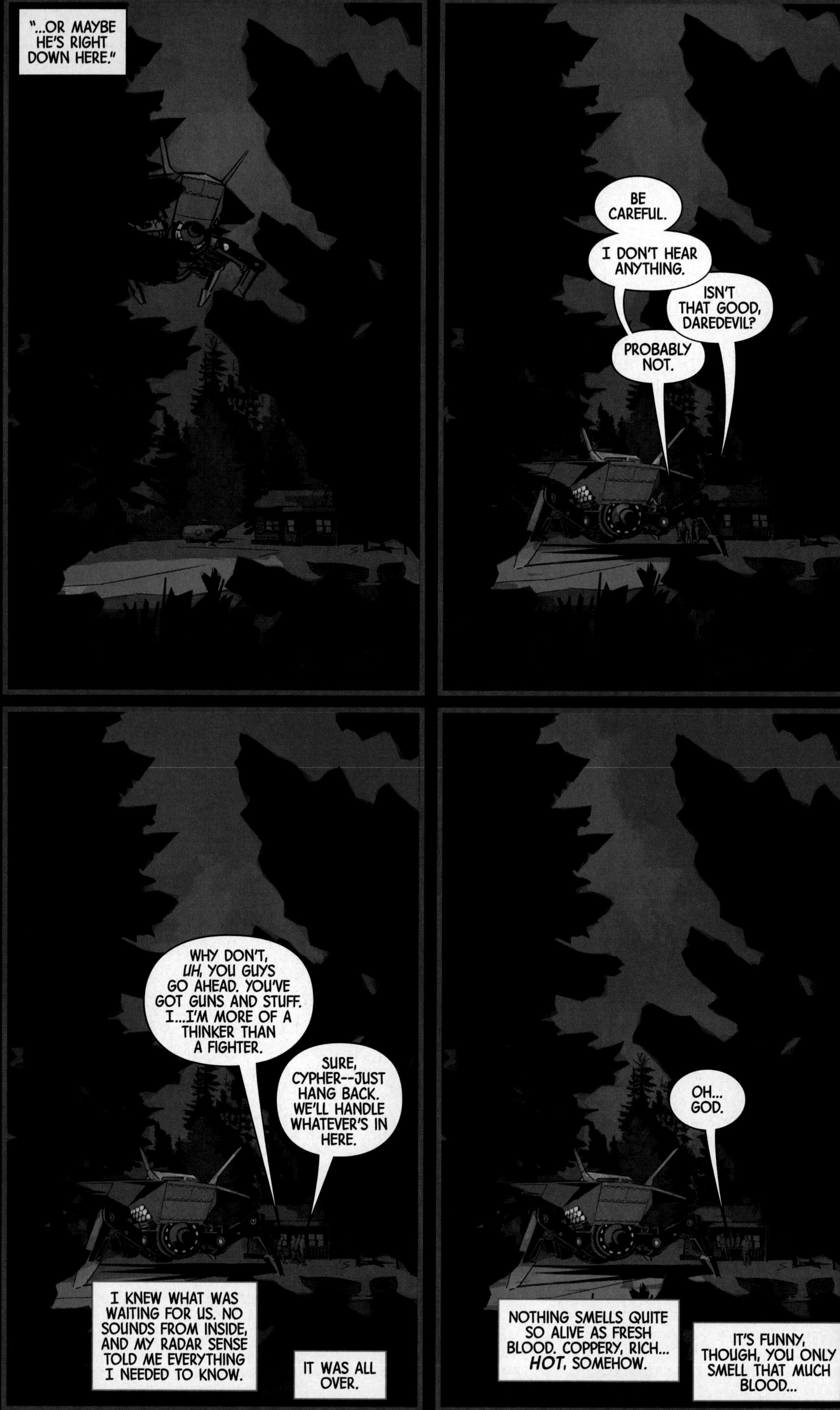
"...OR MAYBE HE'S RIGHT DOWN HERE."
BE CAREFUL.
I DON'T HEAR ANYTHING.
ISN'T THAT GOOD, DAREDEVIL?
PROBABLY NOT.
WHY DON'T, UH, YOU GUYS GO AHEAD. YOU'VE GOT GUNS AND STUFF. I...I'M MORE OF A THINKER THAN A FIGHTER.
SURE, CYPHER--JUST HANG BACK. WE'LL HANDLE WHATEVER'S IN HERE.
I KNEW WHAT WAS WAITING FOR US. NO SOUNDS FROM INSIDE, AND MY RADAR SENSE TOLD ME EVERYTHING I NEEDED TO KNOW.
IT WAS ALL OVER.
OH... GOD.
NOTHING SMELLS QUITE SO ALIVE AS FRESH BLOOD. COPPERY, RICH... HOT, SOMEHOW.
IT'S FUNNY, THOUGH, YOU ONLY SMELL THAT MUCH BLOOD...

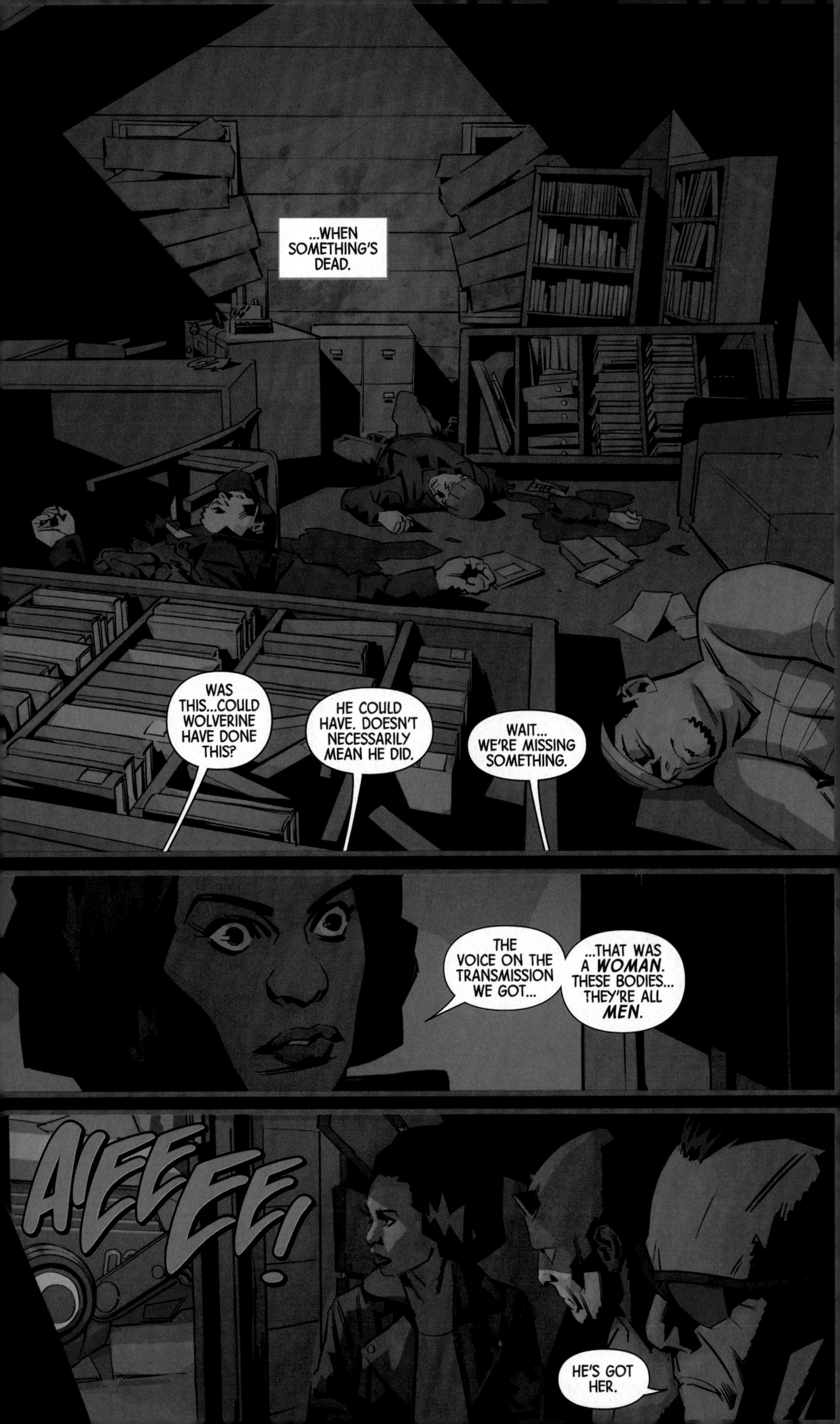
...WHEN SOMETHING'S DEAD.
WAS THIS...COULD WOLVERINE HAVE DONE THIS?
HE COULD HAVE. DOESN'T NECESSARILY MEAN HE DID.
WAIT... WE'RE MISSING SOMETHING.
THE VOICE ON THE TRANSMISSION WE GOT...
...THAT WAS A *WOMAN*. THESE BODIES... THEY'RE ALL *MEN*.
AIEEEE!
HE'S GOT HER.

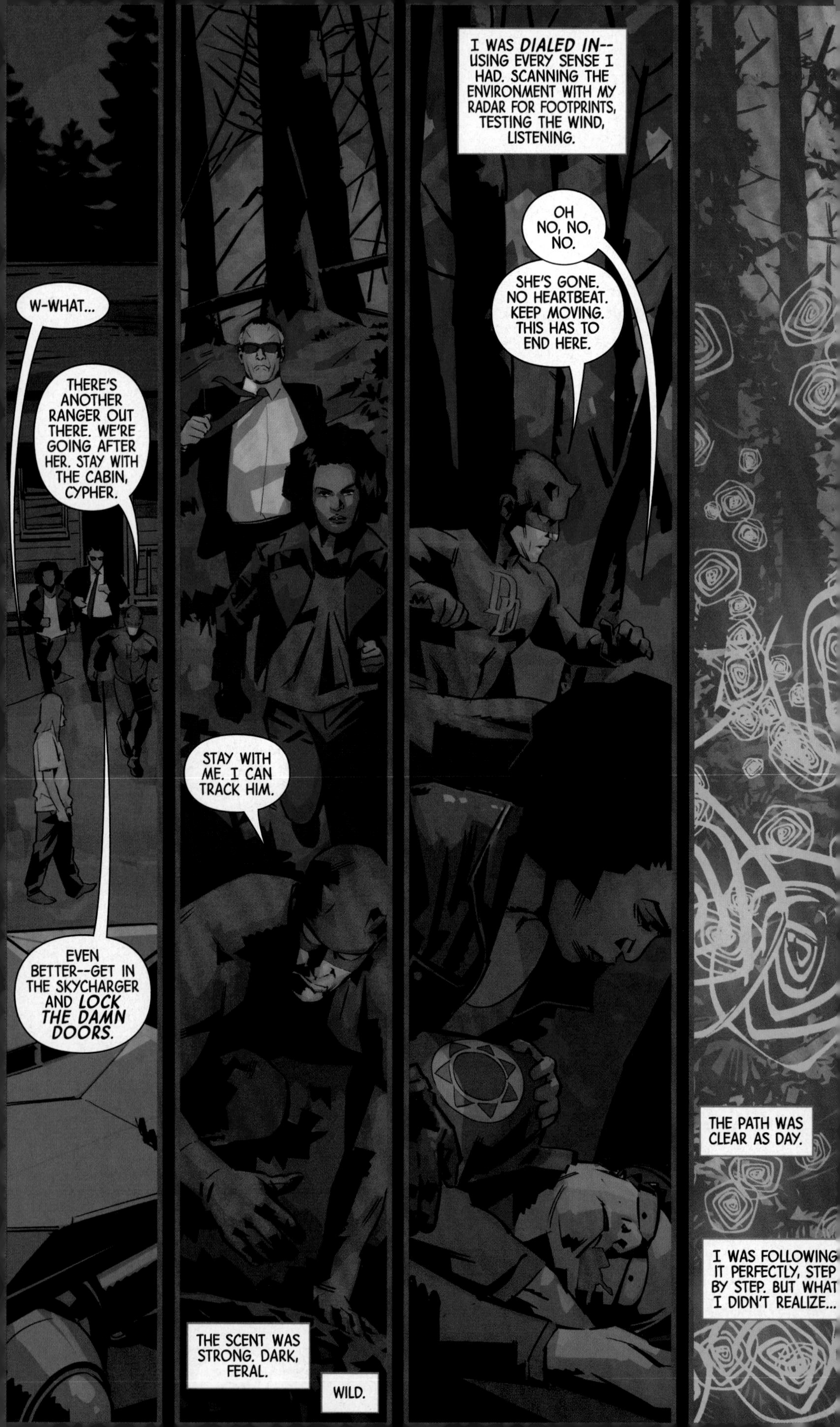
W-WHAT...
THERE'S ANOTHER RANGER OUT THERE. WE'RE GOING AFTER HER. STAY WITH THE CABIN, CYPHER.
EVEN BETTER--GET IN THE SKYCHARGER AND *LOCK THE DAMN DOORS.*
STAY WITH ME. I CAN TRACK HIM.
THE SCENT WAS STRONG. DARK, FERAL.
WILD.
I WAS *DIALED IN*--USING EVERY SENSE I HAD. SCANNING THE ENVIRONMENT WITH MY RADAR FOR FOOTPRINTS, TESTING THE WIND, LISTENING.
OH NO, NO, NO.
SHE'S GONE. NO HEARTBEAT. KEEP MOVING. THIS HAS TO END HERE.
THE PATH WAS CLEAR AS DAY.
I WAS FOLLOWING IT PERFECTLY, STEP BY STEP. BUT WHAT I DIDN'T REALIZE...

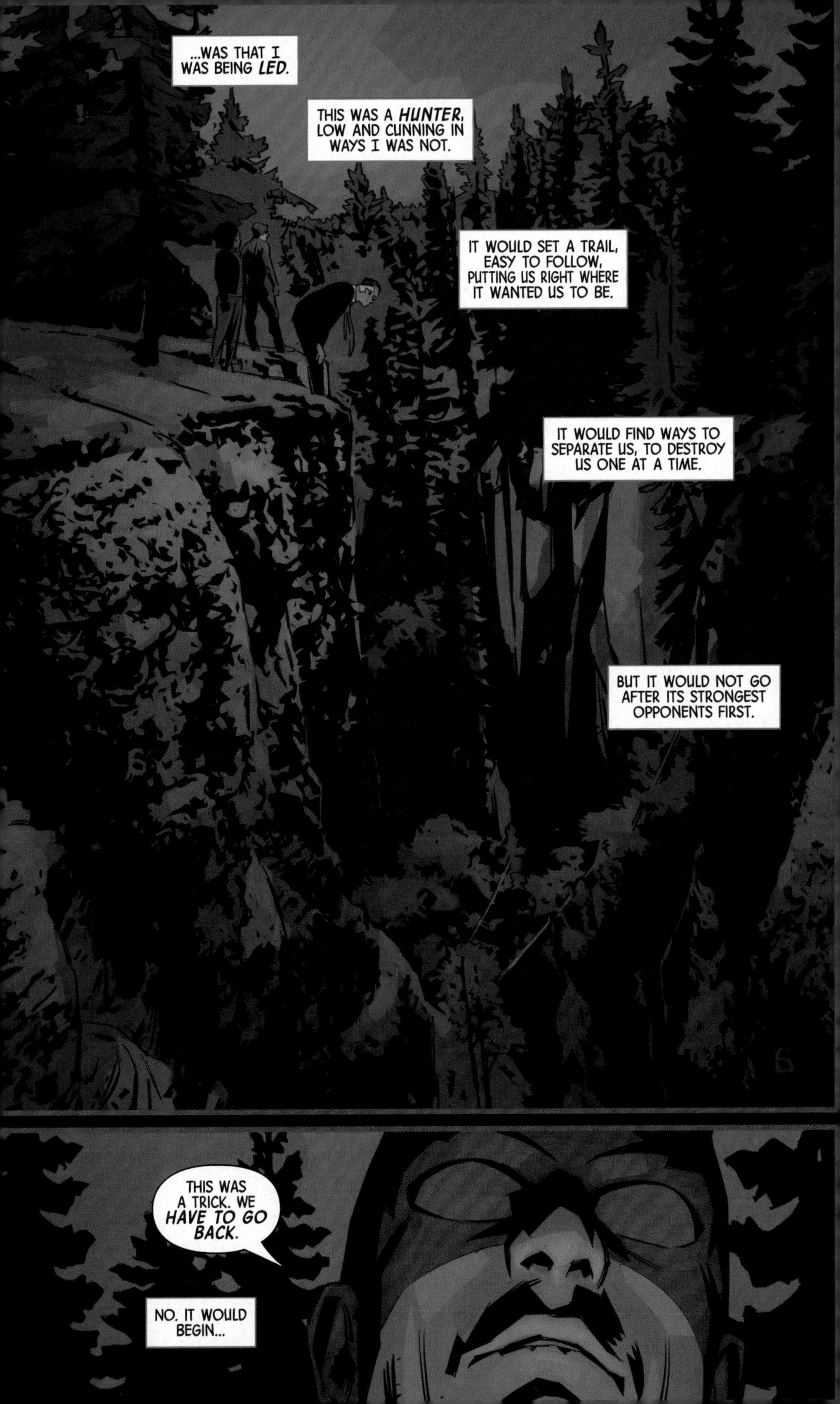
...WAS THAT I WAS BEING *LED*.
THIS WAS A *HUNTER*, LOW AND CUNNING IN WAYS I WAS NOT.
IT WOULD SET A TRAIL, EASY TO FOLLOW, PUTTING US RIGHT WHERE IT WANTED US TO BE.
IT WOULD FIND WAYS TO SEPARATE US, TO DESTROY US ONE AT A TIME.
BUT IT WOULD NOT GO AFTER ITS STRONGEST OPPONENTS FIRST.
THIS WAS A TRICK. WE *HAVE TO GO BACK*.
NO. IT WOULD BEGIN...

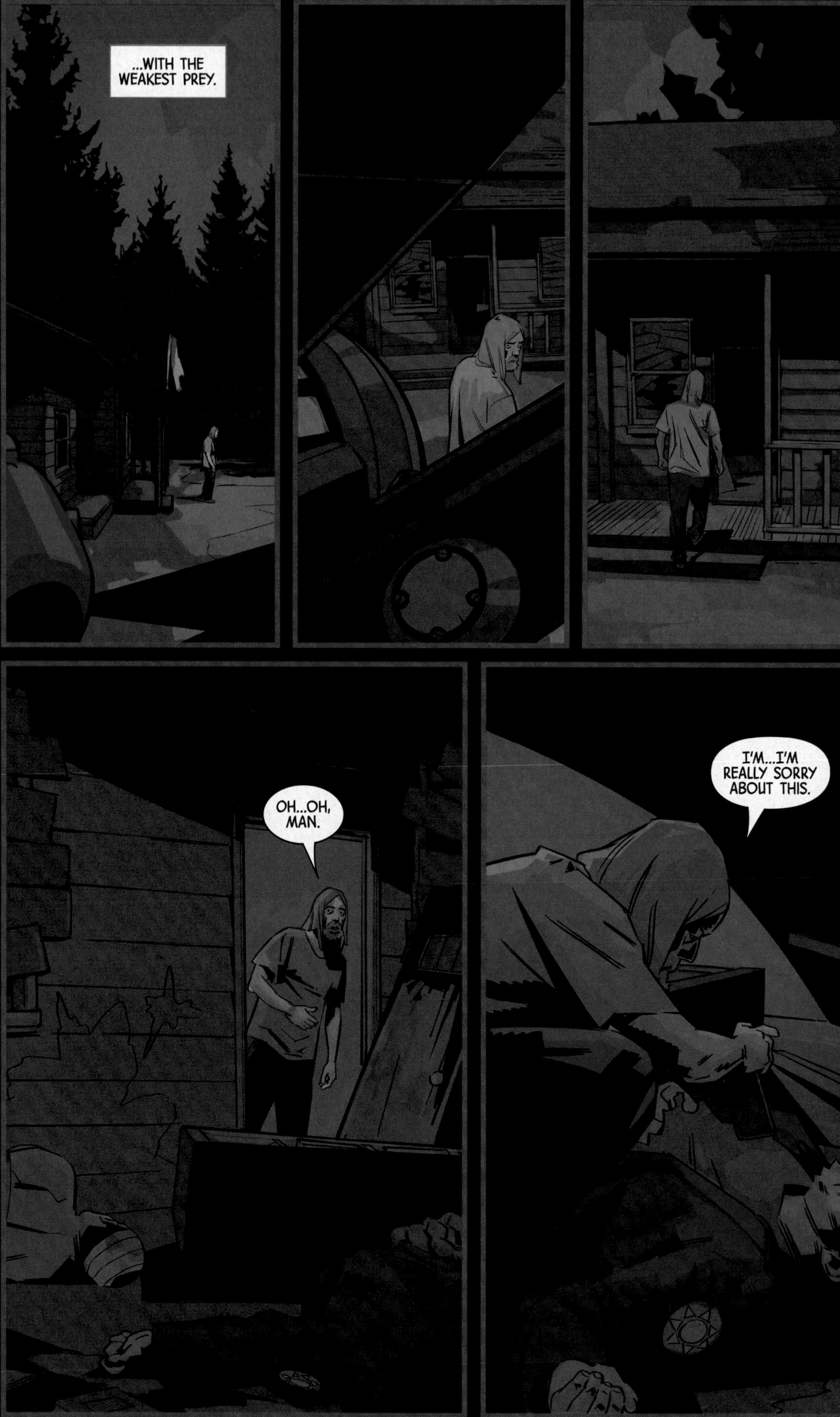
...WITH THE WEAKEST PREY.
OH...OH, MAN.
I'M...I'M REALLY SORRY ABOUT THIS.

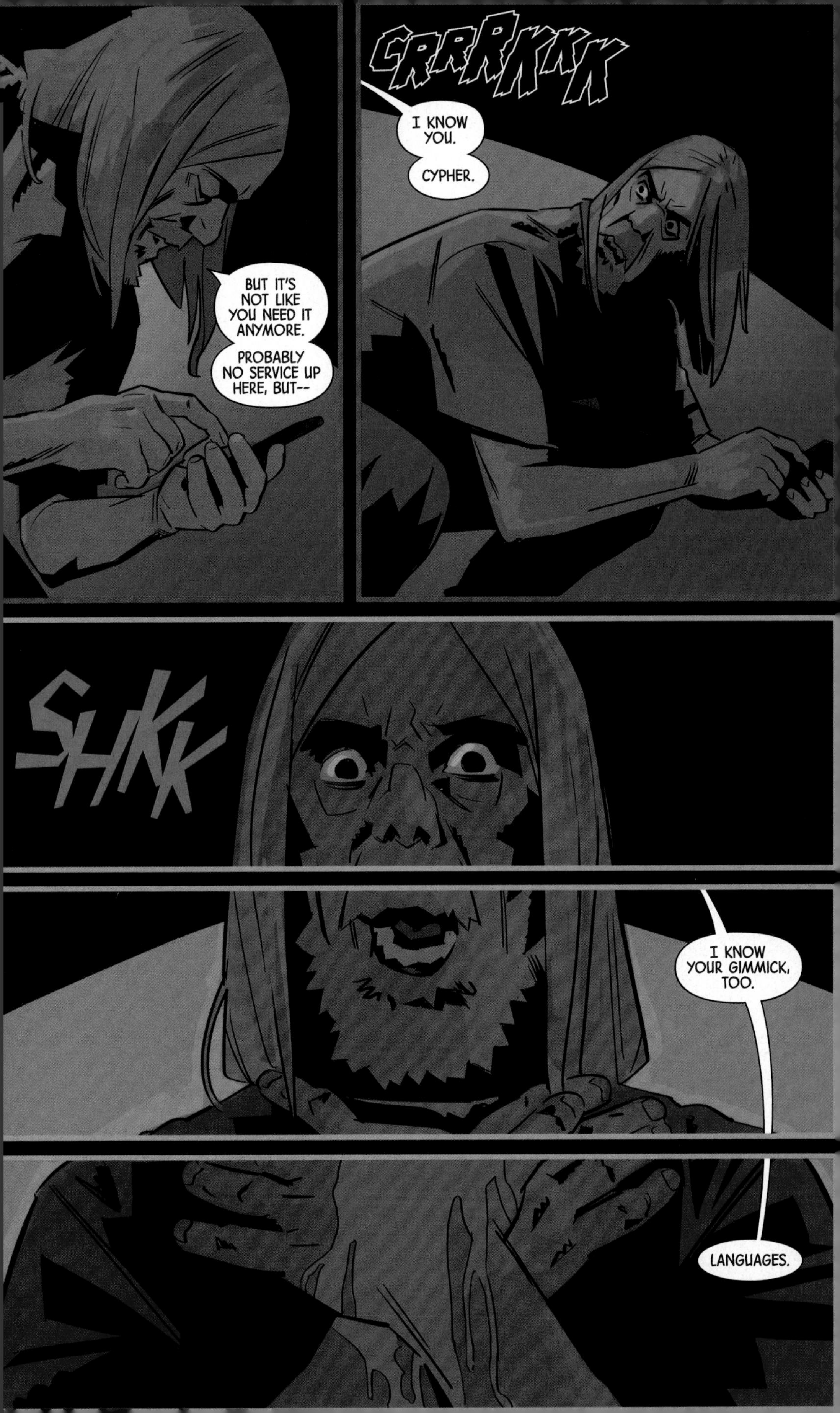
BUT IT'S NOT LIKE YOU NEED IT ANYMORE.
PROBABLY NO SERVICE UP HERE, BUT--
CRRRKKK
I KNOW YOU.
CYPHER.
SHKK
I KNOW YOUR GIMMICK, TOO.
LANGUAGES.

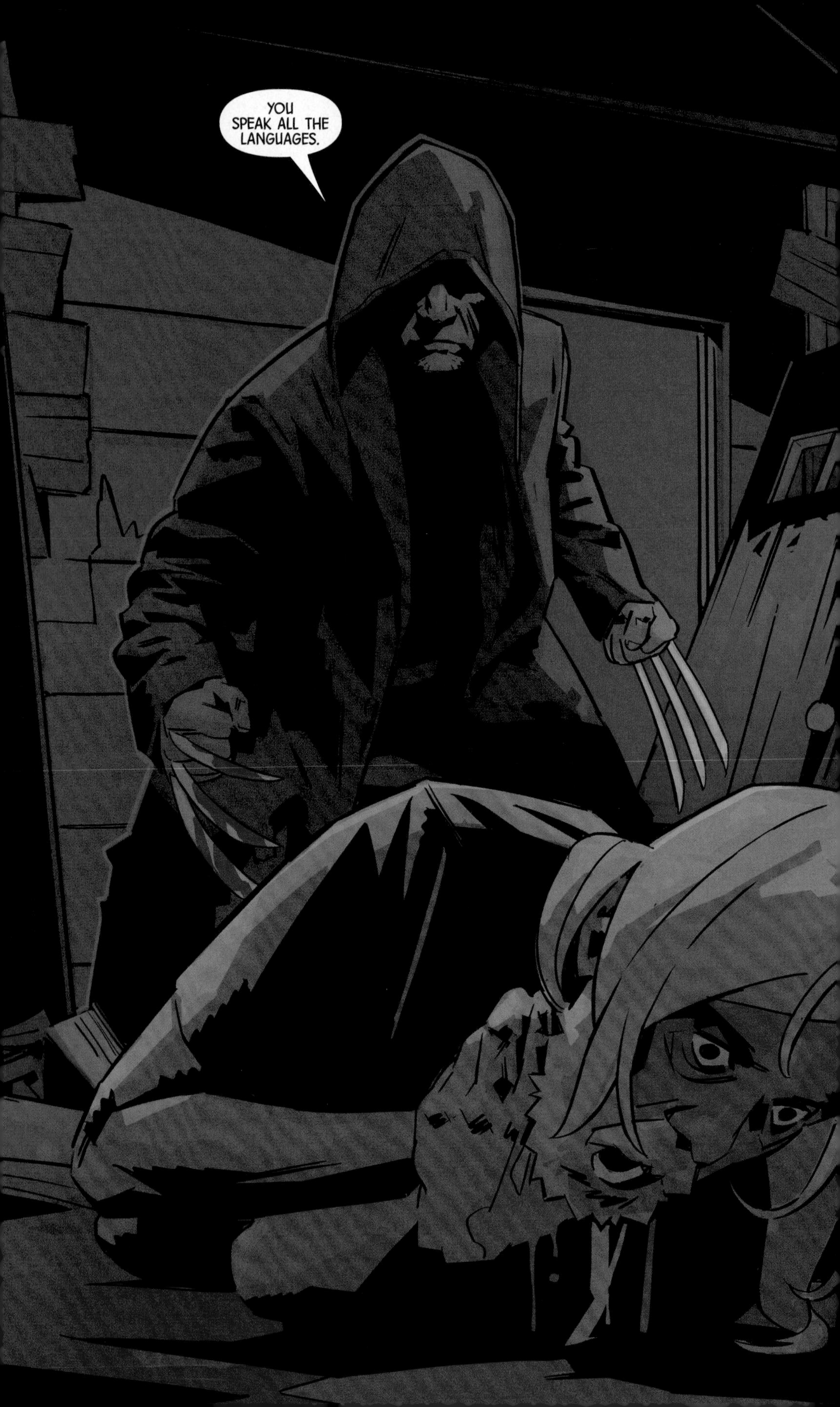
YOU SPEAK ALL THE LANGUAGES.

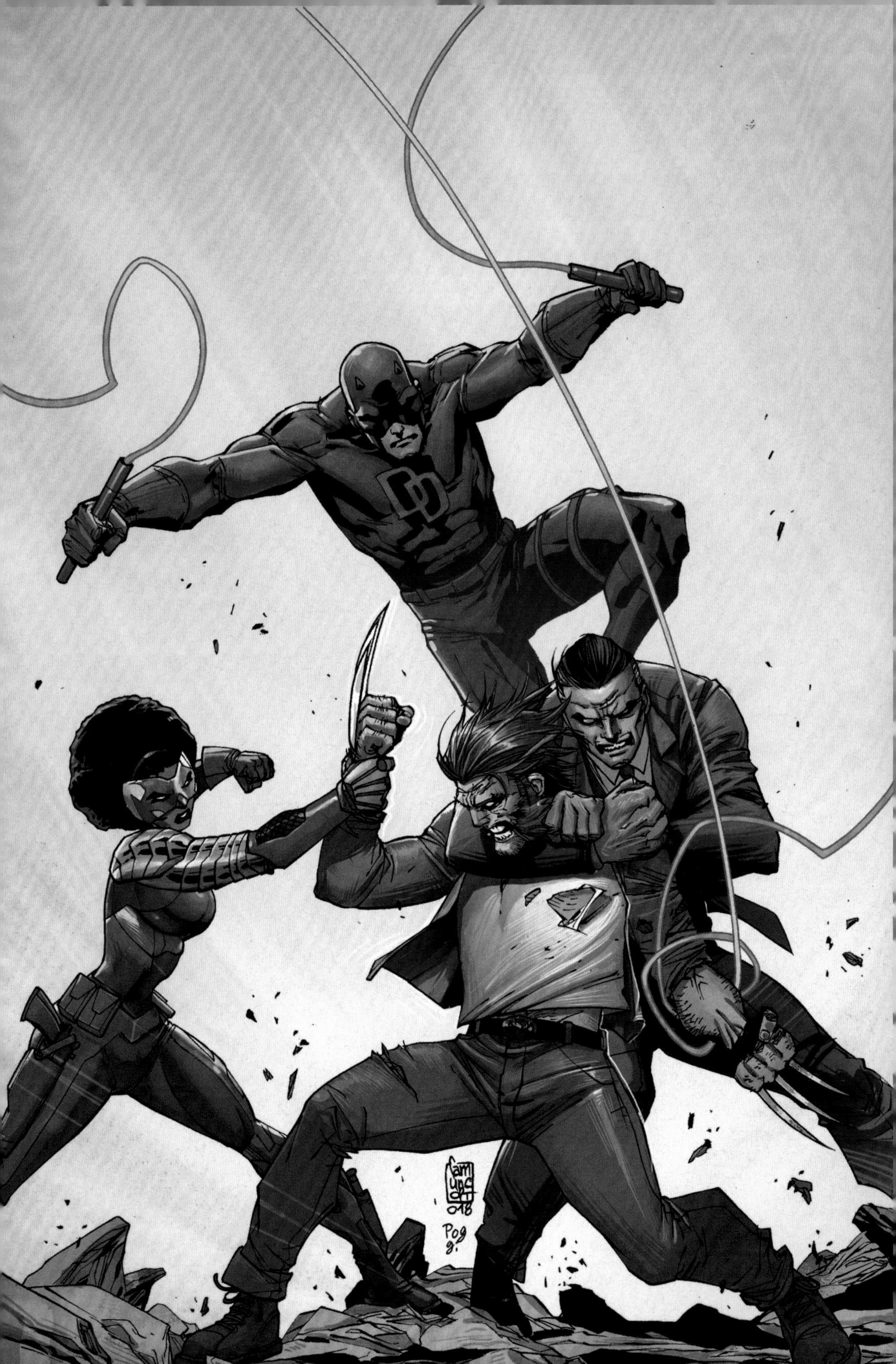

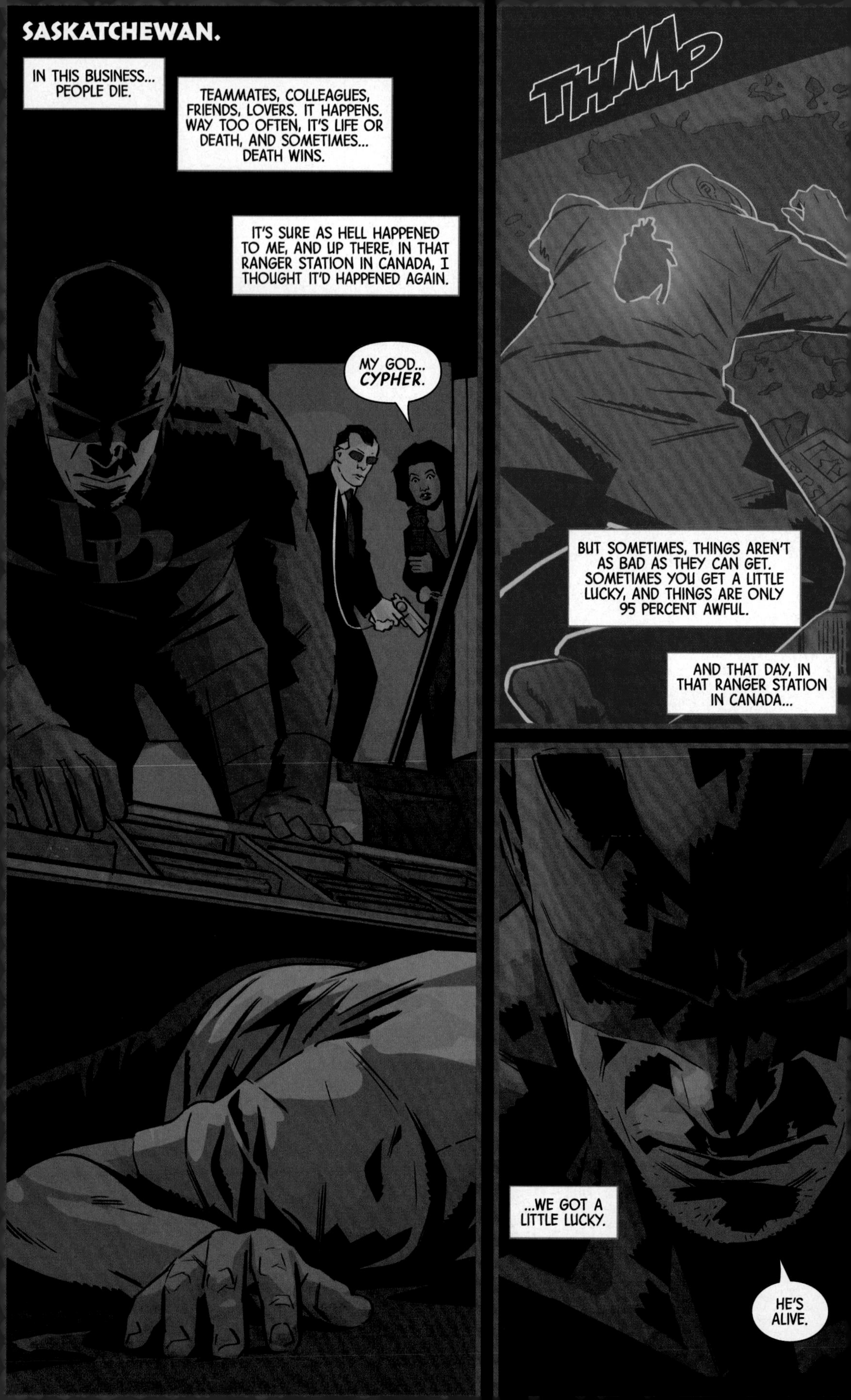
SASKATCHEWAN.
IN THIS BUSINESS... PEOPLE DIE.
TEAMMATES, COLLEAGUES, FRIENDS, LOVERS. IT HAPPENS. WAY TOO OFTEN, IT'S LIFE OR DEATH, AND SOMETIMES... DEATH WINS.
IT'S SURE AS HELL HAPPENED TO ME, AND UP THERE, IN THAT RANGER STATION IN CANADA, I THOUGHT IT'D HAPPENED AGAIN.
MY GOD... CYPHER.
THMP
BUT SOMETIMES, THINGS AREN'T AS BAD AS THEY CAN GET. SOMETIMES YOU GET A LITTLE LUCKY, AND THINGS ARE ONLY 95 PERCENT AWFUL.
AND THAT DAY, IN THAT RANGER STATION IN CANADA...
...WE GOT A LITTLE LUCKY.
HE'S ALIVE.

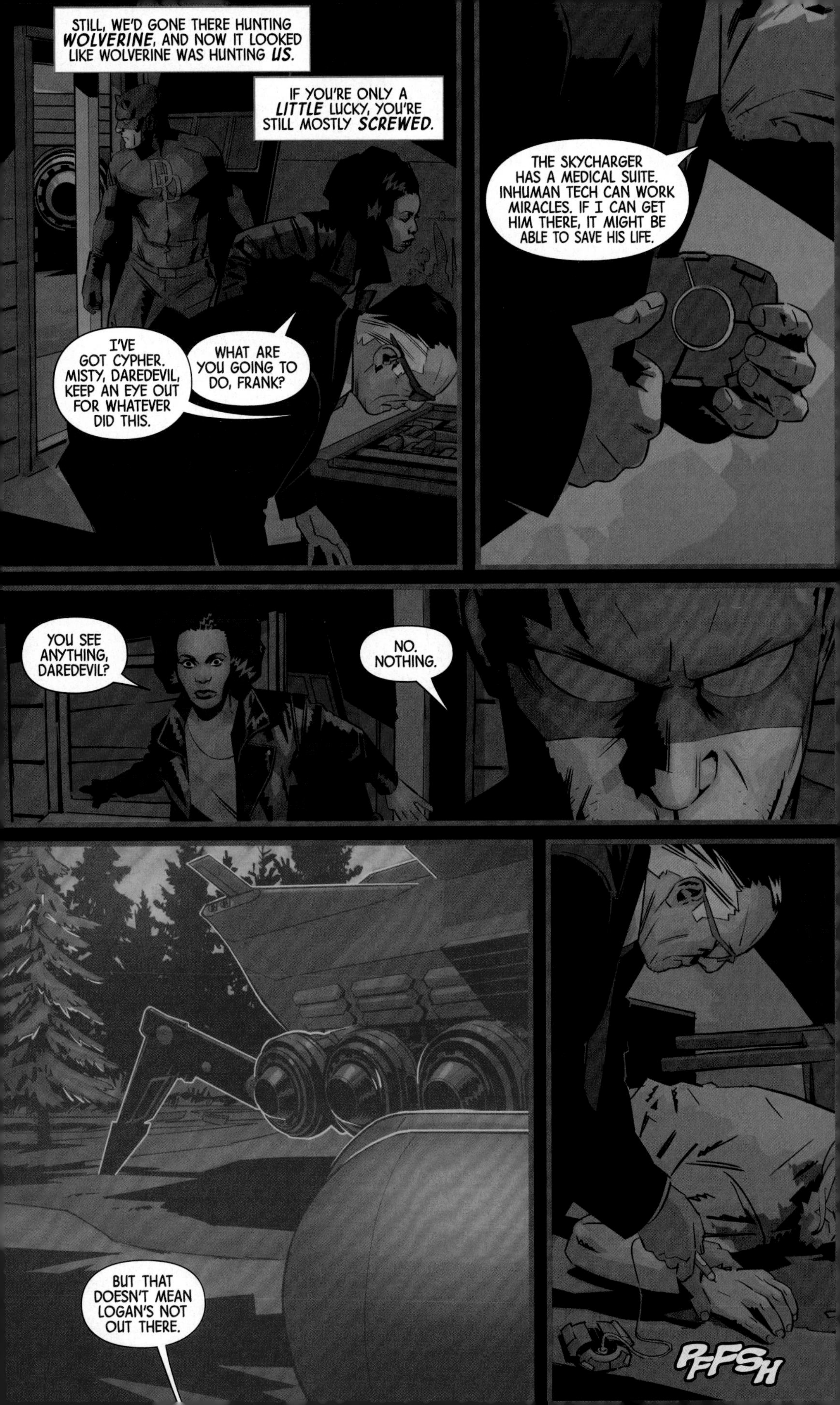
STILL, WE'D GONE THERE HUNTING *WOLVERINE*, AND NOW IT LOOKED LIKE WOLVERINE WAS HUNTING *US*.
IF YOU'RE ONLY A *LITTLE* LUCKY, YOU'RE STILL MOSTLY *SCREWED*.
WHAT ARE YOU GOING TO DO, FRANK?
I'VE GOT CYPHER. MISTY, DAREDEVIL, KEEP AN EYE OUT FOR WHATEVER DID THIS.
THE SKYCHARGER HAS A MEDICAL SUITE. INHUMAN TECH CAN WORK MIRACLES. IF I CAN GET HIM THERE, IT MIGHT BE ABLE TO SAVE HIS LIFE.
YOU SEE ANYTHING, DAREDEVIL?
NO. NOTHING.
BUT THAT DOESN'T MEAN LOGAN'S NOT OUT THERE.
PFFSH

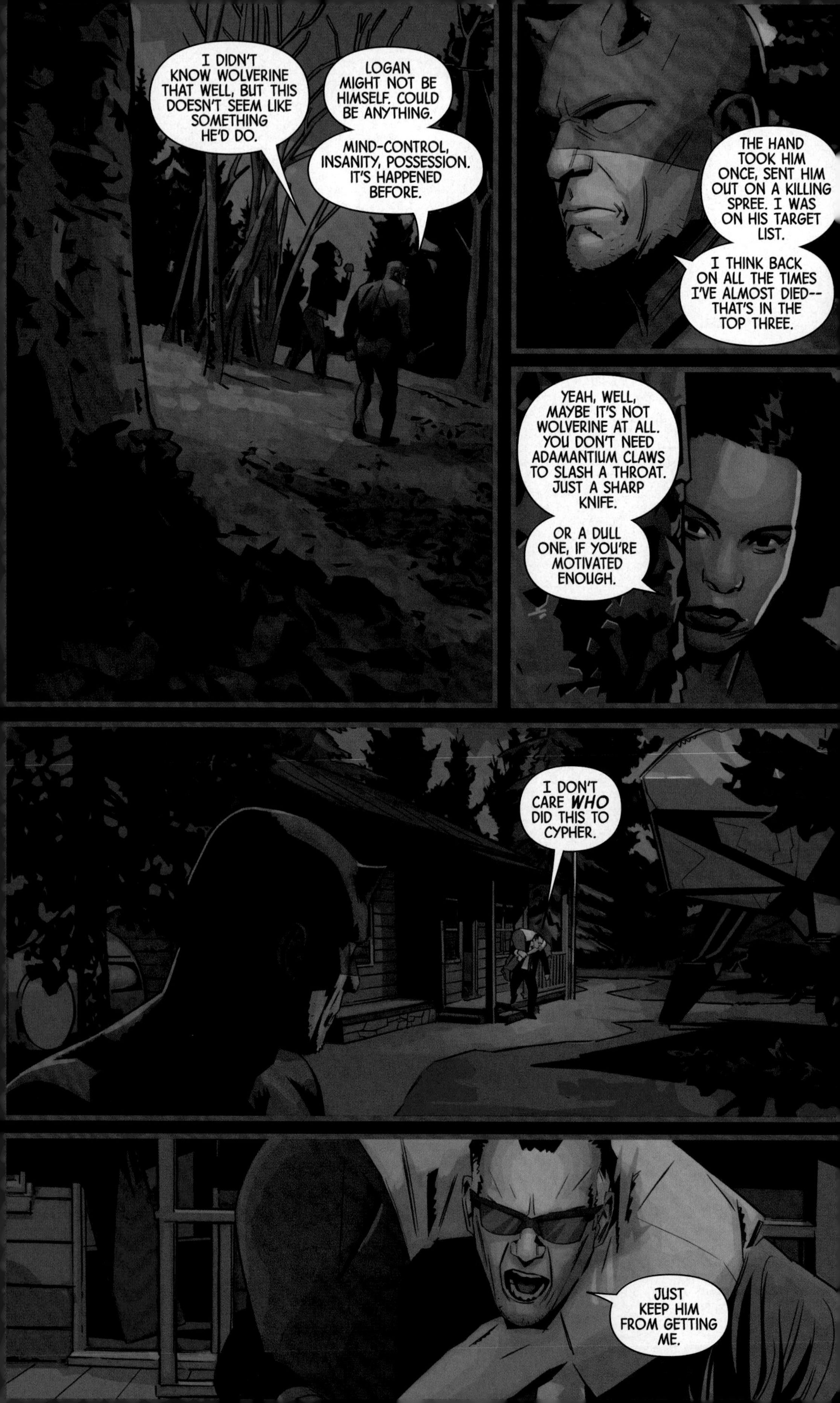

I DIDN'T KNOW WOLVERINE THAT WELL, BUT THIS DOESN'T SEEM LIKE SOMETHING HE'D DO.
LOGAN MIGHT NOT BE HIMSELF. COULD BE ANYTHING.
MIND-CONTROL, INSANITY, POSSESSION. IT'S HAPPENED BEFORE.
THE HAND TOOK HIM ONCE, SENT HIM OUT ON A KILLING SPREE. I WAS ON HIS TARGET LIST.
I THINK BACK ON ALL THE TIMES I'VE ALMOST DIED-- THAT'S IN THE TOP THREE.
YEAH, WELL, MAYBE IT'S NOT WOLVERINE AT ALL. YOU DON'T NEED ADAMANTIUM CLAWS TO SLASH A THROAT. JUST A SHARP KNIFE.
OR A DULL ONE, IF YOU'RE MOTIVATED ENOUGH.
I DON'T CARE *WHO* DID THIS TO CYPHER.
JUST KEEP HIM FROM GETTING ME.

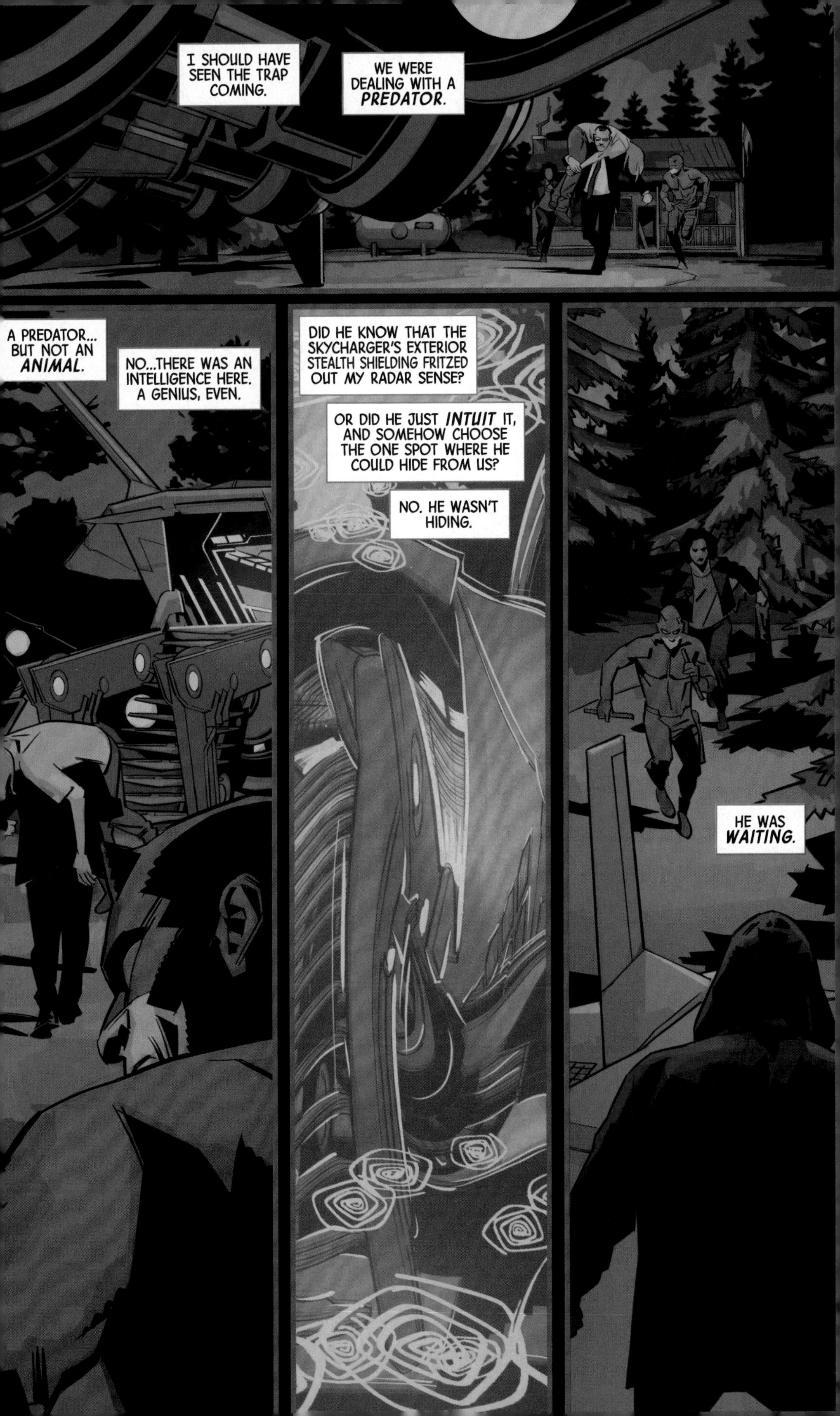
I SHOULD HAVE SEEN THE TRAP COMING.
WE WERE DEALING WITH A *PREDATOR*.
A PREDATOR... BUT NOT AN *ANIMAL*.
NO...THERE WAS AN INTELLIGENCE HERE. A GENIUS, EVEN.
DID HE KNOW THAT THE SKYCHARGER'S EXTERIOR STEALTH SHIELDING FRITZED OUT MY RADAR SENSE?
OR DID HE JUST *INTUIT* IT, AND SOMEHOW CHOOSE THE ONE SPOT WHERE HE COULD HIDE FROM US?
NO. HE WASN'T HIDING.
HE WAS *WAITING*.

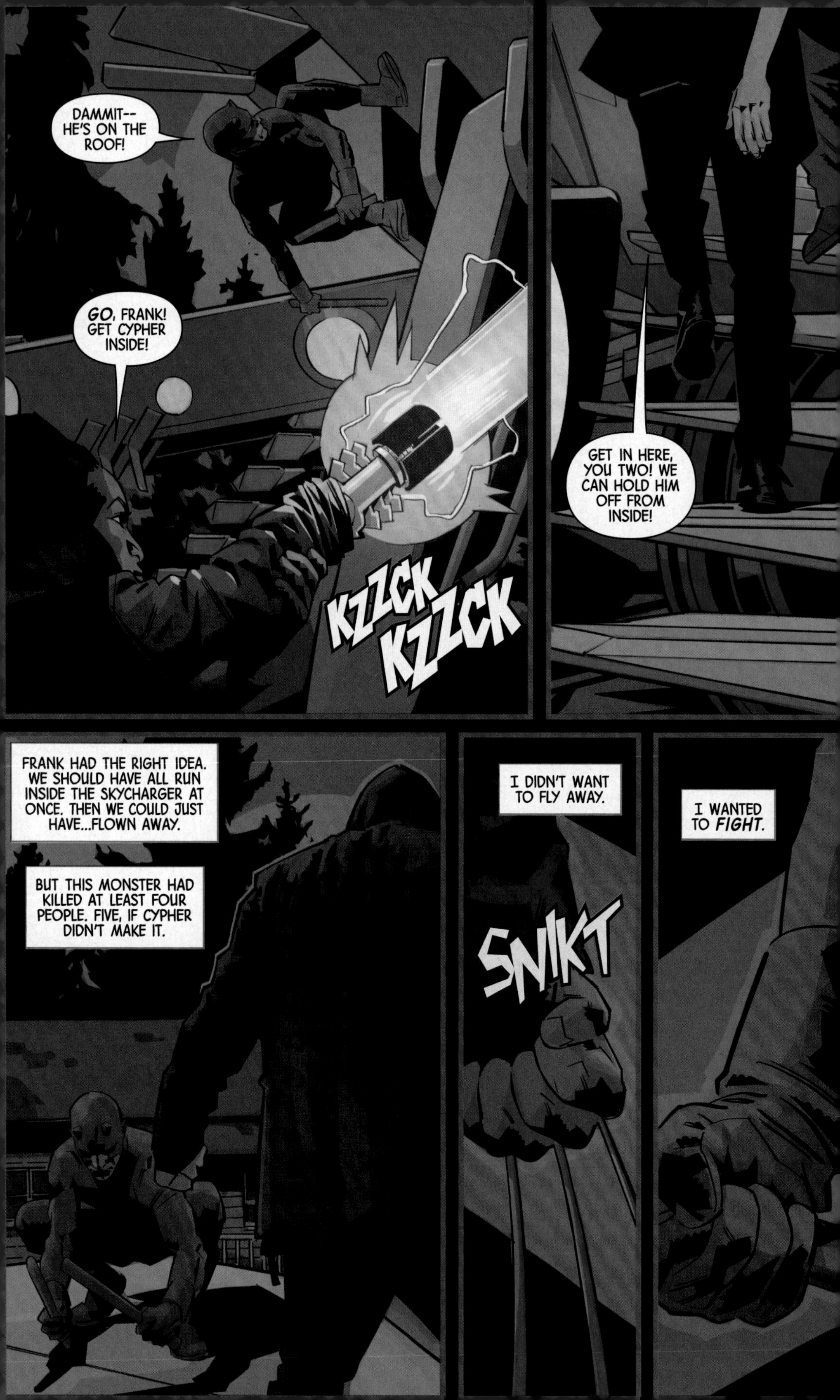
DAMMIT-- HE'S ON THE ROOF!
GO, FRANK! GET CYPHER INSIDE!
KZZCK KZZCK
GET IN HERE, YOU TWO! WE CAN HOLD HIM OFF FROM INSIDE!
FRANK HAD THE RIGHT IDEA. WE SHOULD HAVE ALL RUN INSIDE THE SKYCHARGER AT ONCE. THEN WE COULD JUST HAVE...FLOWN AWAY.
BUT THIS MONSTER HAD KILLED AT LEAST FOUR PEOPLE. FIVE, IF CYPHER DIDN'T MAKE IT.
I DIDN'T WANT TO FLY AWAY.
SNIKT
I WANTED TO FIGHT.

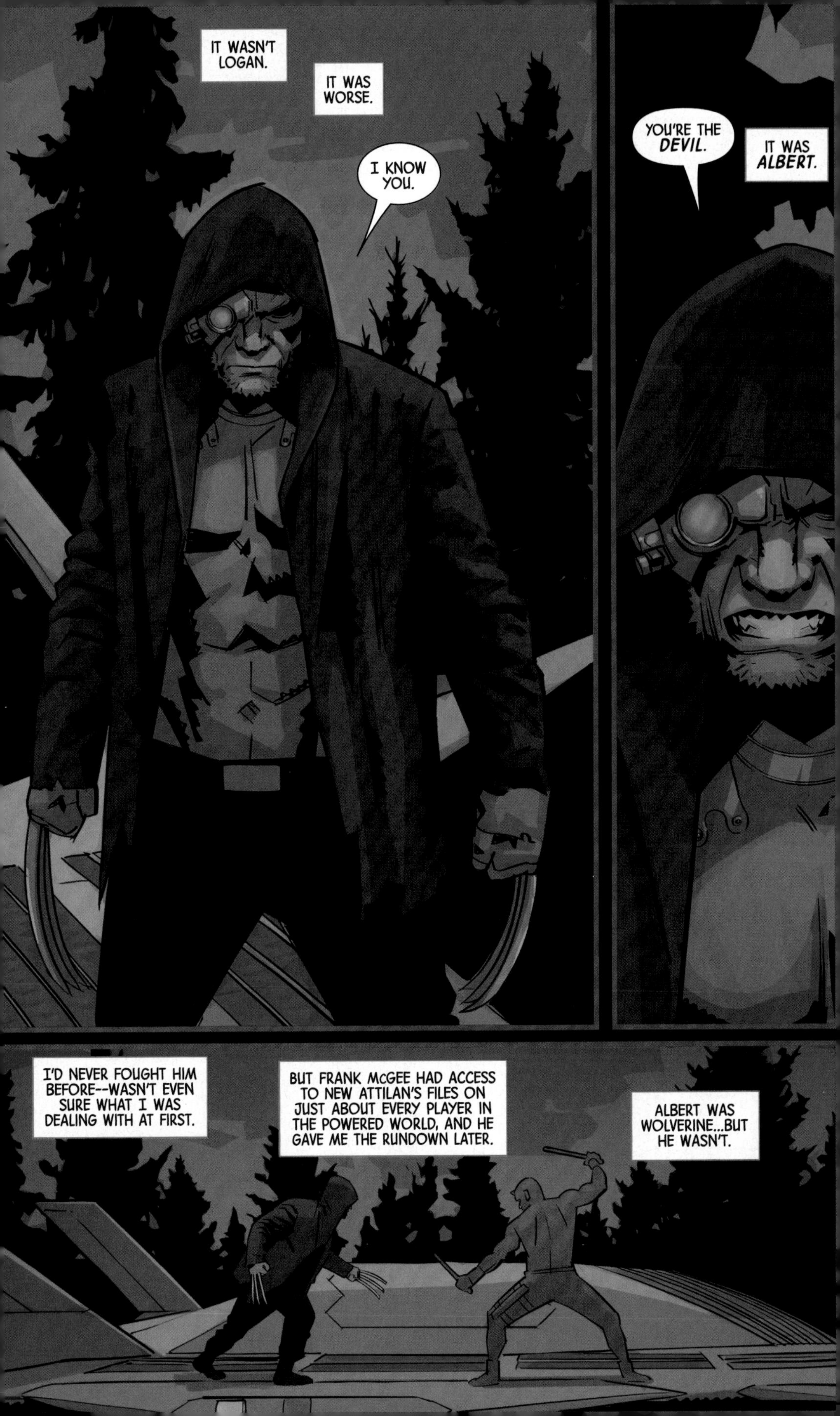
IT WASN'T LOGAN.
IT WAS WORSE.
I KNOW YOU.
YOU'RE THE DEVIL.
IT WAS ALBERT.
I'D NEVER FOUGHT HIM BEFORE--WASN'T EVEN SURE WHAT I WAS DEALING WITH AT FIRST.
BUT FRANK McGEE HAD ACCESS TO NEW ATTILAN'S FILES ON JUST ABOUT EVERY PLAYER IN THE POWERED WORLD, AND HE GAVE ME THE RUNDOWN LATER.
ALBERT WAS WOLVERINE...BUT HE WASN'T.

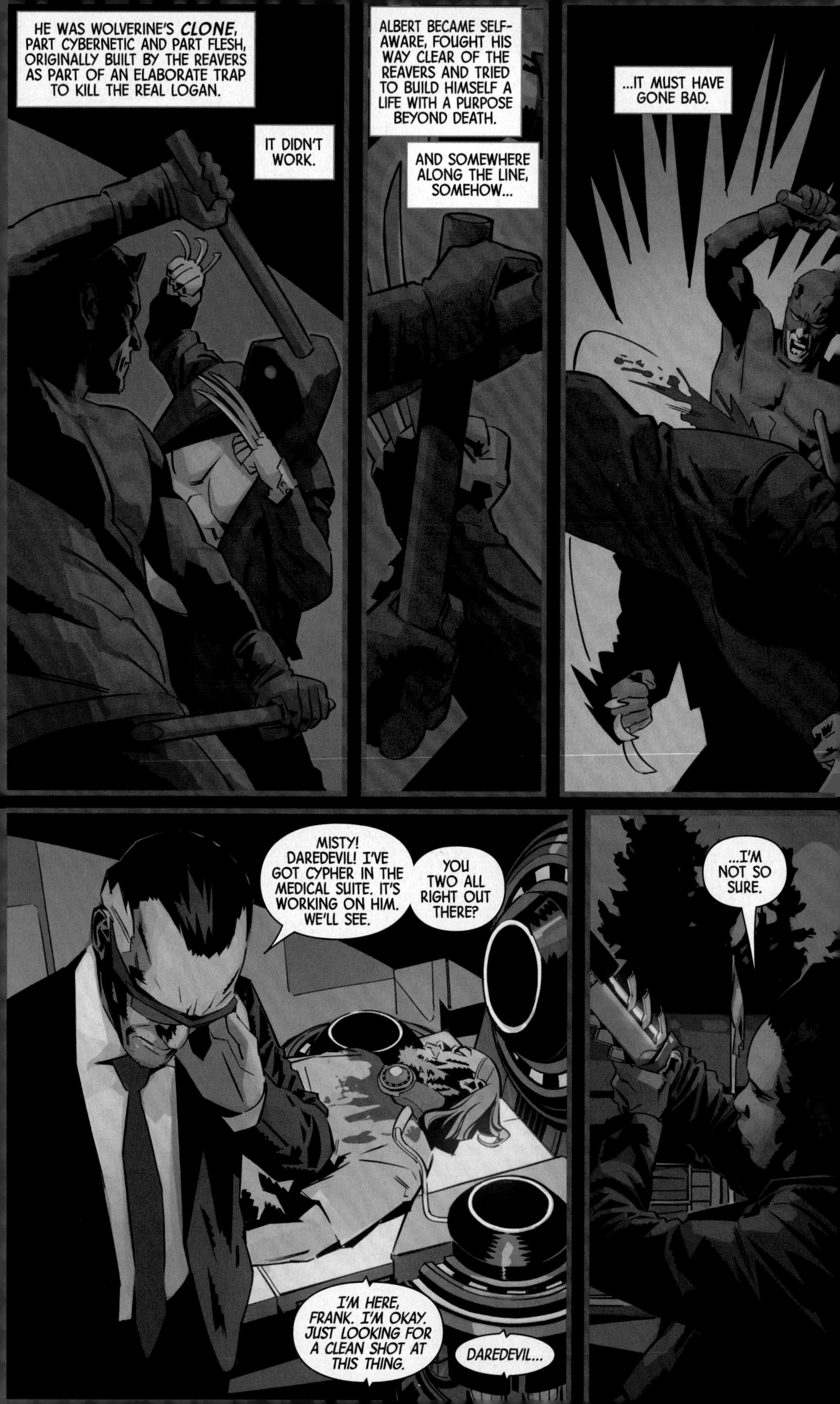
HE WAS WOLVERINE'S CLONE, PART CYBERNETIC AND PART FLESH, ORIGINALLY BUILT BY THE REAVERS AS PART OF AN ELABORATE TRAP TO KILL THE REAL LOGAN.
IT DIDN'T WORK.
ALBERT BECAME SELF-AWARE, FOUGHT HIS WAY CLEAR OF THE REAVERS AND TRIED TO BUILD HIMSELF A LIFE WITH A PURPOSE BEYOND DEATH.
AND SOMEWHERE ALONG THE LINE, SOMEHOW...
...IT MUST HAVE GONE BAD.
MISTY! DAREDEVIL! I'VE GOT CYPHER IN THE MEDICAL SUITE. IT'S WORKING ON HIM. WE'LL SEE.
YOU TWO ALL RIGHT OUT THERE?
I'M HERE, FRANK. I'M OKAY. JUST LOOKING FOR A CLEAN SHOT AT THIS THING.
DAREDEVIL...
...I'M NOT SO SURE.

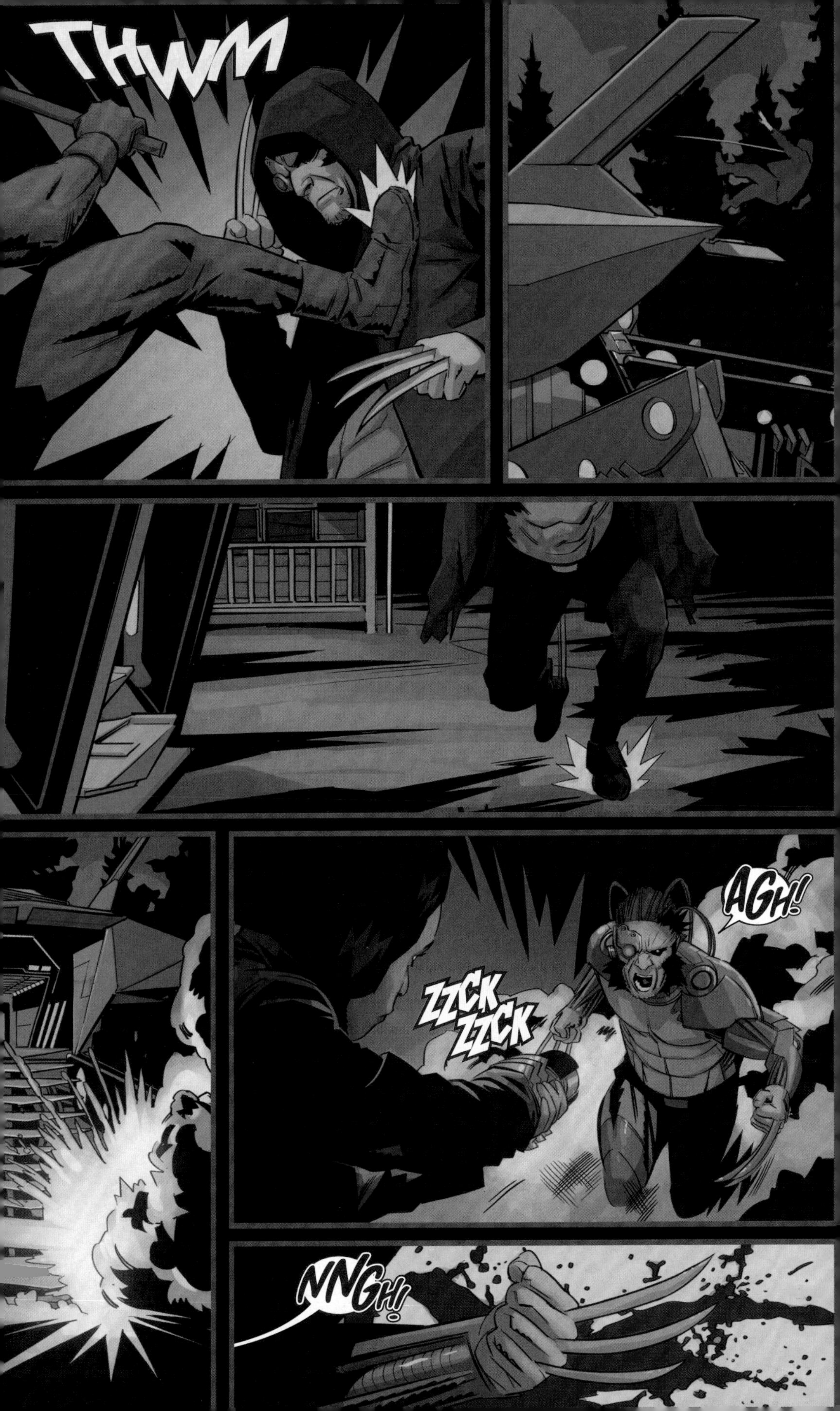
THWM
AGH!
ZZCK ZZCK
NNGH!

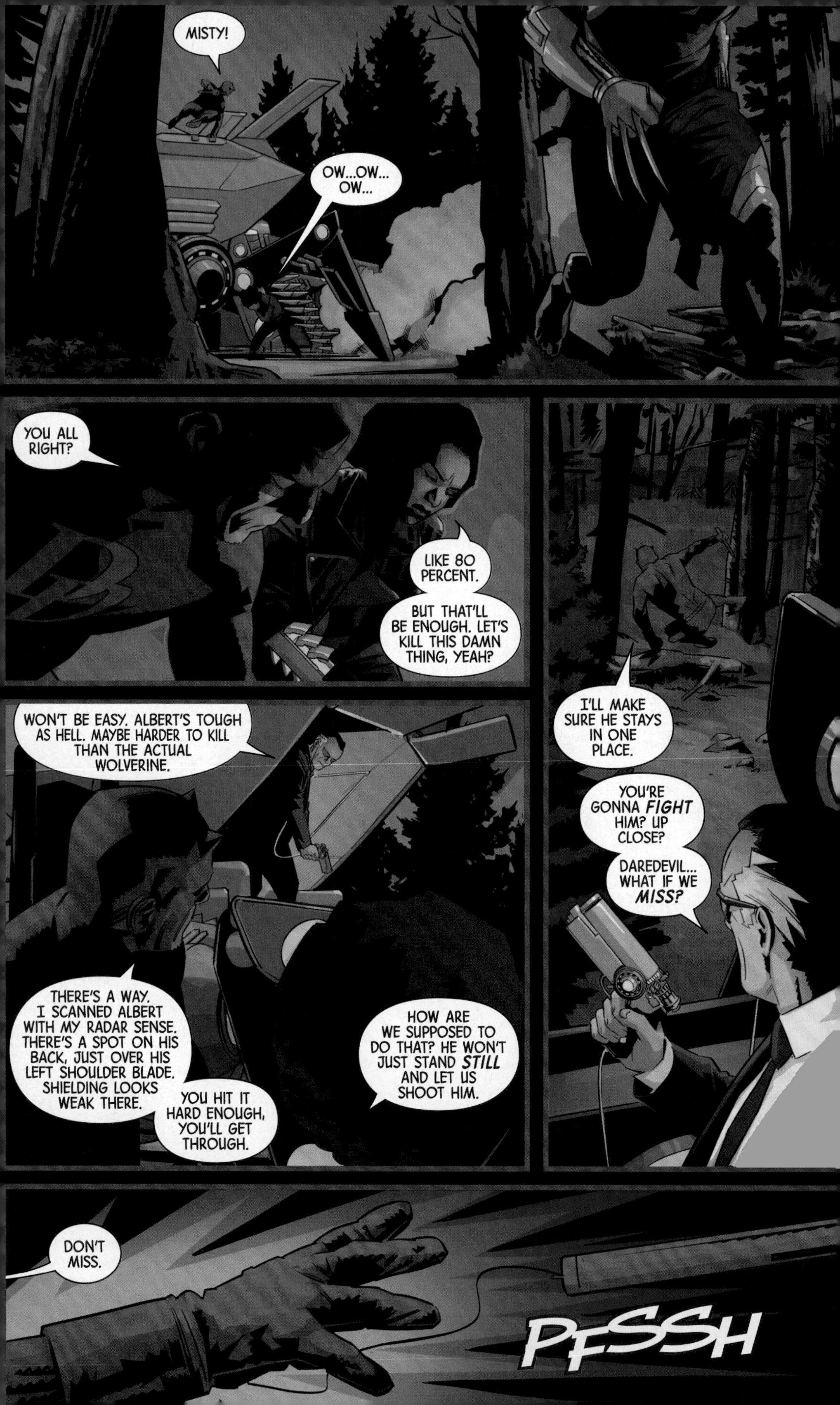
MISTY!
OW...OW... OW...
YOU ALL RIGHT?
LIKE 80 PERCENT.
BUT THAT'LL BE ENOUGH. LET'S KILL THIS DAMN THING, YEAH?
WON'T BE EASY. ALBERT'S TOUGH AS HELL. MAYBE HARDER TO KILL THAN THE ACTUAL WOLVERINE.
THERE'S A WAY. I SCANNED ALBERT WITH MY RADAR SENSE. THERE'S A SPOT ON HIS BACK, JUST OVER HIS LEFT SHOULDER BLADE. SHIELDING LOOKS WEAK THERE.
YOU HIT IT HARD ENOUGH, YOU'LL GET THROUGH.
HOW ARE WE SUPPOSED TO DO THAT? HE WON'T JUST STAND *STILL* AND LET US SHOOT HIM.
I'LL MAKE SURE HE STAYS IN ONE PLACE.
YOU'RE GONNA *FIGHT* HIM? UP CLOSE?
DAREDEVIL... WHAT IF WE *MISS?*
DON'T MISS.
PFSSH

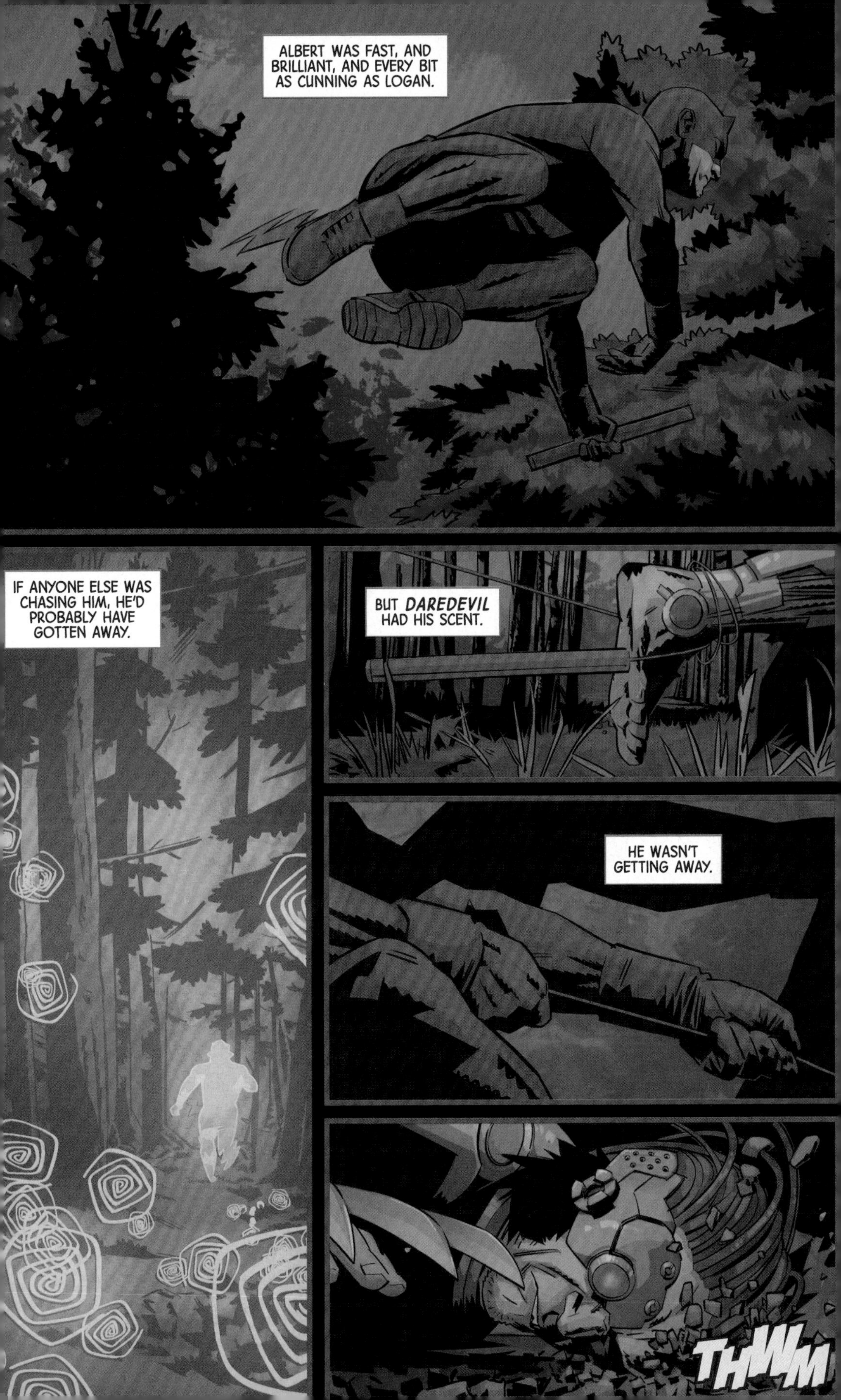
ALBERT WAS FAST, AND BRILLIANT, AND EVERY BIT AS CUNNING AS LOGAN.
IF ANYONE ELSE WAS CHASING HIM, HE'D PROBABLY HAVE GOTTEN AWAY.
BUT DAREDEVIL HAD HIS SCENT.
HE WASN'T GETTING AWAY.
THWM

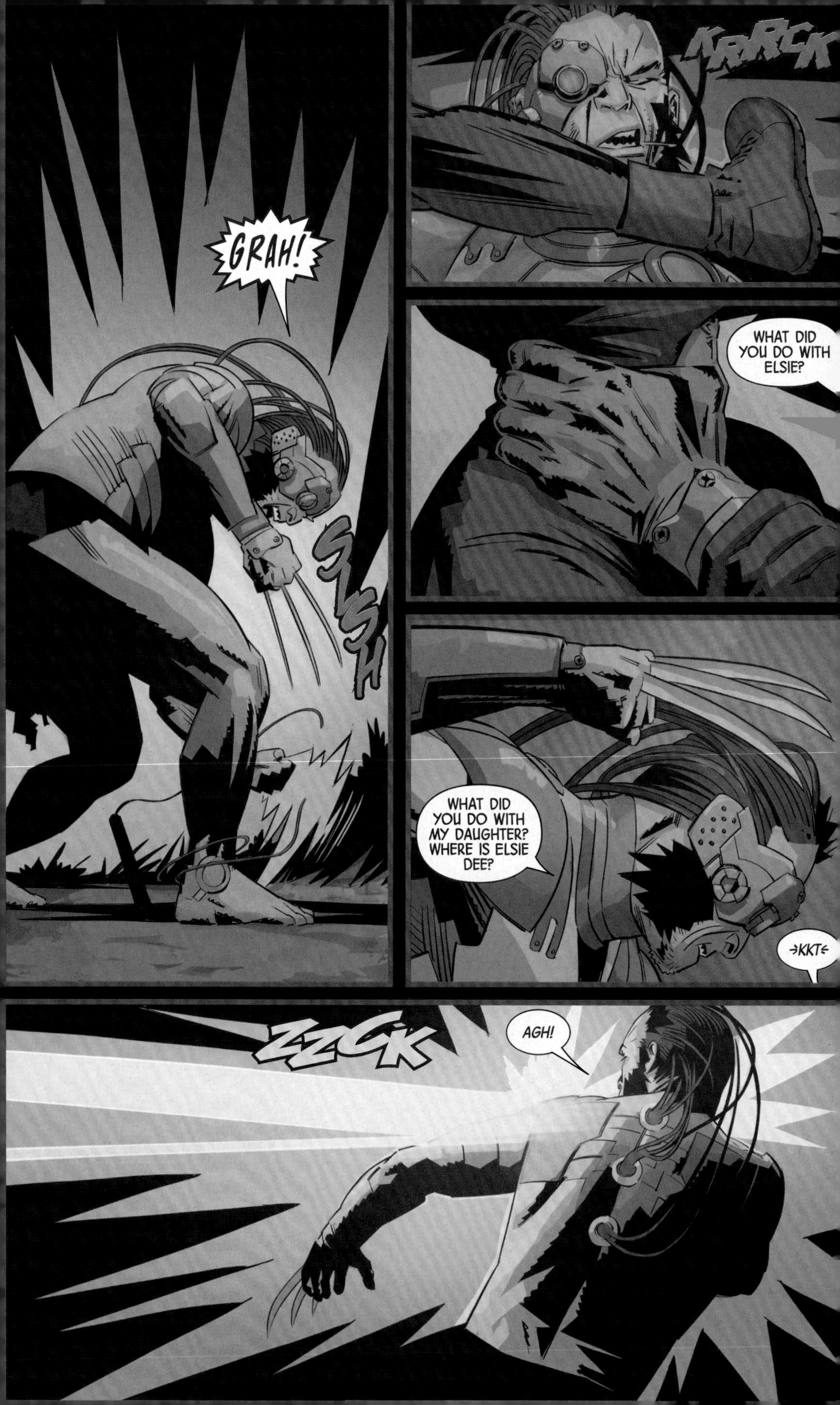
GRAH!
SNSH
KRRCK
WHAT DID YOU DO WITH ELSIE?
WHAT DID YOU DO WITH MY DAUGHTER? WHERE IS ELSIE DEE?
KKT
ZZCK
AGH!

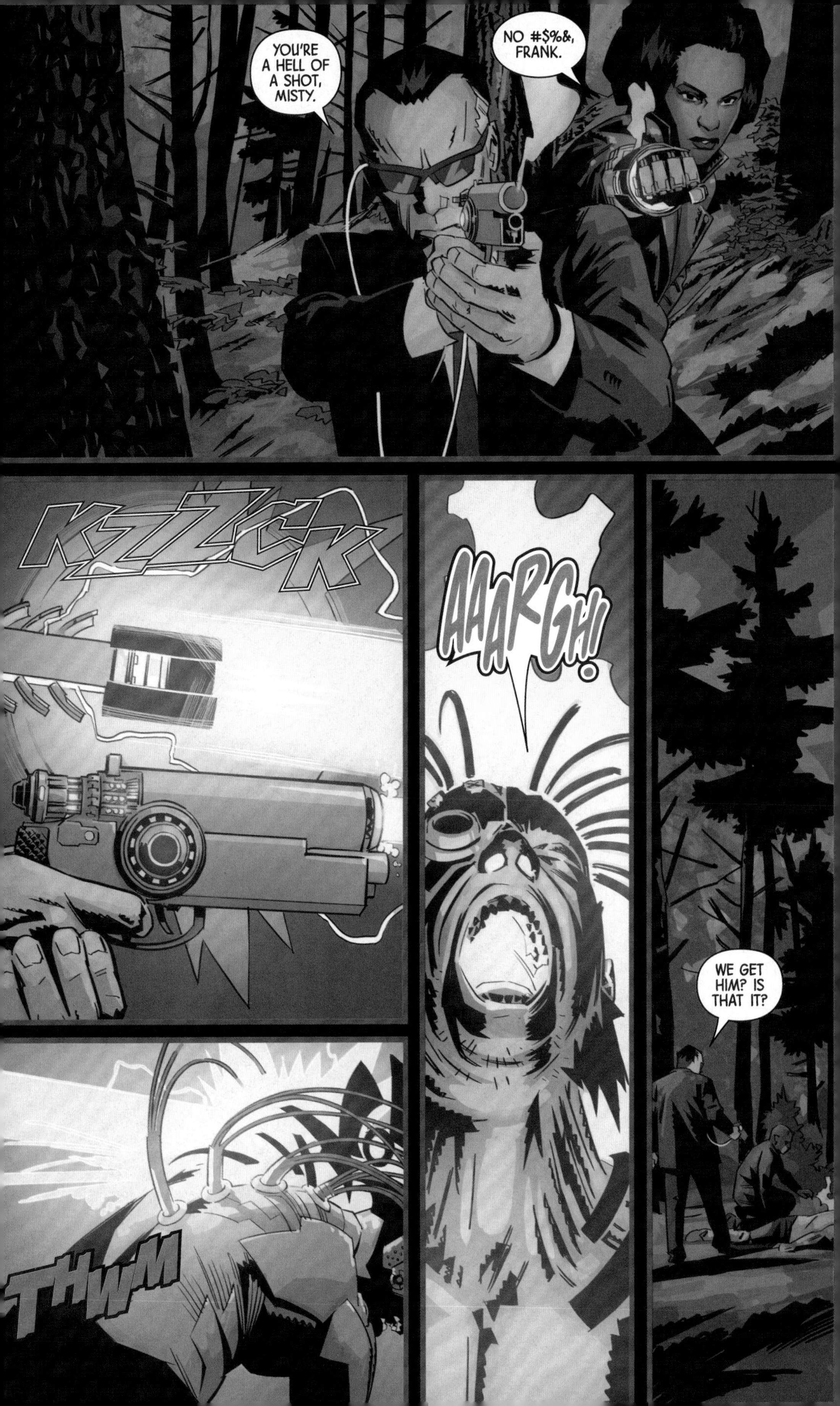
YOU'RE A HELL OF A SHOT, MISTY.
NO #$%&, FRANK.
KZZCK
THWM
AAARGH!
WE GET HIM? IS THAT IT?

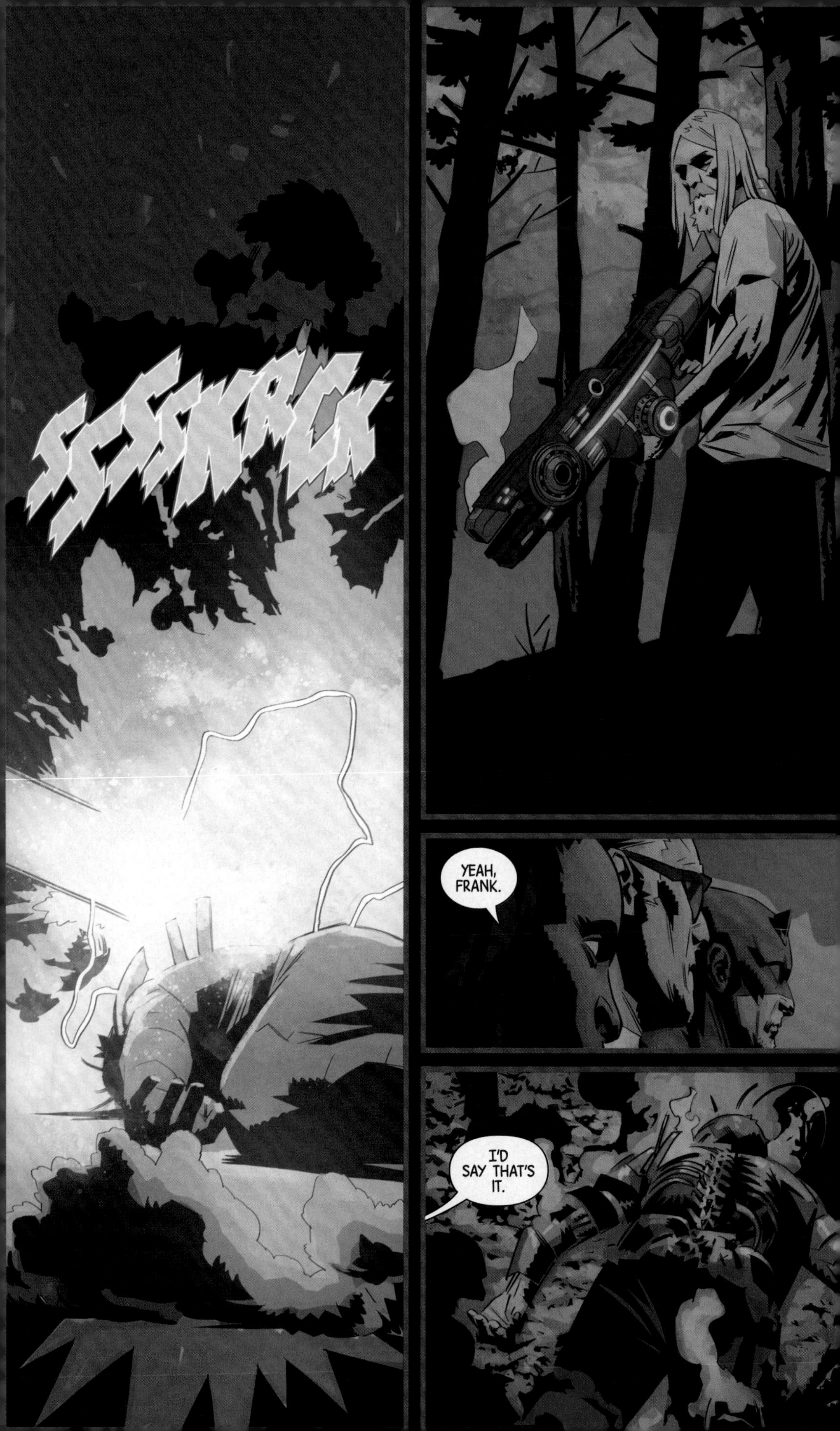
YEAH, FRANK.
I'D SAY THAT'S IT.

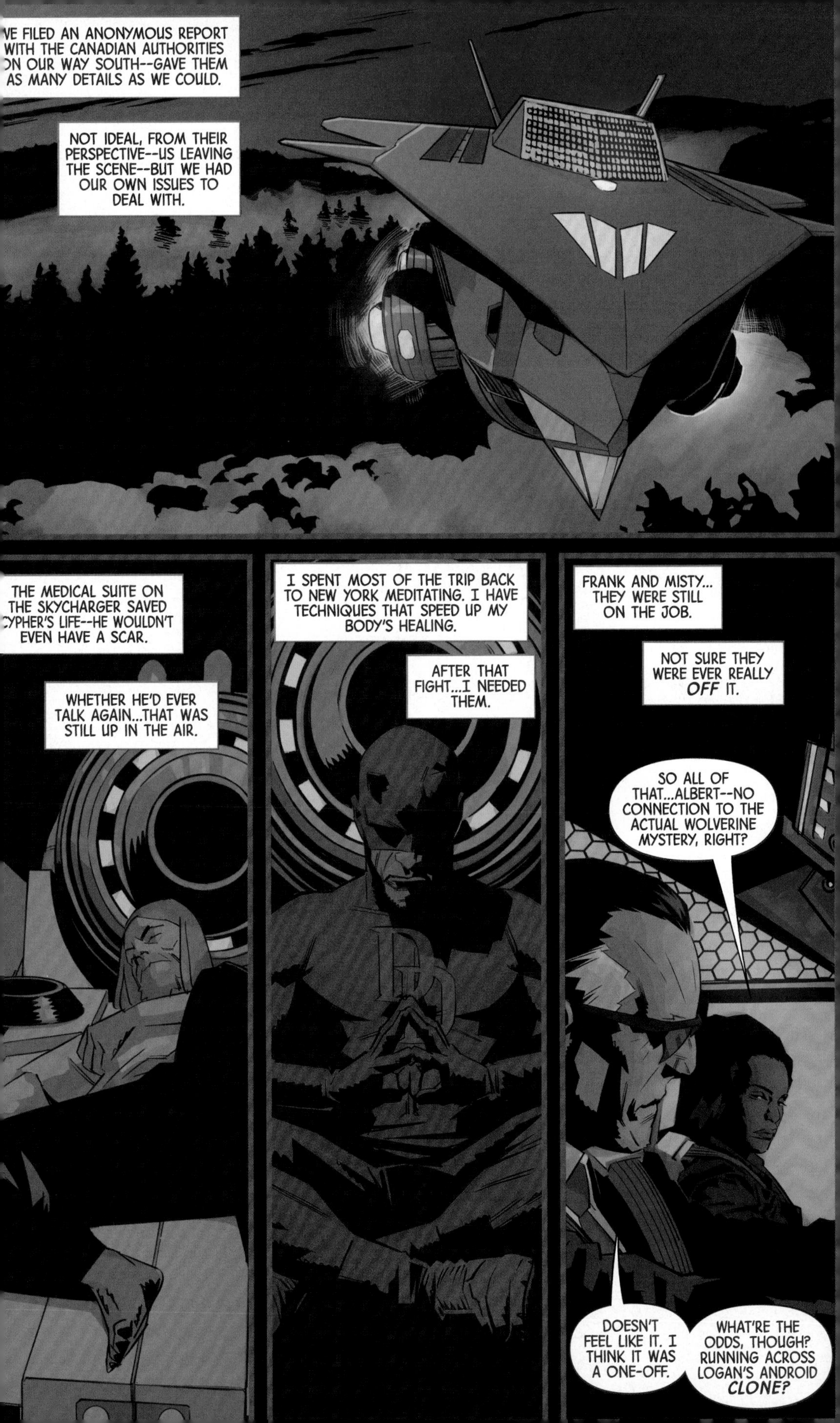

WE FILED AN ANONYMOUS REPORT WITH THE CANADIAN AUTHORITIES ON OUR WAY SOUTH--GAVE THEM AS MANY DETAILS AS WE COULD.
NOT IDEAL, FROM THEIR PERSPECTIVE--US LEAVING THE SCENE--BUT WE HAD OUR OWN ISSUES TO DEAL WITH.
THE MEDICAL SUITE ON THE SKYCHARGER SAVED CYPHER'S LIFE--HE WOULDN'T EVEN HAVE A SCAR.
WHETHER HE'D EVER TALK AGAIN...THAT WAS STILL UP IN THE AIR.
I SPENT MOST OF THE TRIP BACK TO NEW YORK MEDITATING. I HAVE TECHNIQUES THAT SPEED UP MY BODY'S HEALING.
AFTER THAT FIGHT...I NEEDED THEM.
FRANK AND MISTY... THEY WERE STILL ON THE JOB.
NOT SURE THEY WERE EVER REALLY *OFF* IT.
SO ALL OF THAT...ALBERT--NO CONNECTION TO THE ACTUAL WOLVERINE MYSTERY, RIGHT?
DOESN'T FEEL LIKE IT. I THINK IT WAS A ONE-OFF.
WHAT'RE THE ODDS, THOUGH? RUNNING ACROSS LOGAN'S ANDROID *CLONE?*

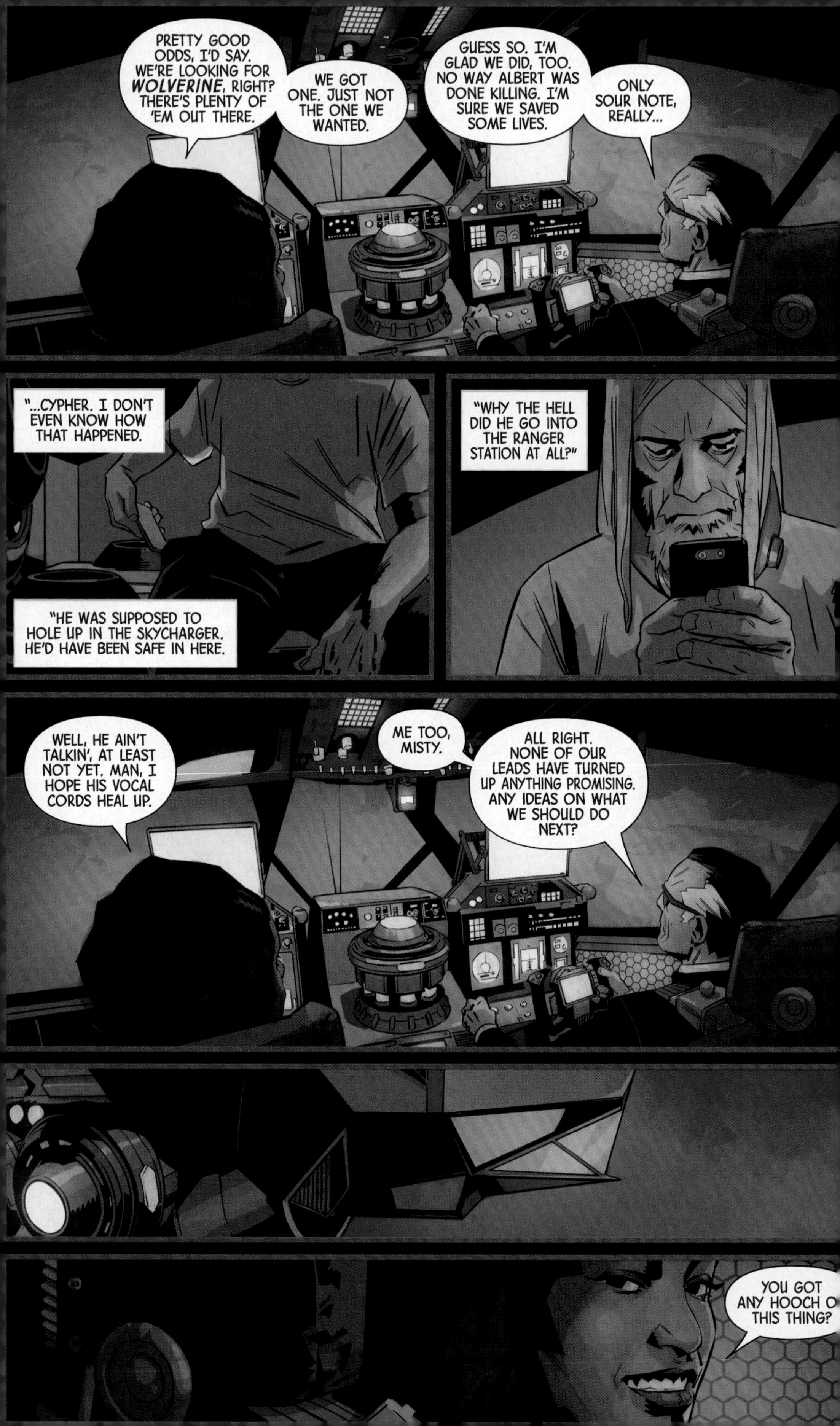
PRETTY GOOD ODDS, I'D SAY. WE'RE LOOKING FOR WOLVERINE, RIGHT? THERE'S PLENTY OF 'EM OUT THERE.
WE GOT ONE. JUST NOT THE ONE WE WANTED.
GUESS SO. I'M GLAD WE DID, TOO. NO WAY ALBERT WAS DONE KILLING. I'M SURE WE SAVED SOME LIVES.
ONLY SOUR NOTE, REALLY...
"...CYPHER. I DON'T EVEN KNOW HOW THAT HAPPENED.
"HE WAS SUPPOSED TO HOLE UP IN THE SKYCHARGER. HE'D HAVE BEEN SAFE IN HERE.
"WHY THE HELL DID HE GO INTO THE RANGER STATION AT ALL?"
WELL, HE AIN'T TALKIN', AT LEAST NOT YET. MAN, I HOPE HIS VOCAL CORDS HEAL UP.
ME TOO, MISTY.
ALL RIGHT. NONE OF OUR LEADS HAVE TURNED UP ANYTHING PROMISING. ANY IDEAS ON WHAT WE SHOULD DO NEXT?
YOU GOT ANY HOOCH O THIS THING?

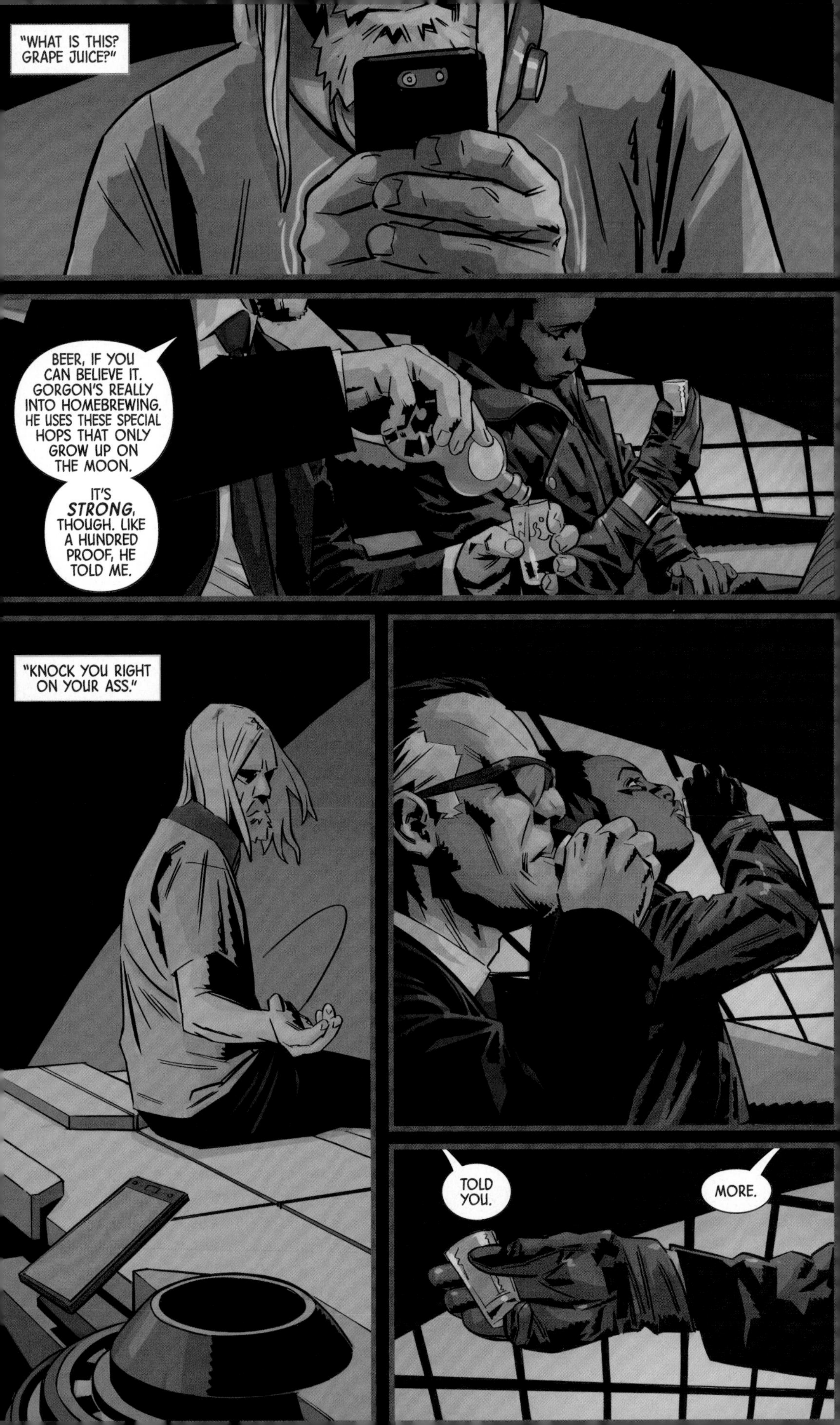
"WHAT IS THIS? GRAPE JUICE?"
BEER, IF YOU CAN BELIEVE IT. GORGON'S REALLY INTO HOMEBREWING. HE USES THESE SPECIAL HOPS THAT ONLY GROW UP ON THE MOON.
IT'S *STRONG*, THOUGH. LIKE A HUNDRED PROOF, HE TOLD ME.
"KNOCK YOU RIGHT ON YOUR ASS."
TOLD YOU.
MORE.

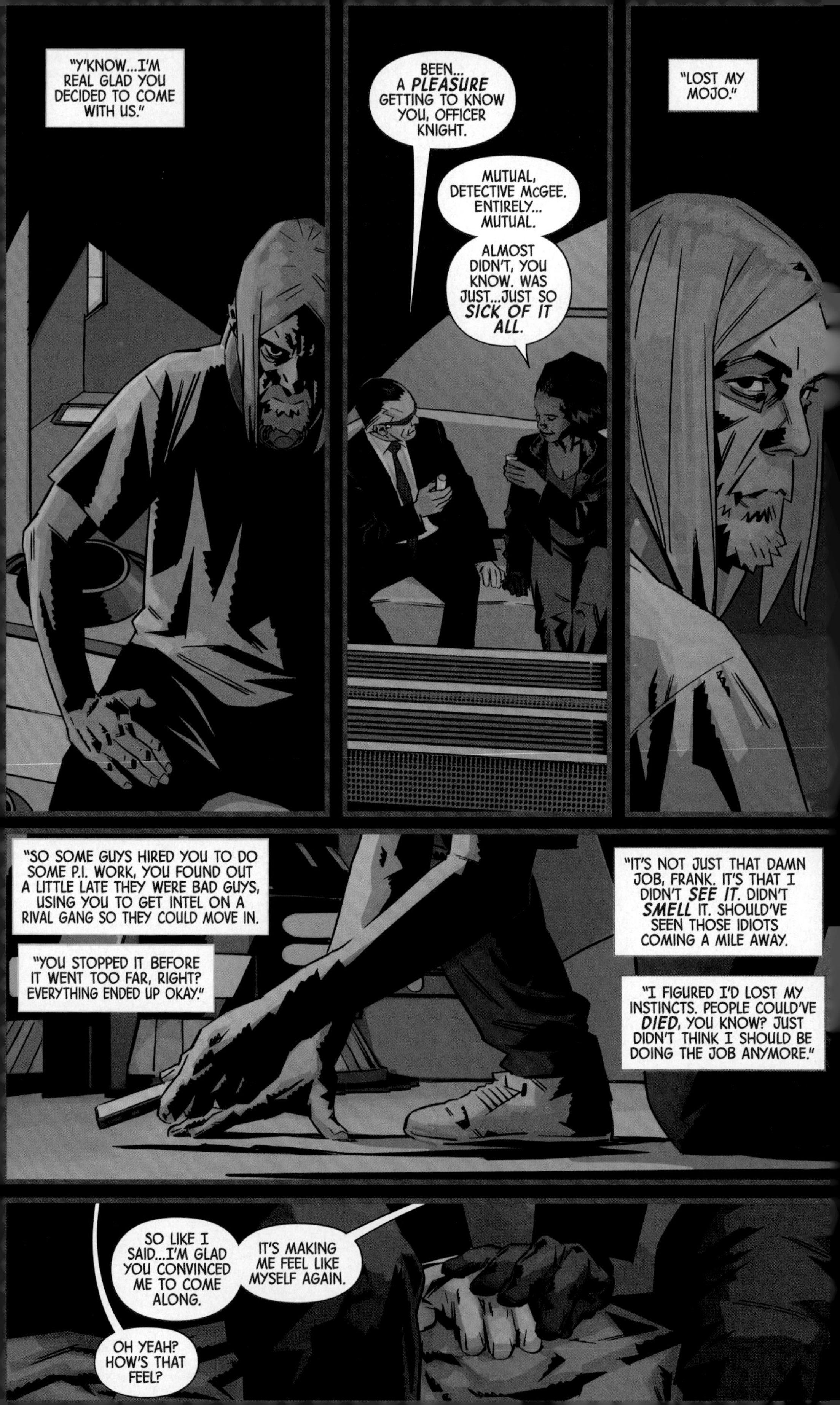
"Y'KNOW...I'M REAL GLAD YOU DECIDED TO COME WITH US."
BEEN... A PLEASURE GETTING TO KNOW YOU, OFFICER KNIGHT.
MUTUAL, DETECTIVE McGEE. ENTIRELY... MUTUAL.
ALMOST DIDN'T, YOU KNOW. WAS JUST...JUST SO SICK OF IT ALL.
"LOST MY MOJO."
"SO SOME GUYS HIRED YOU TO DO SOME P.I. WORK, YOU FOUND OUT A LITTLE LATE THEY WERE BAD GUYS, USING YOU TO GET INTEL ON A RIVAL GANG SO THEY COULD MOVE IN.
"YOU STOPPED IT BEFORE IT WENT TOO FAR, RIGHT? EVERYTHING ENDED UP OKAY."
"IT'S NOT JUST THAT DAMN JOB, FRANK. IT'S THAT I DIDN'T SEE IT. DIDN'T SMELL IT. SHOULD'VE SEEN THOSE IDIOTS COMING A MILE AWAY.
"I FIGURED I'D LOST MY INSTINCTS. PEOPLE COULD'VE DIED, YOU KNOW? JUST DIDN'T THINK I SHOULD BE DOING THE JOB ANYMORE."
SO LIKE I SAID...I'M GLAD YOU CONVINCED ME TO COME ALONG.
IT'S MAKING ME FEEL LIKE MYSELF AGAIN.
OH YEAH? HOW'S THAT FEEL?

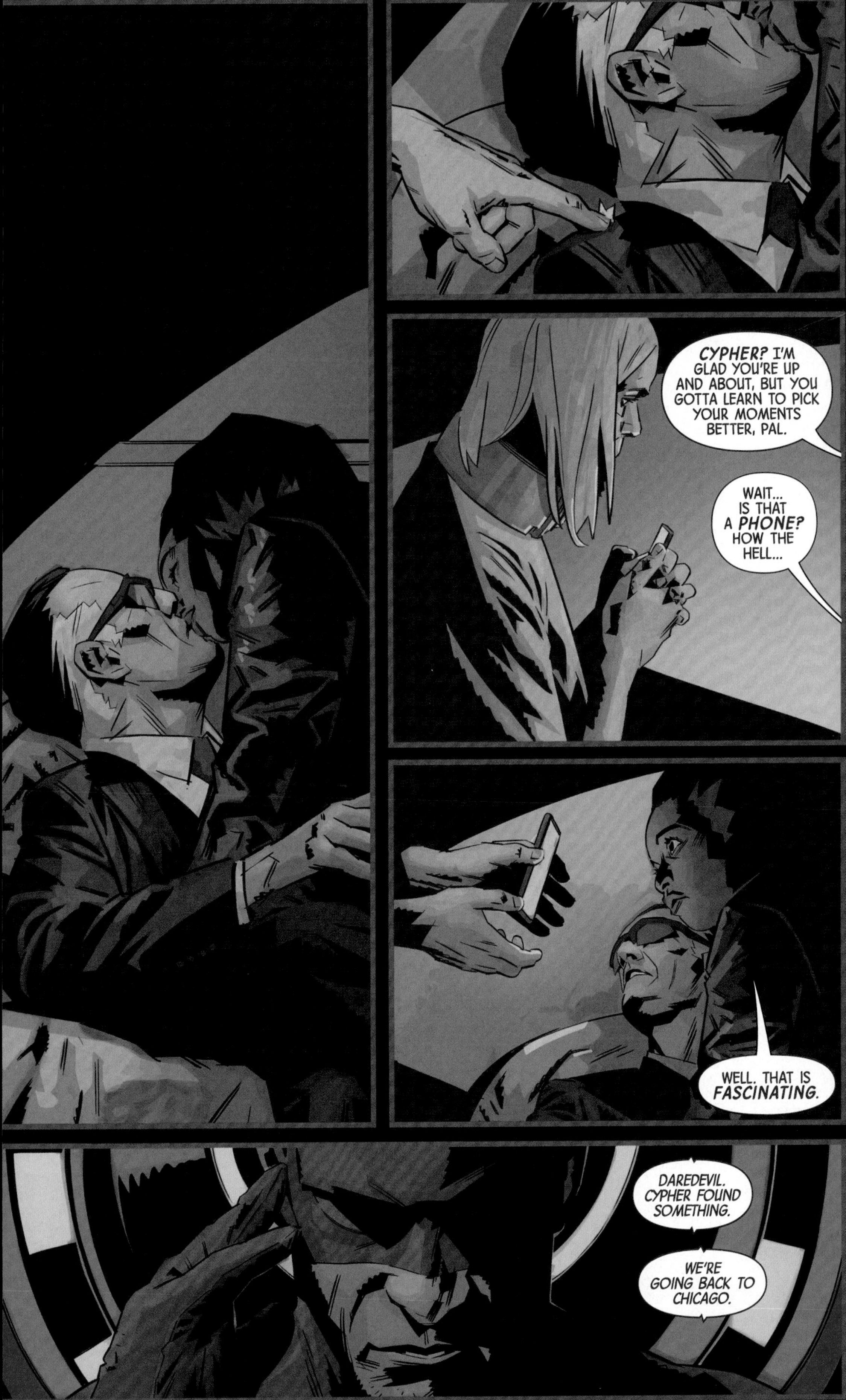
CYPHER? I'M GLAD YOU'RE UP AND ABOUT, BUT YOU GOTTA LEARN TO PICK YOUR MOMENTS BETTER, PAL.
WAIT... IS THAT A PHONE? HOW THE HELL...
WELL, THAT IS FASCINATING.
DAREDEVIL. CYPHER FOUND SOMETHING.
WE'RE GOING BACK TO CHICAGO.

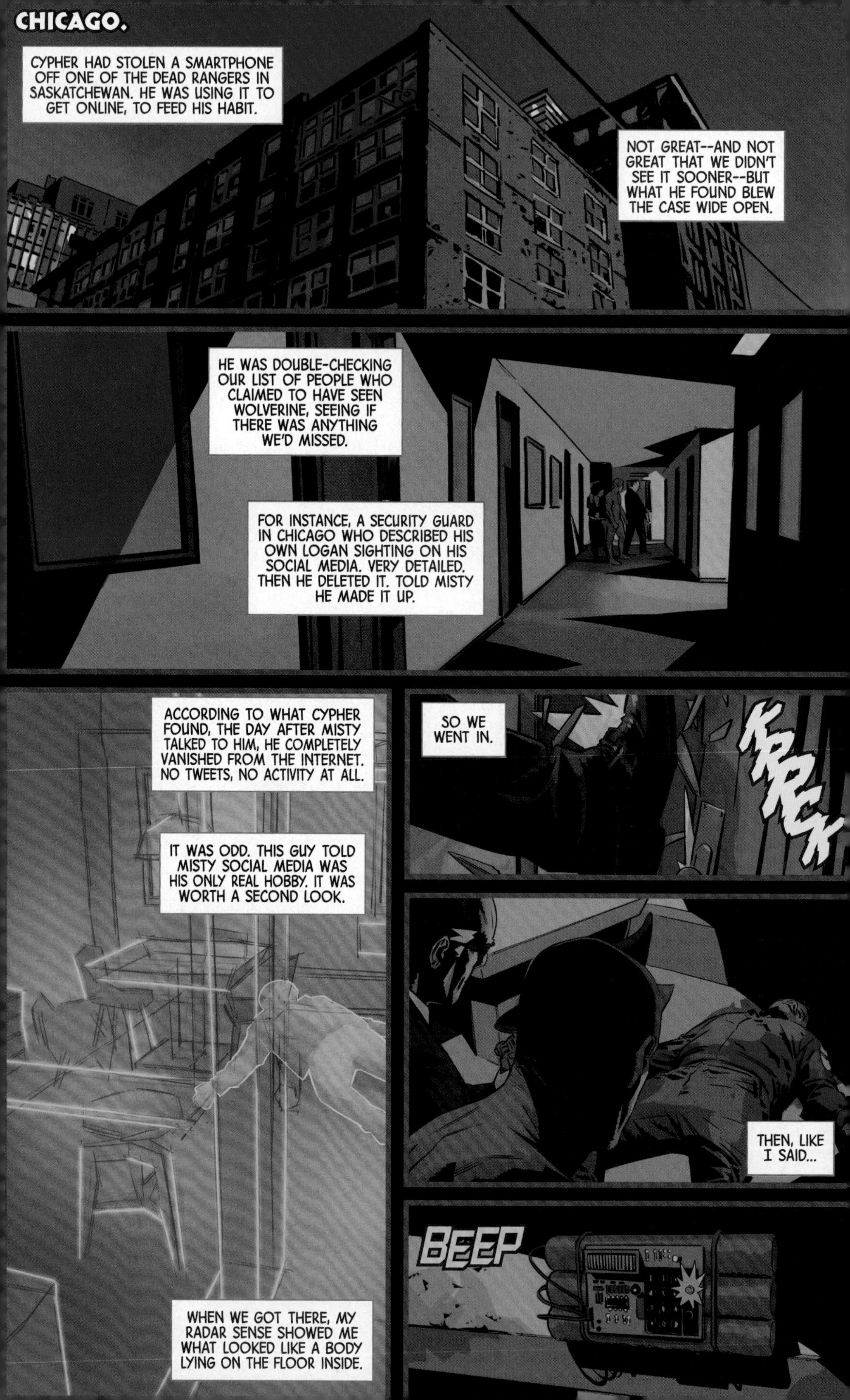
CHICAGO.
CYPHER HAD STOLEN A SMARTPHONE OFF ONE OF THE DEAD RANGERS IN SASKATCHEWAN. HE WAS USING IT TO GET ONLINE, TO FEED HIS HABIT.
NOT GREAT--AND NOT GREAT THAT WE DIDN'T SEE IT SOONER--BUT WHAT HE FOUND BLEW THE CASE WIDE OPEN.
HE WAS DOUBLE-CHECKING OUR LIST OF PEOPLE WHO CLAIMED TO HAVE SEEN WOLVERINE, SEEING IF THERE WAS ANYTHING WE'D MISSED.
FOR INSTANCE, A SECURITY GUARD IN CHICAGO WHO DESCRIBED HIS OWN LOGAN SIGHTING ON HIS SOCIAL MEDIA. VERY DETAILED. THEN HE DELETED IT. TOLD MISTY HE MADE IT UP.
ACCORDING TO WHAT CYPHER FOUND, THE DAY AFTER MISTY TALKED TO HIM, HE COMPLETELY VANISHED FROM THE INTERNET. NO TWEETS, NO ACTIVITY AT ALL.
IT WAS ODD. THIS GUY TOLD MISTY SOCIAL MEDIA WAS HIS ONLY REAL HOBBY. IT WAS WORTH A SECOND LOOK.
WHEN WE GOT THERE, MY RADAR SENSE SHOWED ME WHAT LOOKED LIKE A BODY LYING ON THE FLOOR INSIDE.
SO WE WENT IN.
KRRCK
THEN, LIKE I SAID...
BEEP

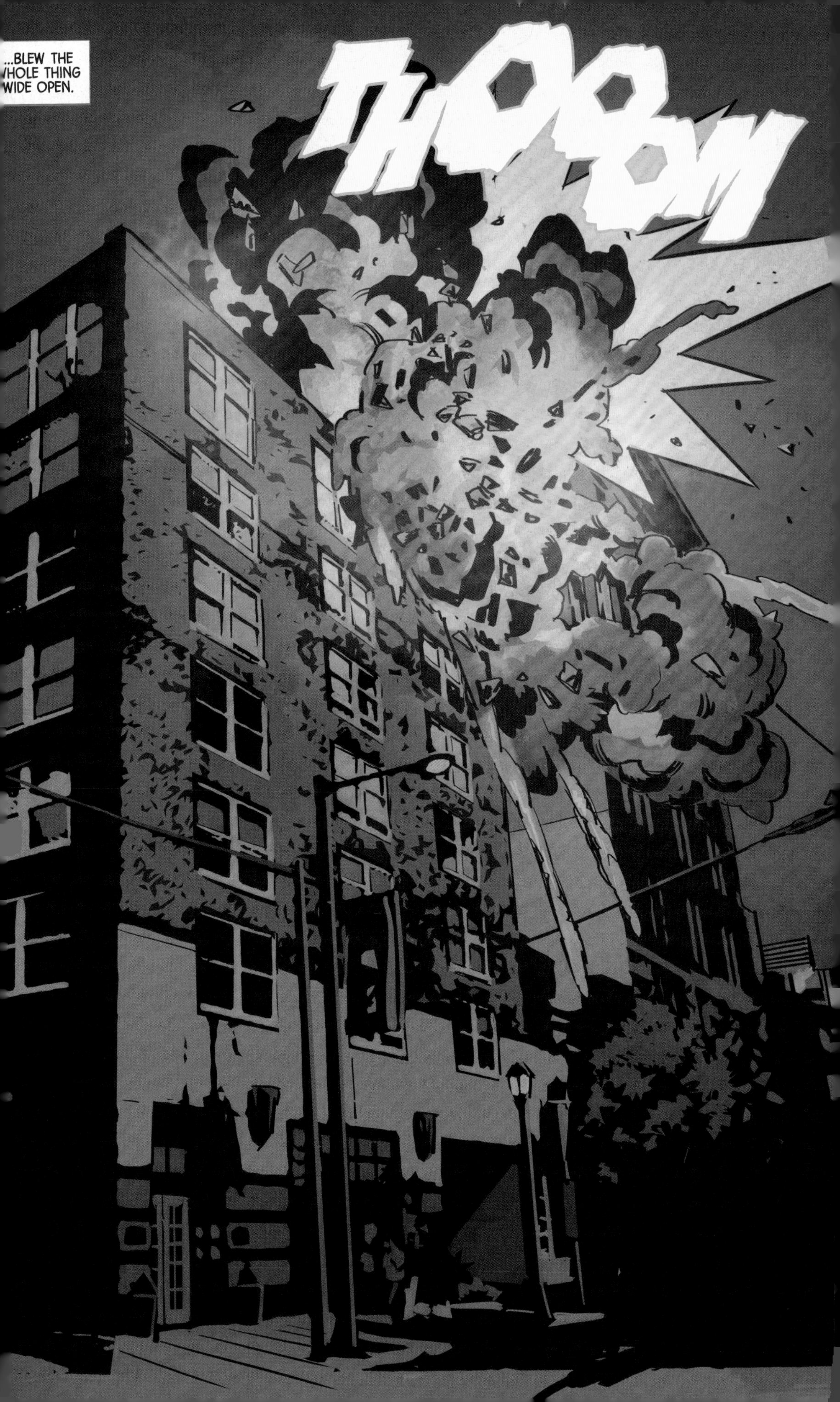
...BLEW THE
WHOLE THING
WIDE OPEN.
THOOOM

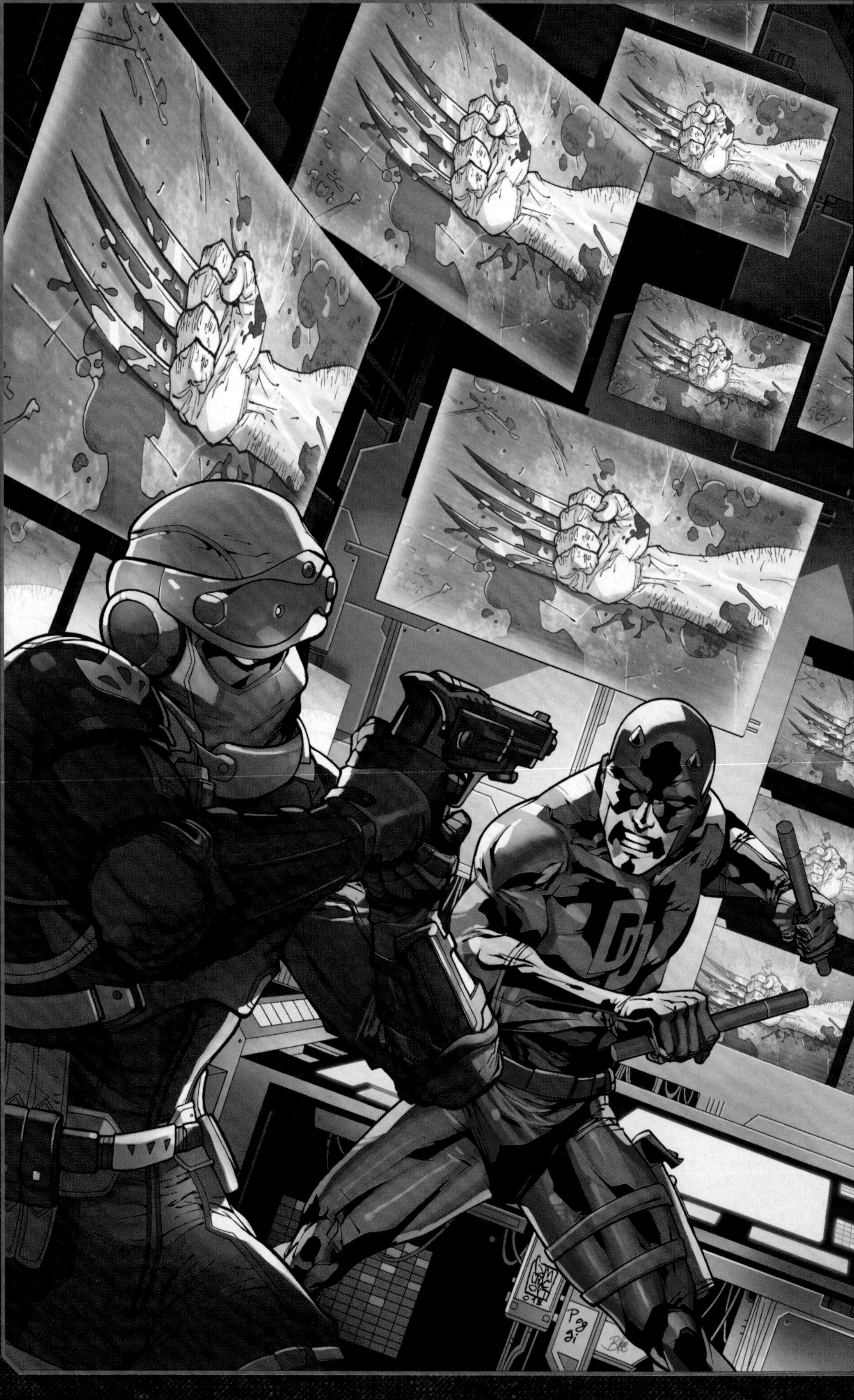

WEAPON LOST 4

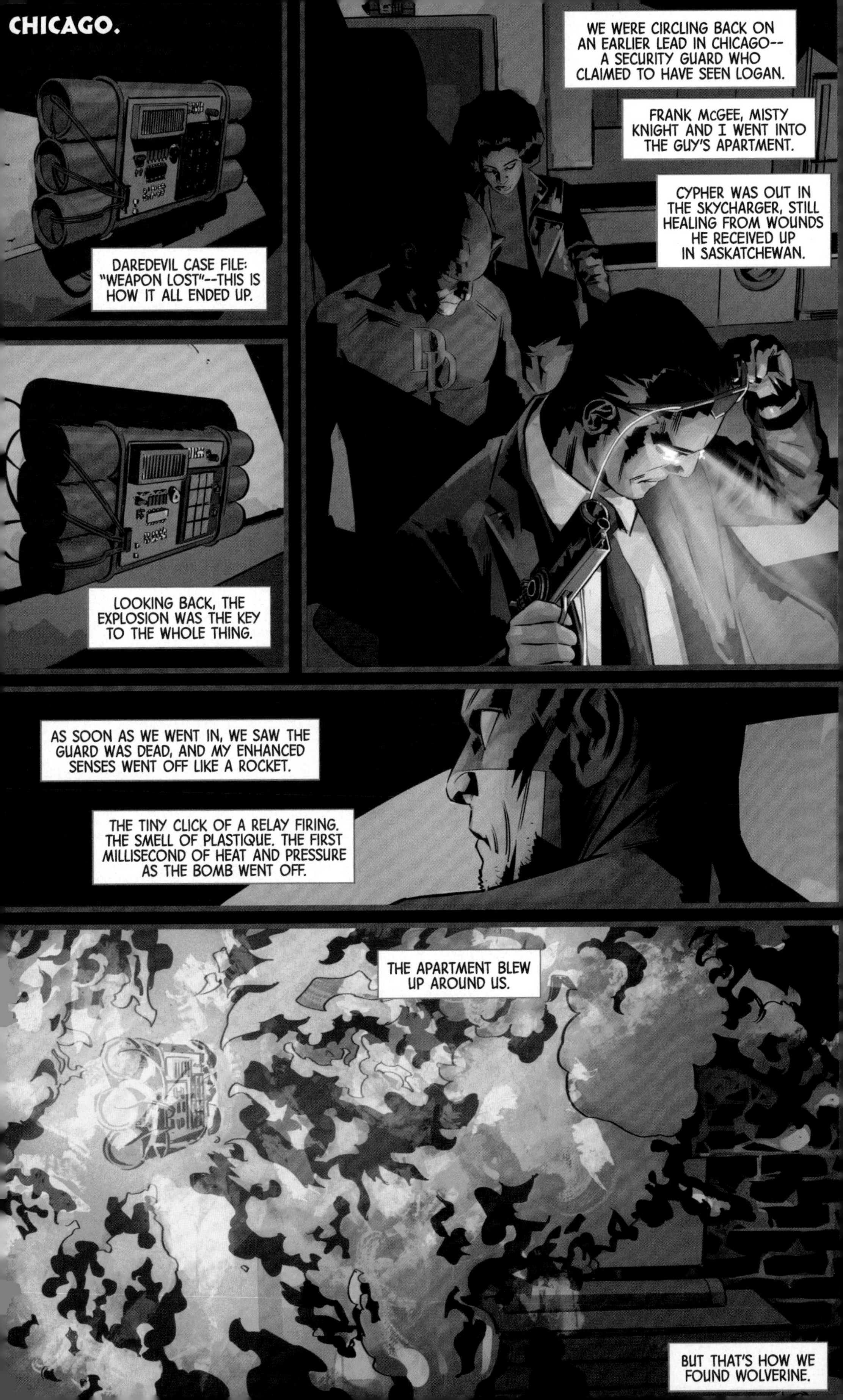
CHICAGO.
DAREDEVIL CASE FILE: "WEAPON LOST"--THIS IS HOW IT ALL ENDED UP.
LOOKING BACK, THE EXPLOSION WAS THE KEY TO THE WHOLE THING.
WE WERE CIRCLING BACK ON AN EARLIER LEAD IN CHICAGO-- A SECURITY GUARD WHO CLAIMED TO HAVE SEEN LOGAN.
FRANK McGEE, MISTY KNIGHT AND I WENT INTO THE GUY'S APARTMENT.
CYPHER WAS OUT IN THE SKYCHARGER, STILL HEALING FROM WOUNDS HE RECEIVED UP IN SASKATCHEWAN.
AS SOON AS WE WENT IN, WE SAW THE GUARD WAS DEAD, AND MY ENHANCED SENSES WENT OFF LIKE A ROCKET.
THE TINY CLICK OF A RELAY FIRING. THE SMELL OF PLASTIQUE. THE FIRST MILLISECOND OF HEAT AND PRESSURE AS THE BOMB WENT OFF.
THE APARTMENT BLEW UP AROUND US.
BUT THAT'S HOW WE FOUND WOLVERINE.

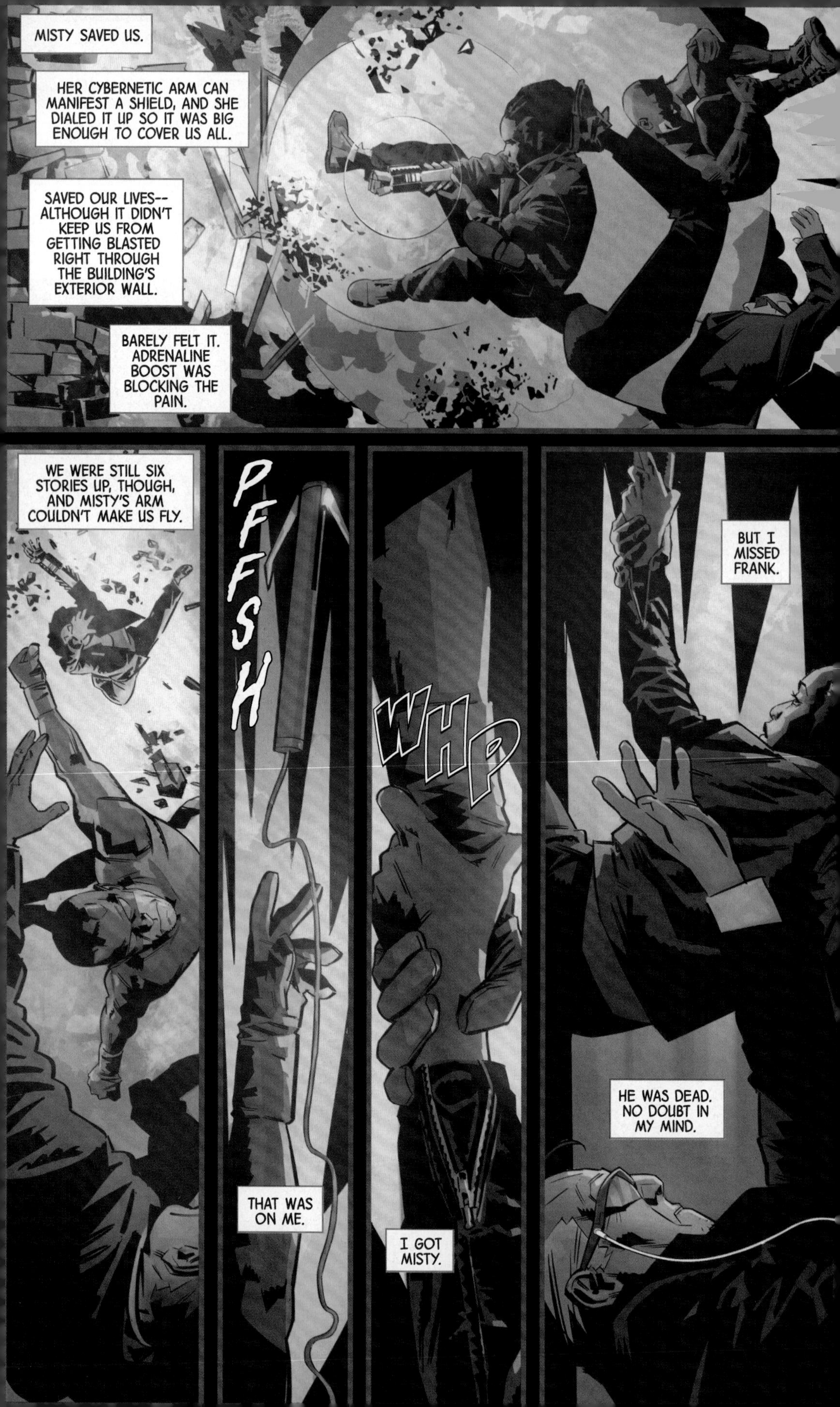
MISTY SAVED US.
HER CYBERNETIC ARM CAN MANIFEST A SHIELD, AND SHE DIALED IT UP SO IT WAS BIG ENOUGH TO COVER US ALL.
SAVED OUR LIVES-- ALTHOUGH IT DIDN'T KEEP US FROM GETTING BLASTED RIGHT THROUGH THE BUILDING'S EXTERIOR WALL.
BARELY FELT IT. ADRENALINE BOOST WAS BLOCKING THE PAIN.
WE WERE STILL SIX STORIES UP, THOUGH, AND MISTY'S ARM COULDN'T MAKE US FLY.
PFFSH
THAT WAS ON ME.
WHP
I GOT MISTY.
BUT I MISSED FRANK.
HE WAS DEAD. NO DOUBT IN MY MIND.

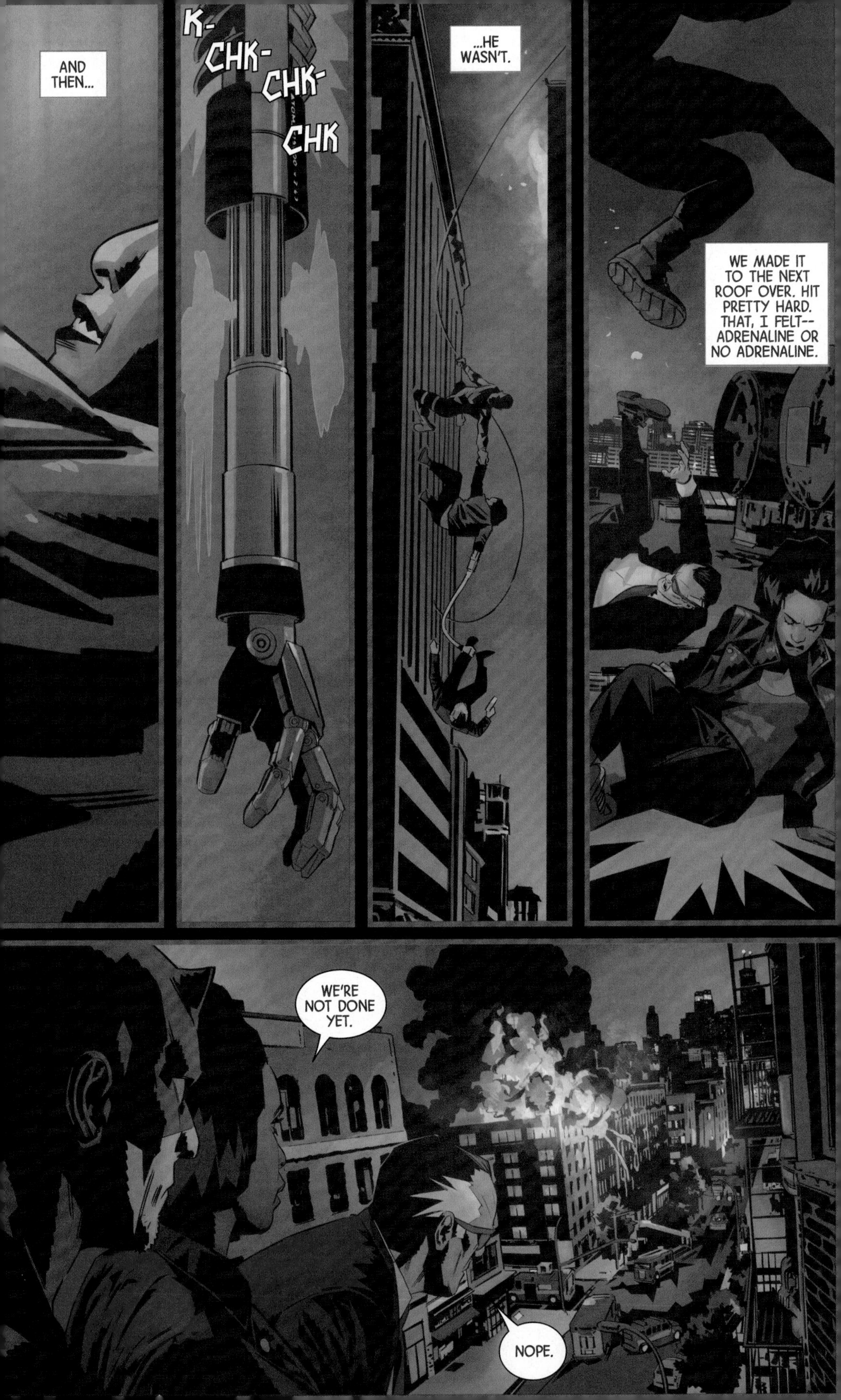
AND THEN...
K-CHK-CHK-CHK
...HE WASN'T.
WE MADE IT TO THE NEXT ROOF OVER. HIT PRETTY HARD. THAT, I FELT--ADRENALINE OR NO ADRENALINE.
WE'RE NOT DONE YET.
NOPE.

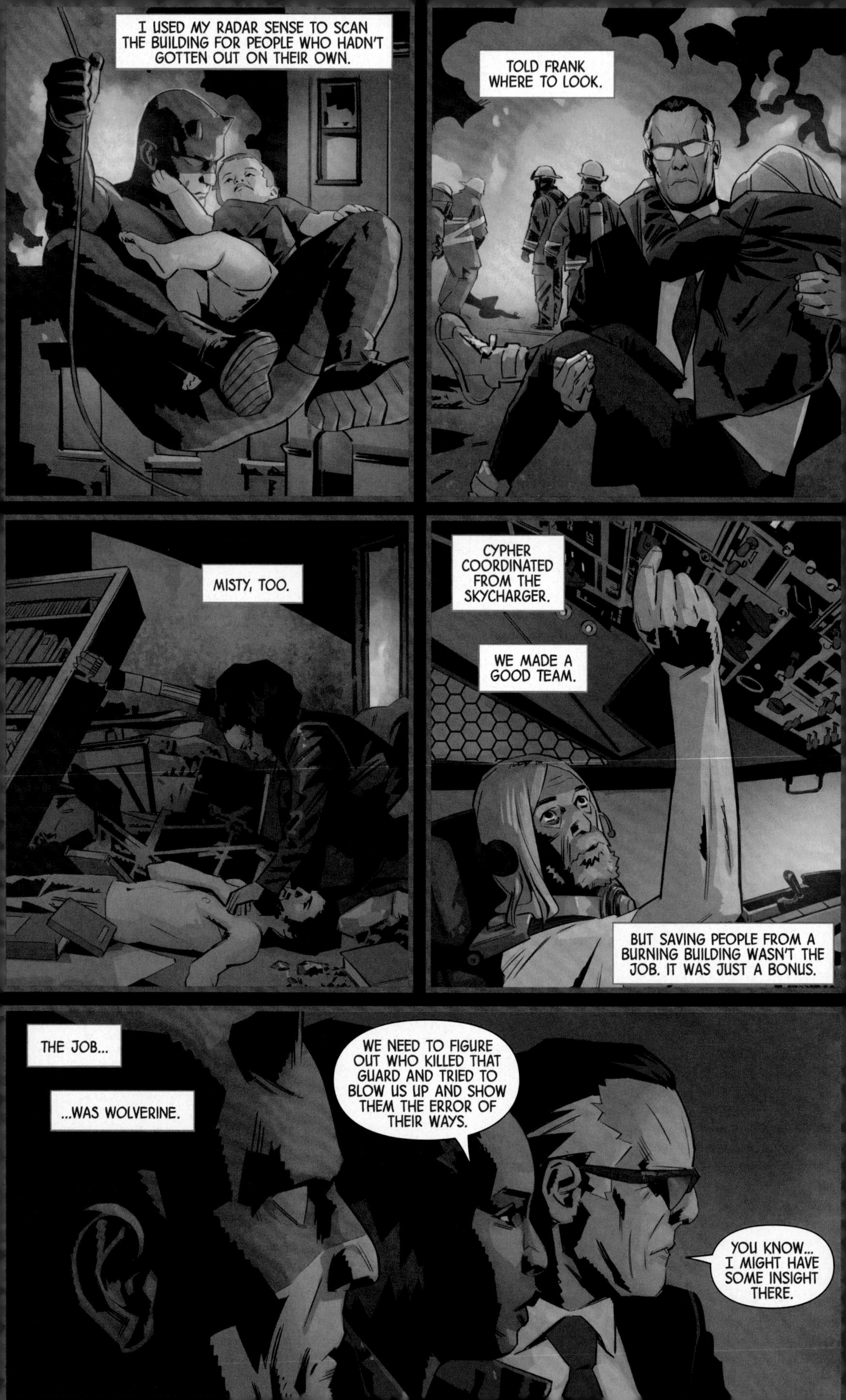

I USED MY RADAR SENSE TO SCAN THE BUILDING FOR PEOPLE WHO HADN'T GOTTEN OUT ON THEIR OWN.
TOLD FRANK WHERE TO LOOK.
MISTY, TOO.
CYPHER COORDINATED FROM THE SKYCHARGER.
WE MADE A GOOD TEAM.
BUT SAVING PEOPLE FROM A BURNING BUILDING WASN'T THE JOB. IT WAS JUST A BONUS.
THE JOB...
...WAS WOLVERINE.
WE NEED TO FIGURE OUT WHO KILLED THAT GUARD AND TRIED TO BLOW US UP AND SHOW THEM THE ERROR OF THEIR WAYS.
YOU KNOW... I MIGHT HAVE SOME INSIGHT THERE.

MY EYES AREN'T JUST GOOD FOR SENDING OUT BLASTS OF LIGHT AND BLINDING PEOPLE. I CAN USE THEM SORT OF LIKE A CAMERA FLASH.

WHEN I DO IT, THE IMAGE GETS STORED IN MY HEAD, AND I CAN ZOOM, ENHANCE, WHATEVER. REAL GOOD FOR CRIME SCENES.

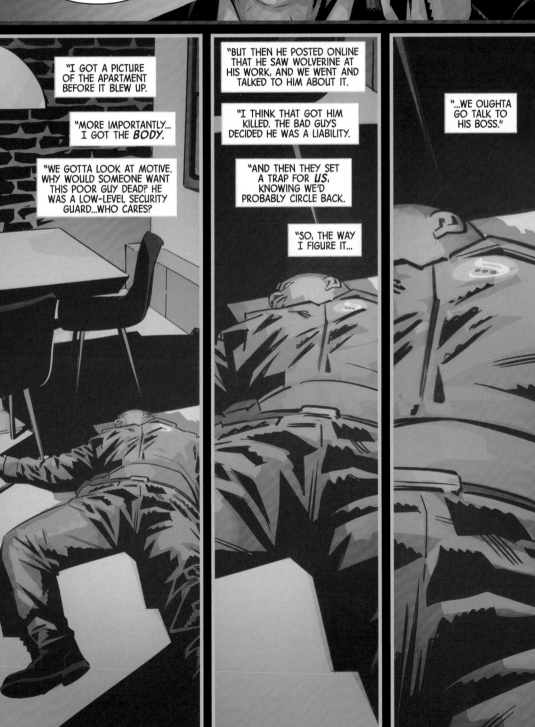

"I GOT A PICTURE OF THE APARTMENT BEFORE IT BLEW UP.

"MORE IMPORTANTLY... I GOT THE *BODY.*

"WE GOTTA LOOK AT MOTIVE. WHY WOULD SOMEONE WANT THIS POOR GUY DEAD? HE WAS A LOW-LEVEL SECURITY GUARD...WHO CARES?

"BUT THEN HE POSTED ONLINE THAT HE SAW WOLVERINE AT HIS WORK, AND WE WENT AND TALKED TO HIM ABOUT IT.

"I THINK THAT GOT HIM KILLED. THE BAD GUYS DECIDED HE WAS A LIABILITY.

"AND THEN THEY SET A TRAP FOR *US,* KNOWING WE'D PROBABLY CIRCLE BACK.

"SO, THE WAY I FIGURE IT...

"...WE OUGHTA GO TALK TO HIS BOSS."

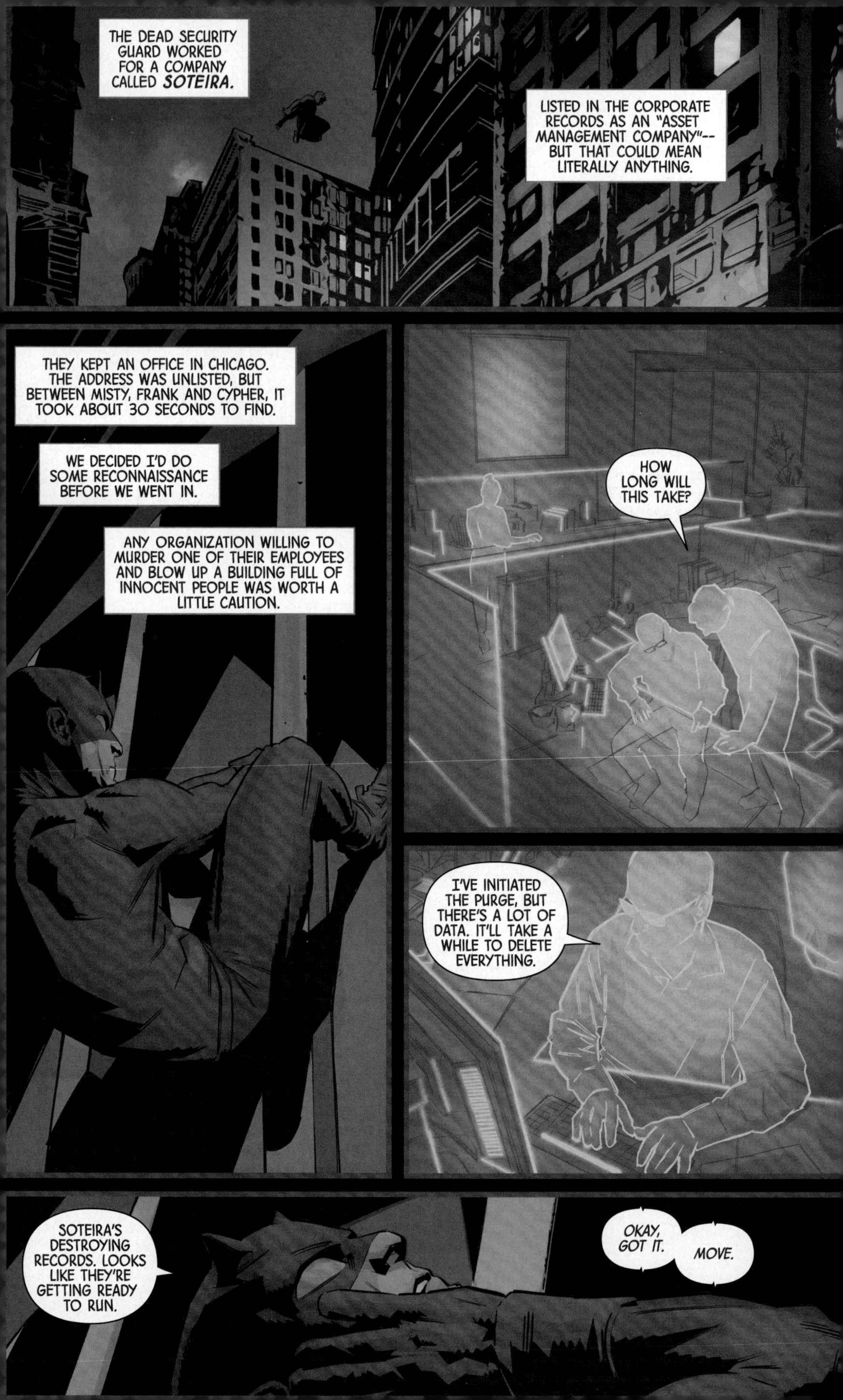
THE DEAD SECURITY GUARD WORKED FOR A COMPANY CALLED SOTEIRA.
LISTED IN THE CORPORATE RECORDS AS AN "ASSET MANAGEMENT COMPANY"-- BUT THAT COULD MEAN LITERALLY ANYTHING.
THEY KEPT AN OFFICE IN CHICAGO. THE ADDRESS WAS UNLISTED, BUT BETWEEN MISTY, FRANK AND CYPHER, IT TOOK ABOUT 30 SECONDS TO FIND.
WE DECIDED I'D DO SOME RECONNAISSANCE BEFORE WE WENT IN.
ANY ORGANIZATION WILLING TO MURDER ONE OF THEIR EMPLOYEES AND BLOW UP A BUILDING FULL OF INNOCENT PEOPLE WAS WORTH A LITTLE CAUTION.
HOW LONG WILL THIS TAKE?
I'VE INITIATED THE PURGE, BUT THERE'S A LOT OF DATA. IT'LL TAKE A WHILE TO DELETE EVERYTHING.
SOTEIRA'S DESTROYING RECORDS. LOOKS LIKE THEY'RE GETTING READY TO RUN.
OKAY, GOT IT.
MOVE.

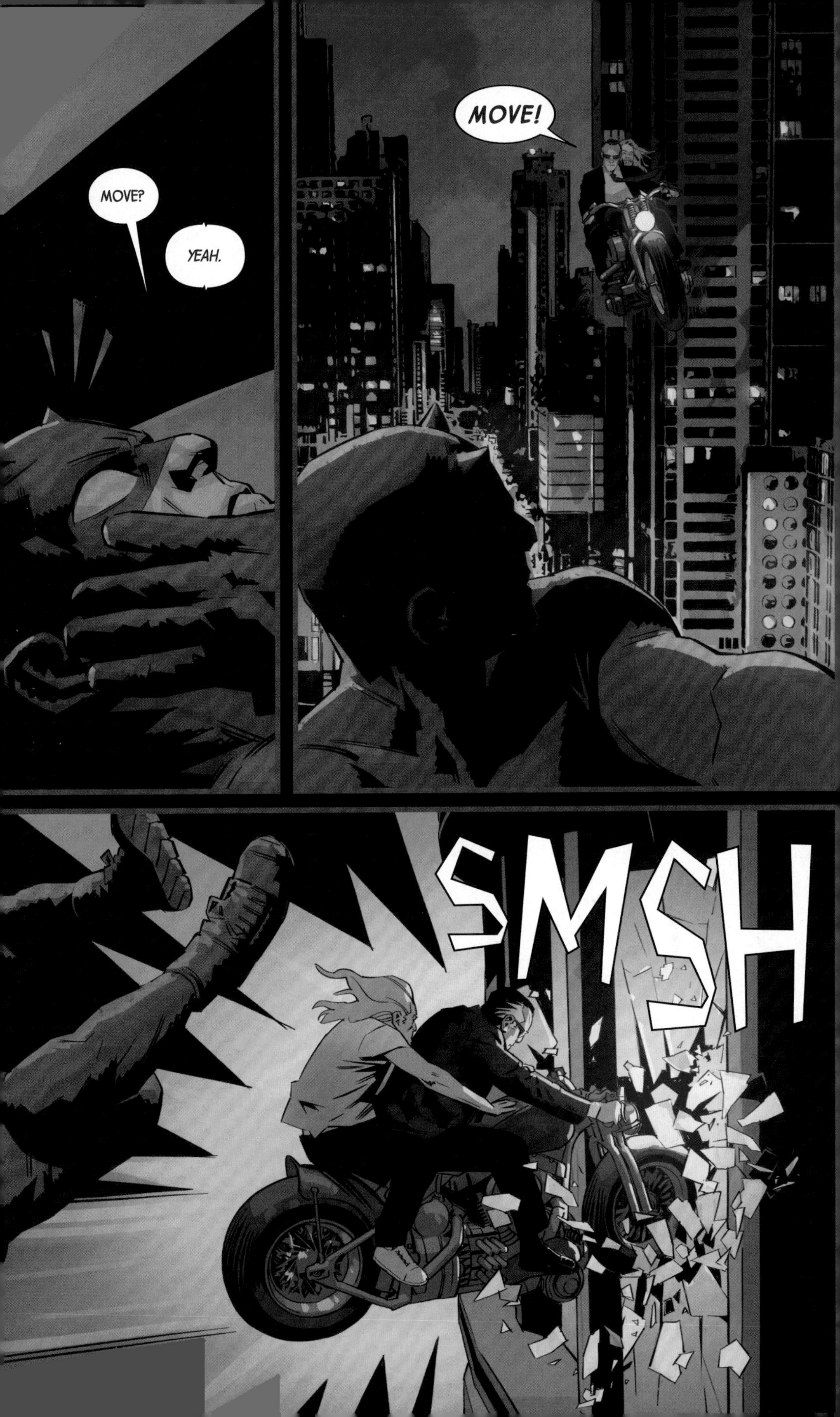
MOVE?
YEAH.
MOVE!
SMSH

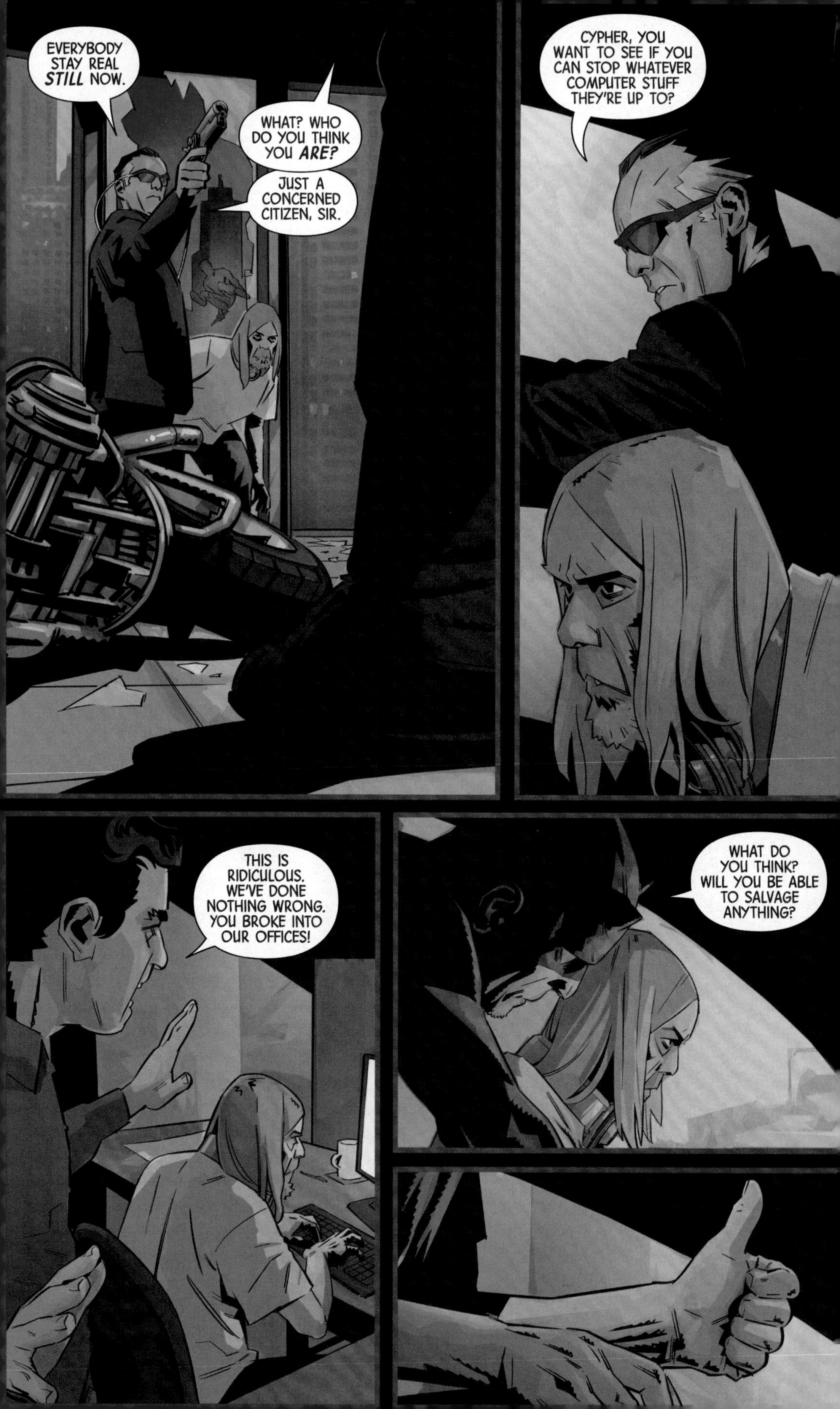
EVERYBODY STAY REAL STILL NOW.
WHAT? WHO DO YOU THINK YOU ARE?
JUST A CONCERNED CITIZEN, SIR.
CYPHER, YOU WANT TO SEE IF YOU CAN STOP WHATEVER COMPUTER STUFF THEY'RE UP TO?
THIS IS RIDICULOUS. WE'VE DONE NOTHING WRONG. YOU BROKE INTO OUR OFFICES!
WHAT DO YOU THINK? WILL YOU BE ABLE TO SALVAGE ANYTHING?

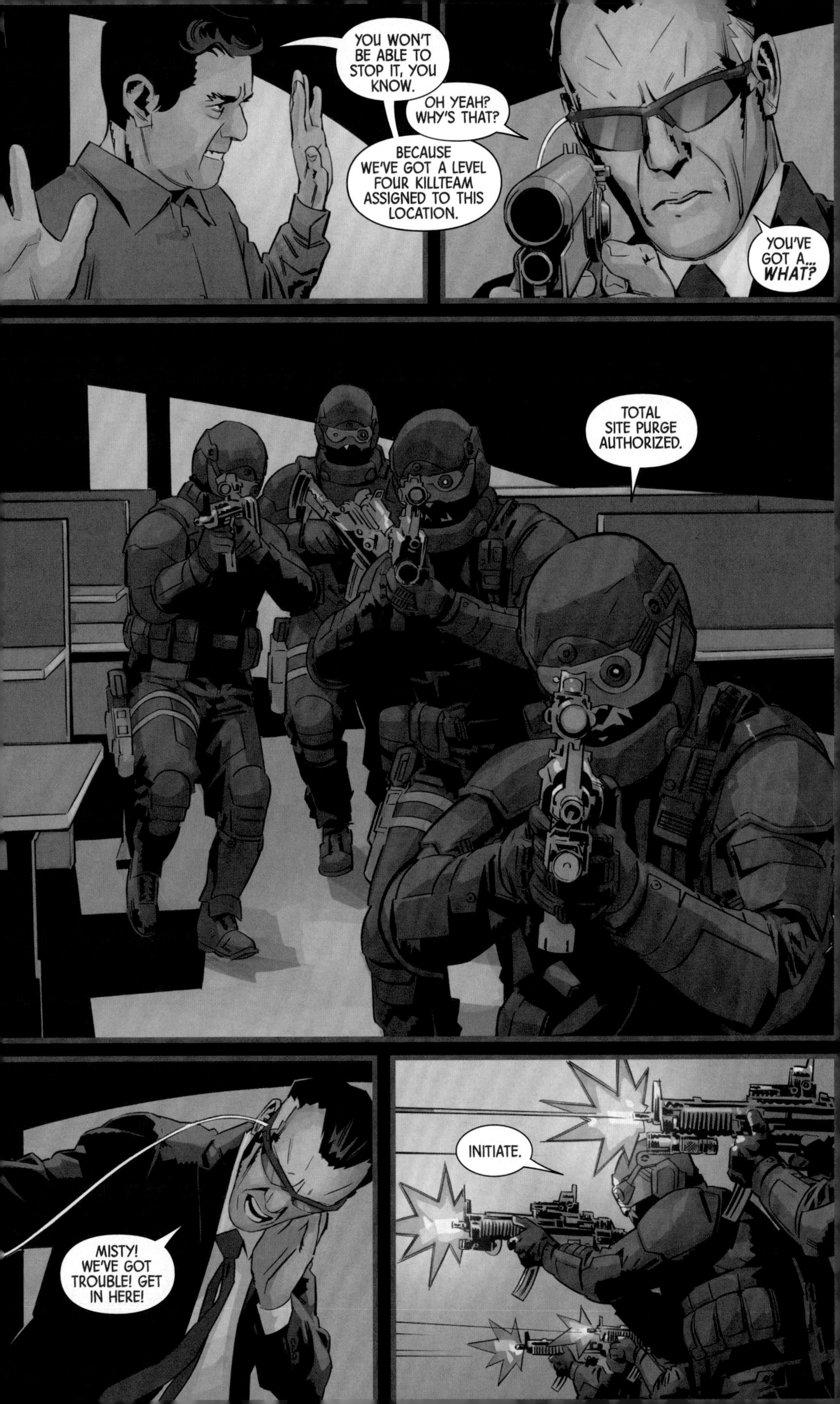

YOU WON'T BE ABLE TO STOP IT, YOU KNOW.
OH YEAH? WHY'S THAT?
BECAUSE WE'VE GOT A LEVEL FOUR KILLTEAM ASSIGNED TO THIS LOCATION.
YOU'VE GOT A... WHAT?
TOTAL SITE PURGE AUTHORIZED.
MISTY! WE'VE GOT TROUBLE! GET IN HERE!
INITIATE.

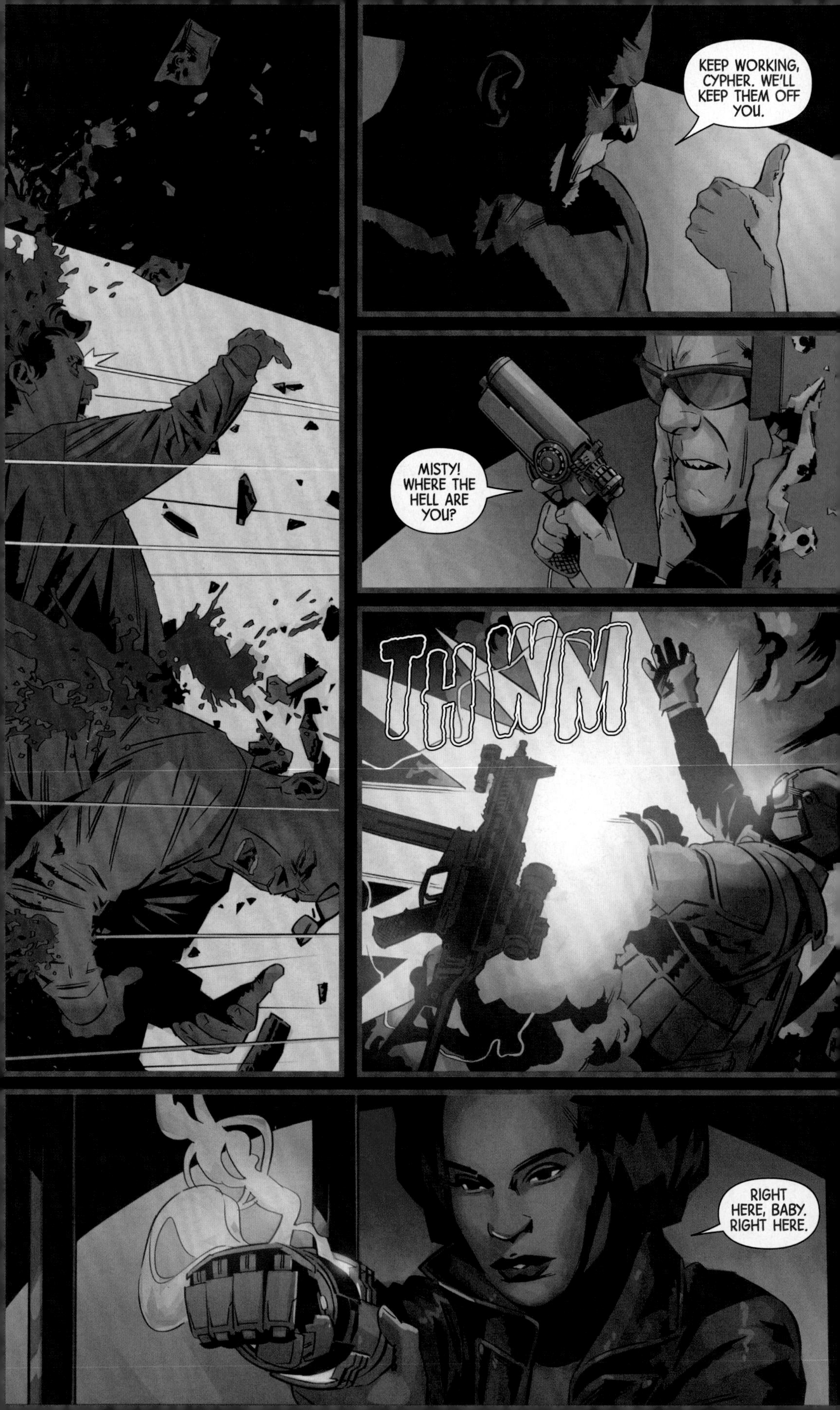
KEEP WORKING, CYPHER. WE'LL KEEP THEM OFF YOU.
MISTY! WHERE THE HELL ARE YOU?
THWM
RIGHT HERE, BABY. RIGHT HERE.

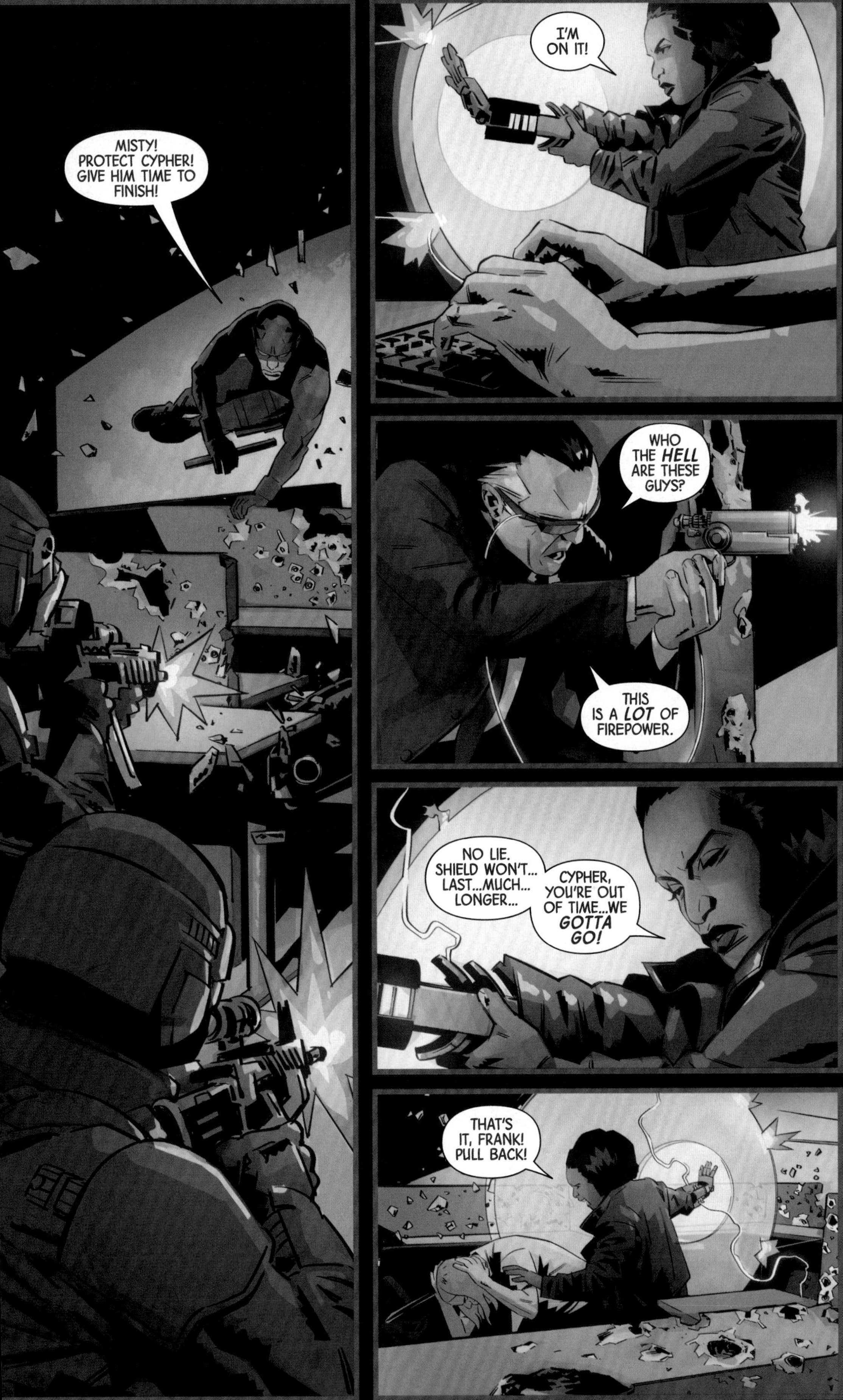
MISTY! PROTECT CYPHER! GIVE HIM TIME TO FINISH!
I'M ON IT!
WHO THE HELL ARE THESE GUYS?
THIS IS A LOT OF FIREPOWER.
NO LIE. SHIELD WON'T... LAST...MUCH... LONGER...
CYPHER, YOU'RE OUT OF TIME...WE GOTTA GO!
THAT'S IT, FRANK! PULL BACK!

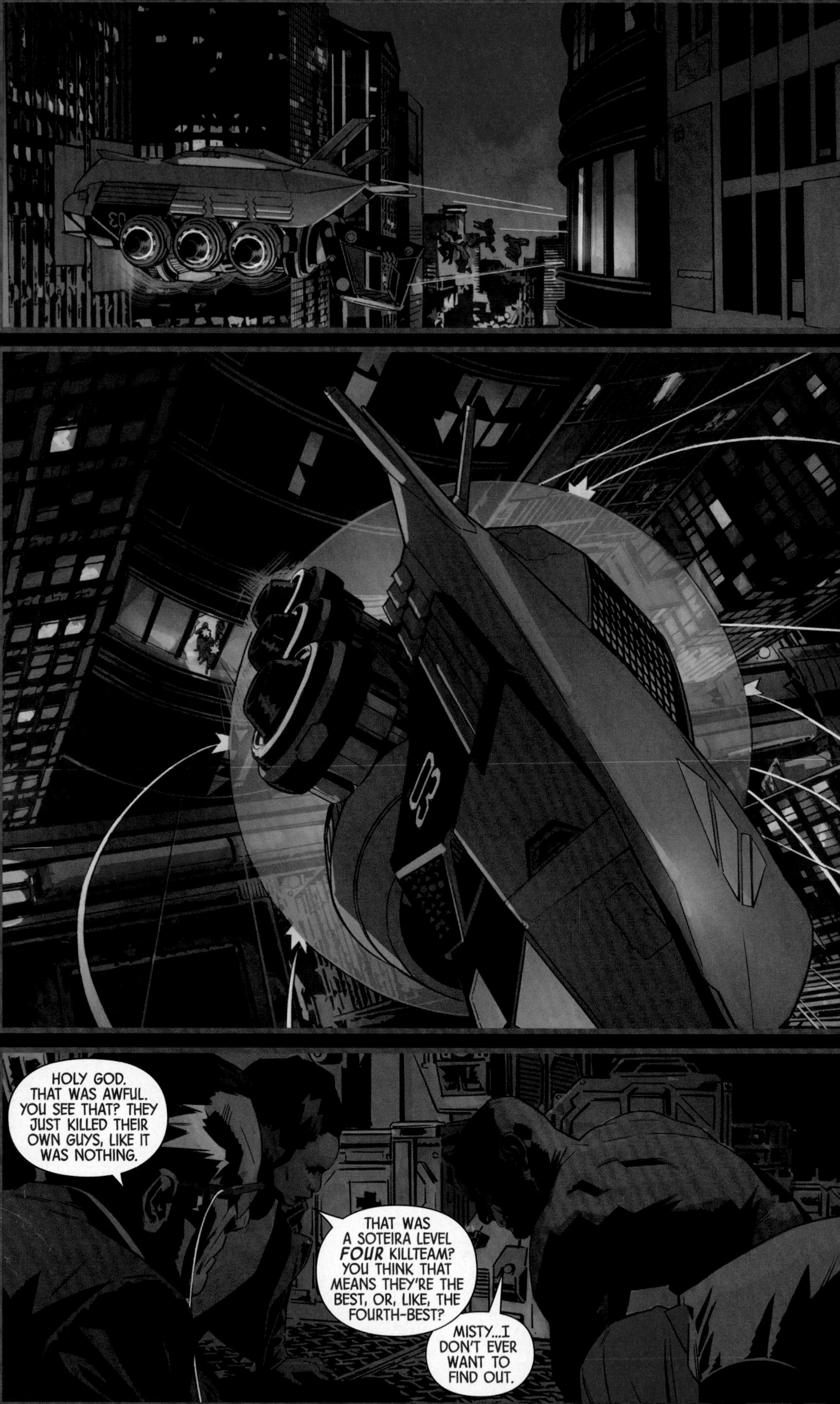
HOLY GOD. THAT WAS AWFUL. YOU SEE THAT? THEY JUST KILLED THEIR OWN GUYS, LIKE IT WAS NOTHING.
THAT WAS A SOTEIRA LEVEL *FOUR* KILLTEAM? YOU THINK THAT MEANS THEY'RE THE BEST, OR, LIKE, THE FOURTH-BEST?
MISTY...I DON'T EVER WANT TO FIND OUT.

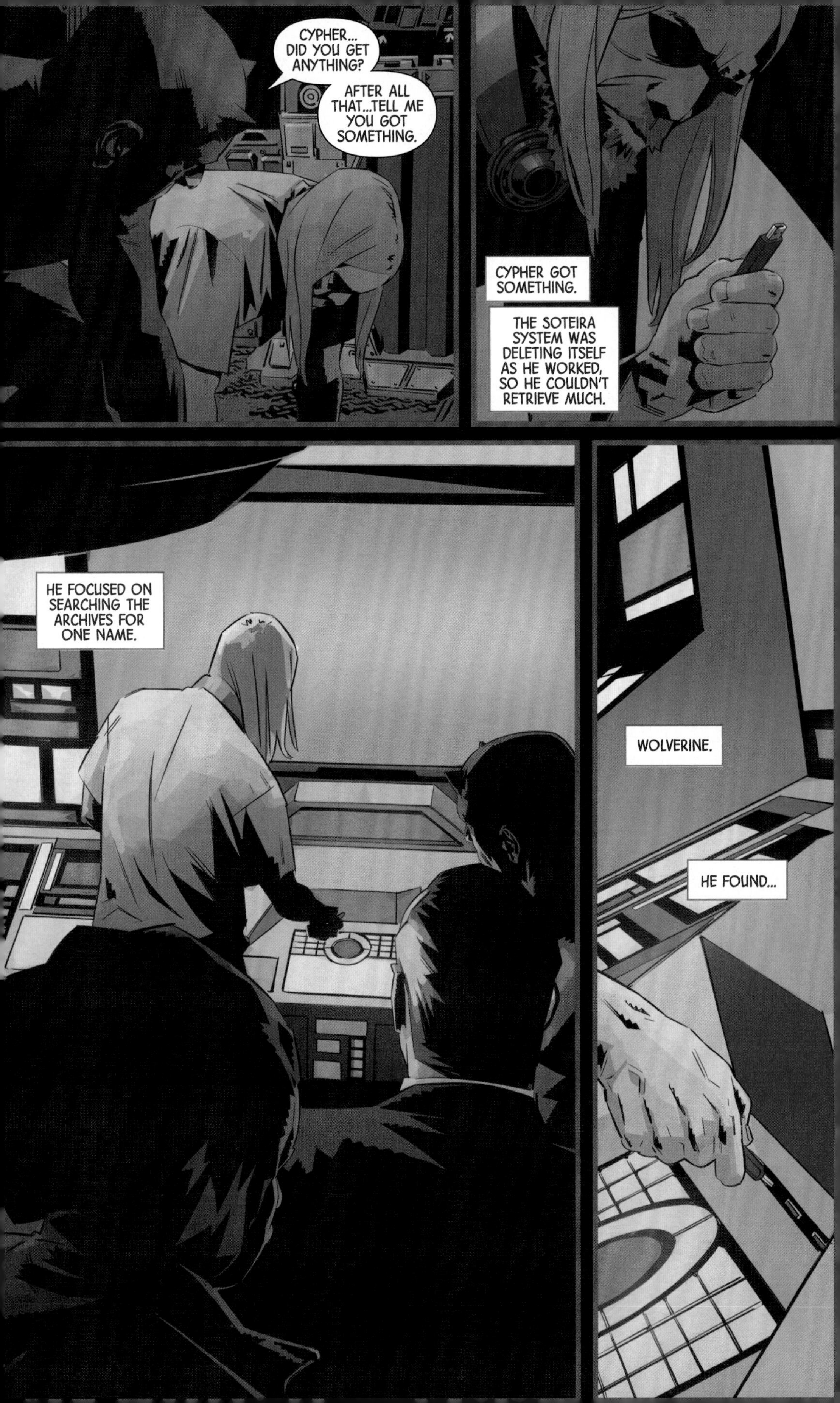
CYPHER... DID YOU GET ANYTHING?
AFTER ALL THAT...TELL ME YOU GOT SOMETHING.
CYPHER GOT SOMETHING.
THE SOTEIRA SYSTEM WAS DELETING ITSELF AS HE WORKED, SO HE COULDN'T RETRIEVE MUCH.
HE FOCUSED ON SEARCHING THE ARCHIVES FOR ONE NAME.
WOLVERINE.
HE FOUND...

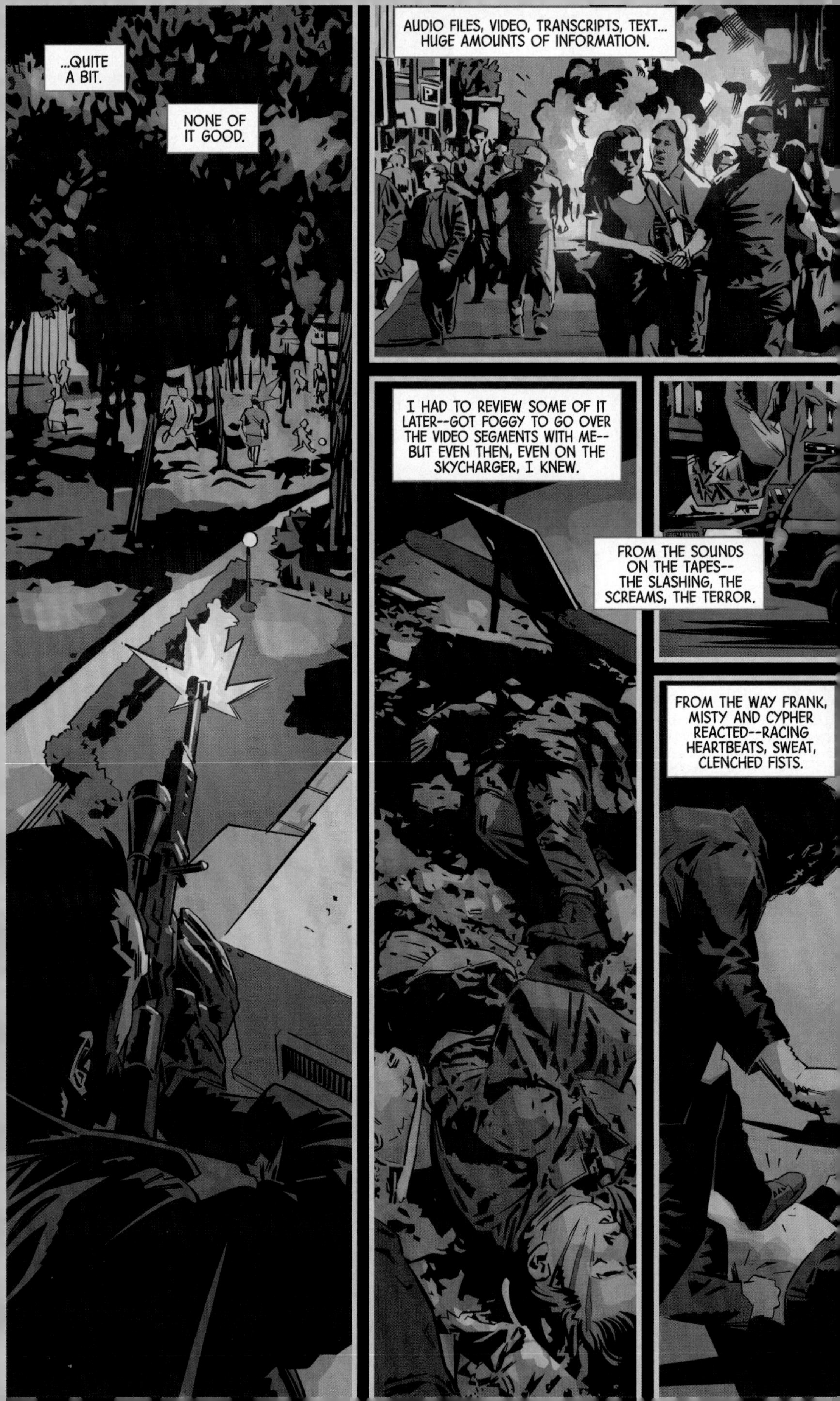
...QUITE A BIT.
NONE OF IT GOOD.
AUDIO FILES, VIDEO, TRANSCRIPTS, TEXT... HUGE AMOUNTS OF INFORMATION.
I HAD TO REVIEW SOME OF IT LATER--GOT FOGGY TO GO OVER THE VIDEO SEGMENTS WITH ME--BUT EVEN THEN, EVEN ON THE SKYCHARGER, I KNEW.
FROM THE SOUNDS ON THE TAPES--THE SLASHING, THE SCREAMS, THE TERROR.
FROM THE WAY FRANK, MISTY AND CYPHER REACTED--RACING HEARTBEATS, SWEAT, CLENCHED FISTS.

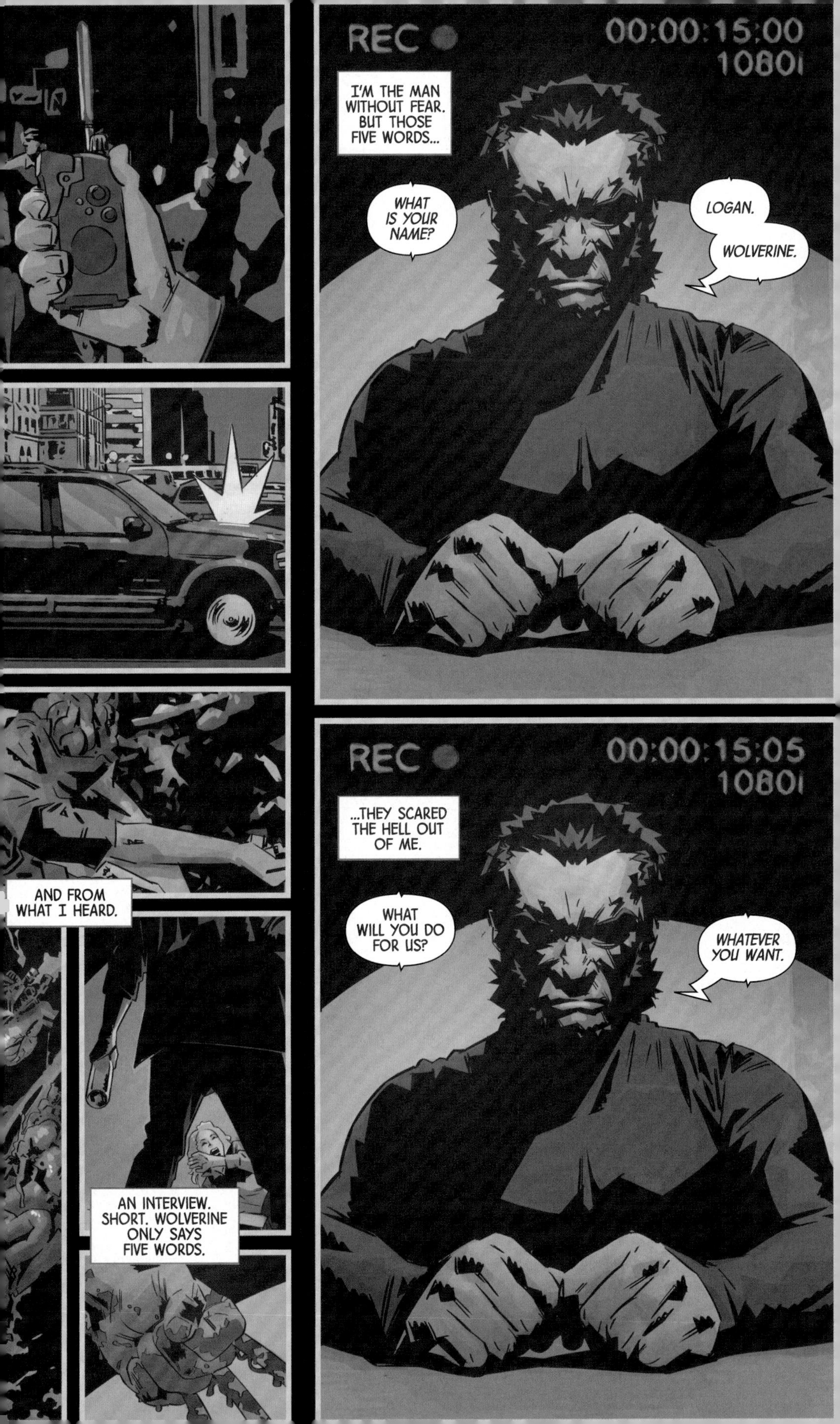
REC
00:00:15:00
1080i
I'M THE MAN WITHOUT FEAR. BUT THOSE FIVE WORDS...
WHAT IS YOUR NAME?
LOGAN.
WOLVERINE.
AND FROM WHAT I HEARD.
AN INTERVIEW. SHORT. WOLVERINE ONLY SAYS FIVE WORDS.
REC
00:00:15:05
1080i
...THEY SCARED THE HELL OUT OF ME.
WHAT WILL YOU DO FOR US?
WHATEVER YOU WANT.

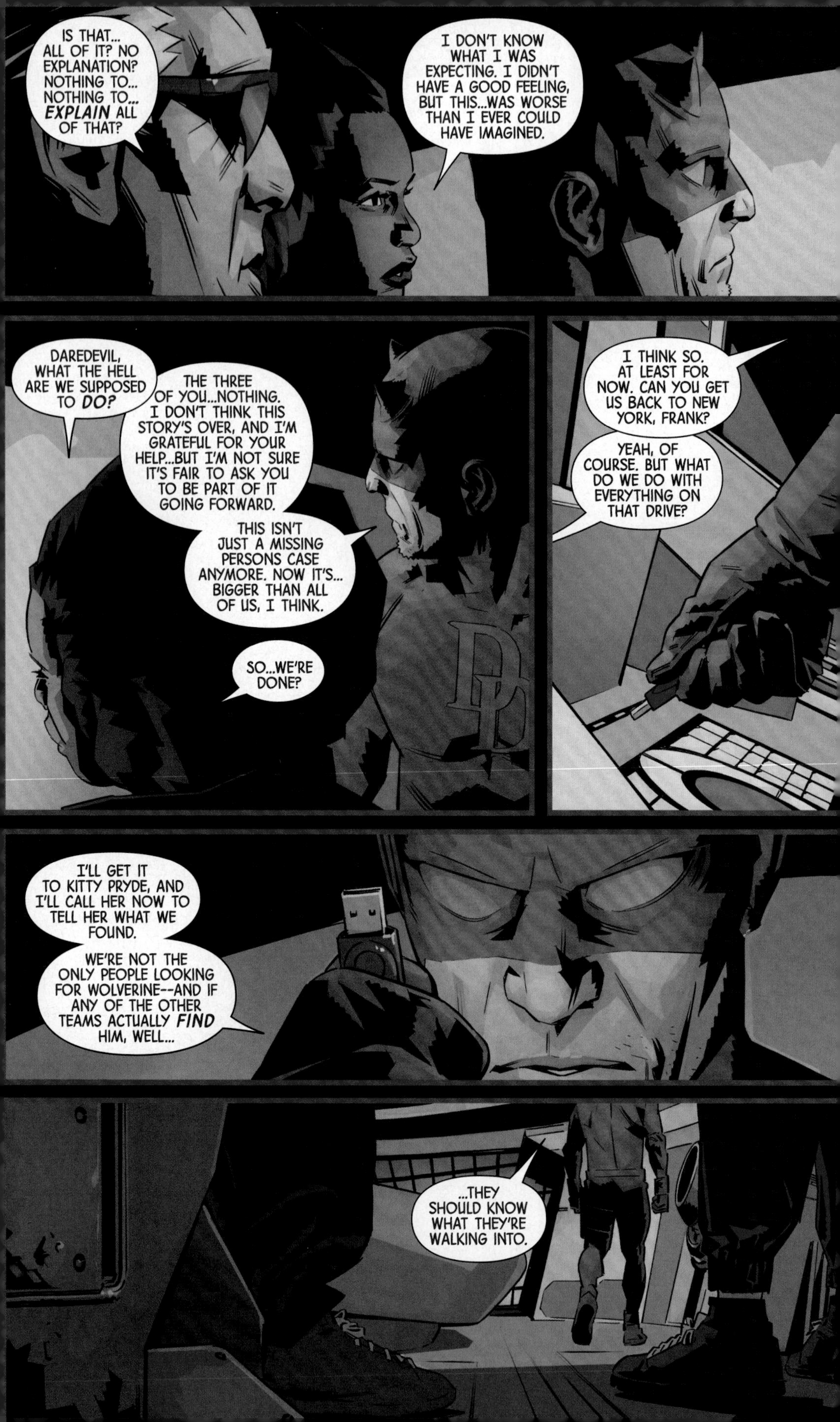
IS THAT... ALL OF IT? NO EXPLANATION? NOTHING TO... NOTHING TO... ***EXPLAIN*** ALL OF THAT?
I DON'T KNOW WHAT I WAS EXPECTING. I DIDN'T HAVE A GOOD FEELING, BUT THIS...WAS WORSE THAN I EVER COULD HAVE IMAGINED.
DAREDEVIL, WHAT THE HELL ARE WE SUPPOSED TO ***DO?***
THE THREE OF YOU...NOTHING. I DON'T THINK THIS STORY'S OVER, AND I'M GRATEFUL FOR YOUR HELP...BUT I'M NOT SURE IT'S FAIR TO ASK YOU TO BE PART OF IT GOING FORWARD.
THIS ISN'T JUST A MISSING PERSONS CASE ANYMORE. NOW IT'S... BIGGER THAN ALL OF US, I THINK.
SO...WE'RE DONE?
I THINK SO. AT LEAST FOR NOW. CAN YOU GET US BACK TO NEW YORK, FRANK?
YEAH, OF COURSE. BUT WHAT DO WE DO WITH EVERYTHING ON THAT DRIVE?
I'LL GET IT TO KITTY PRYDE, AND I'LL CALL HER NOW TO TELL HER WHAT WE FOUND.
WE'RE NOT THE ONLY PEOPLE LOOKING FOR WOLVERINE--AND IF ANY OF THE OTHER TEAMS ACTUALLY ***FIND*** HIM, WELL...
...THEY SHOULD KNOW WHAT THEY'RE WALKING INTO.

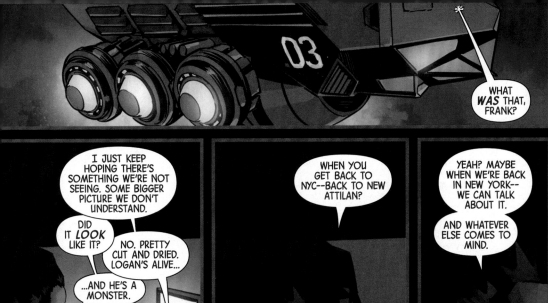

WHAT **WAS** THAT, FRANK?

I JUST KEEP HOPING THERE'S SOMETHING WE'RE NOT SEEING. SOME BIGGER PICTURE WE DON'T UNDERSTAND.

DID IT **LOOK** LIKE IT?

NO. PRETTY CUT AND DRIED. LOGAN'S ALIVE...

...AND HE'S A MONSTER.

WHEN YOU GET BACK TO NYC--BACK TO NEW ATTILAN?

YEAH? MAYBE WHEN WE'RE BACK IN NEW YORK-- WE CAN TALK ABOUT IT.

AND WHATEVER ELSE COMES TO MIND.

YOU KNOW... I'M NOT SURE. GETTING OUT, WORKING A CASE LIKE THIS--REMINDS ME I'M PRETTY GOOD AT HELPING REGULAR PEOPLE TOO, NOT JUST THE INHUMANS.

I MISS THE CITY, TOO. GOOD OLD NYC.

MISTY... LISTEN.

WHEN THIS HAPPENED...THE TERRIGEN...I... WAS MARRIED. MY WIFE...SHE LEFT ME.

AND...I KNOW HOW DUMB THIS SOUNDS, BUT I'M NOT SURE I EVER LEFT HER. NOT IN MY HEART.

YOU KNOW WHAT? I APPRECIATE YOU TELLING ME THAT. LOTTA GUYS WOULD JUST HAVE KEPT ME ON THE SIDE WHILE GOING AFTER WHAT THEY REALLY WANTED.

MAYBE WE'LL CIRCLE BACK AROUND TO EACH OTHER SOMEDAY. WHO KNOWS?

ALL OF THAT ASIDE, I'M GLAD TO HAVE MET YOU, DETECTIVE McGEE. ONE WAY OR ANOTHER, I HOPE THIS ISN'T OUR LAST CASE.

YEAH, OFFICER KNIGHT. ME TOO.

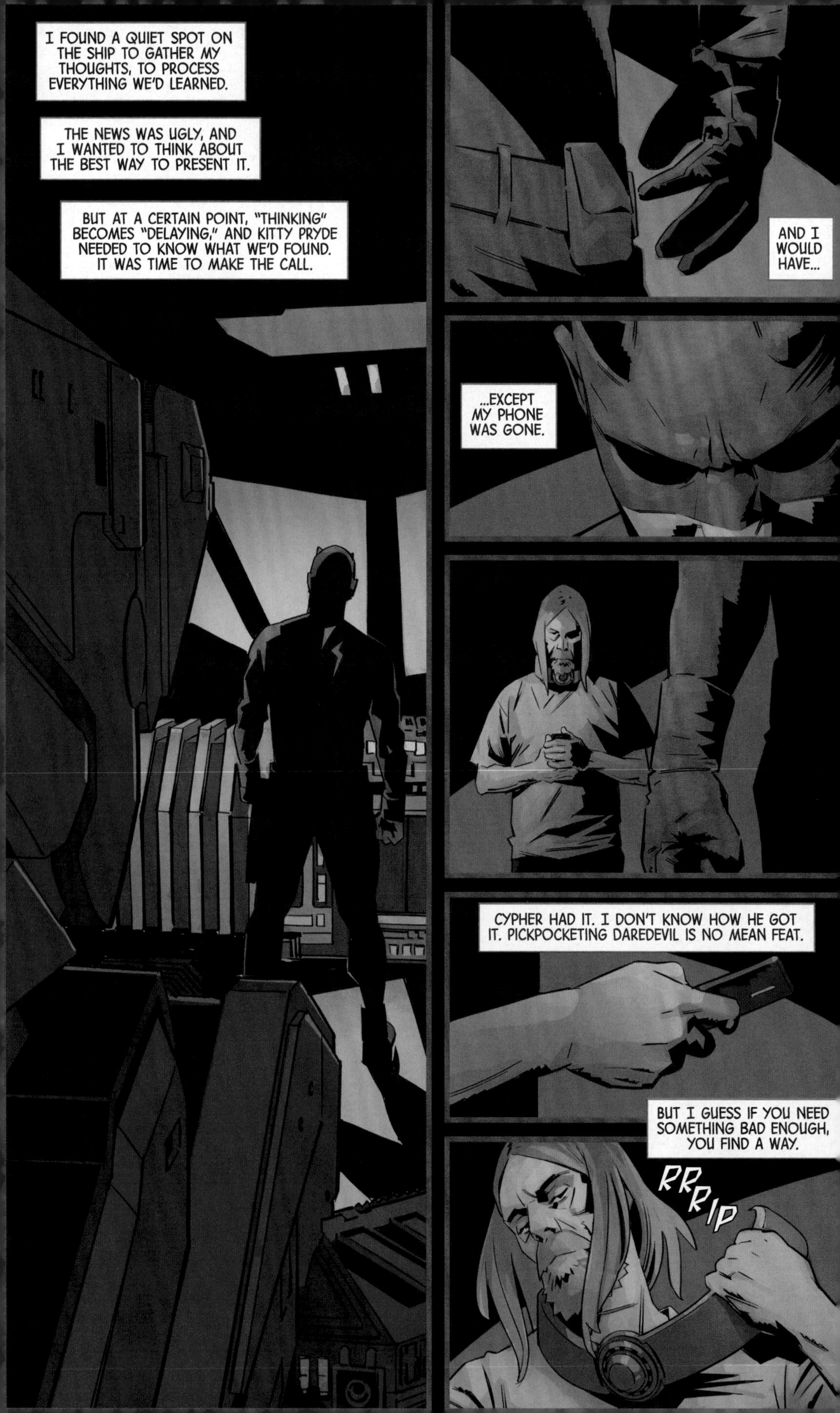
I FOUND A QUIET SPOT ON THE SHIP TO GATHER MY THOUGHTS, TO PROCESS EVERYTHING WE'D LEARNED.
THE NEWS WAS UGLY, AND I WANTED TO THINK ABOUT THE BEST WAY TO PRESENT IT.
BUT AT A CERTAIN POINT, "THINKING" BECOMES "DELAYING," AND KITTY PRYDE NEEDED TO KNOW WHAT WE'D FOUND. IT WAS TIME TO MAKE THE CALL.
AND I WOULD HAVE...
...EXCEPT MY PHONE WAS GONE.
CYPHER HAD IT. I DON'T KNOW HOW HE GOT IT. PICKPOCKETING DAREDEVIL IS NO MEAN FEAT.
BUT I GUESS IF YOU NEED SOMETHING BAD ENOUGH, YOU FIND A WAY.
RRRIP

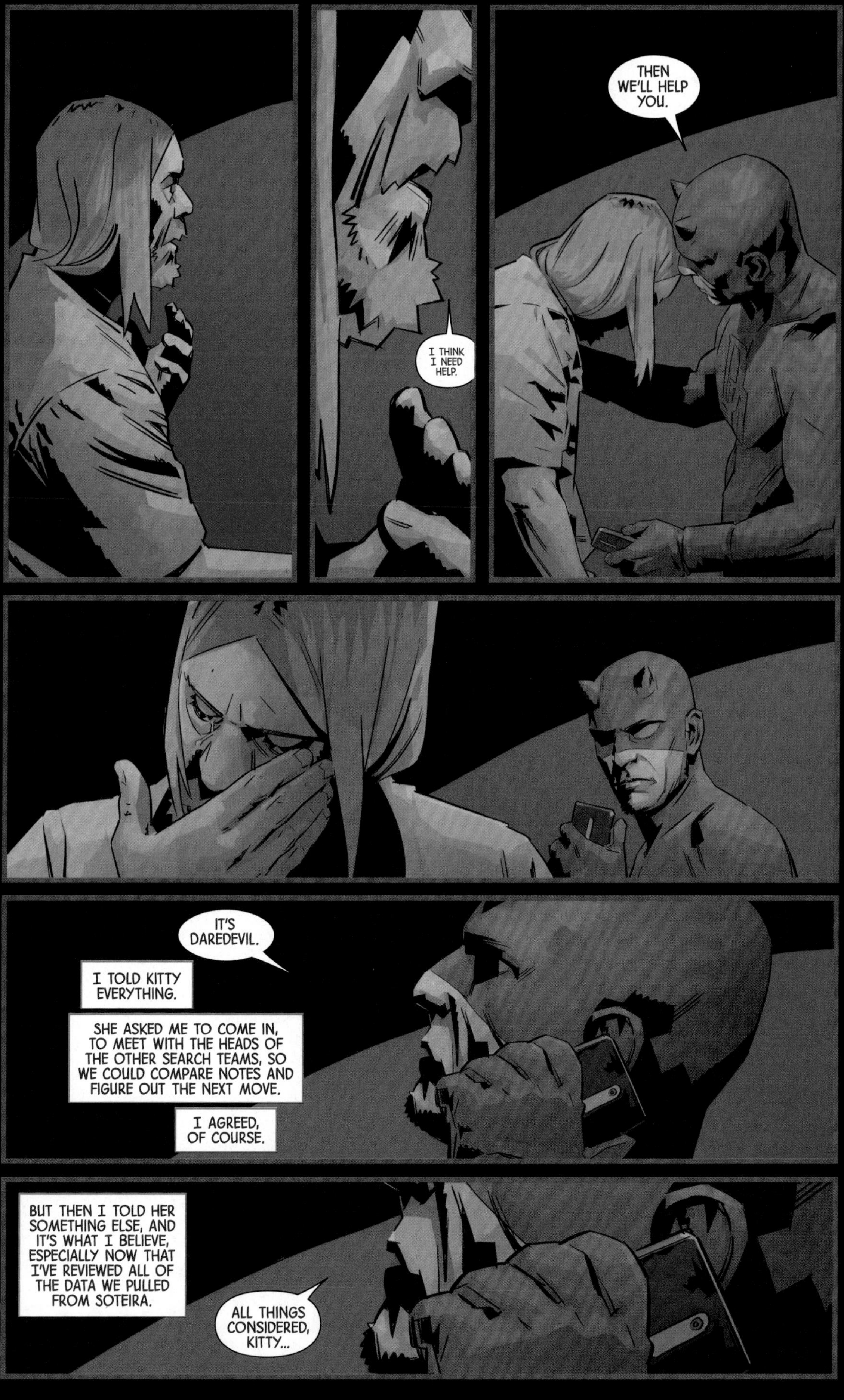
I THINK I NEED HELP.
THEN WE'LL HELP YOU.
IT'S DAREDEVIL.
I TOLD KITTY EVERYTHING.
SHE ASKED ME TO COME IN, TO MEET WITH THE HEADS OF THE OTHER SEARCH TEAMS, SO WE COULD COMPARE NOTES AND FIGURE OUT THE NEXT MOVE.
I AGREED, OF COURSE.
BUT THEN I TOLD HER SOMETHING ELSE, AND IT'S WHAT I BELIEVE, ESPECIALLY NOW THAT I'VE REVIEWED ALL OF THE DATA WE PULLED FROM SOTEIRA.
ALL THINGS CONSIDERED, KITTY...

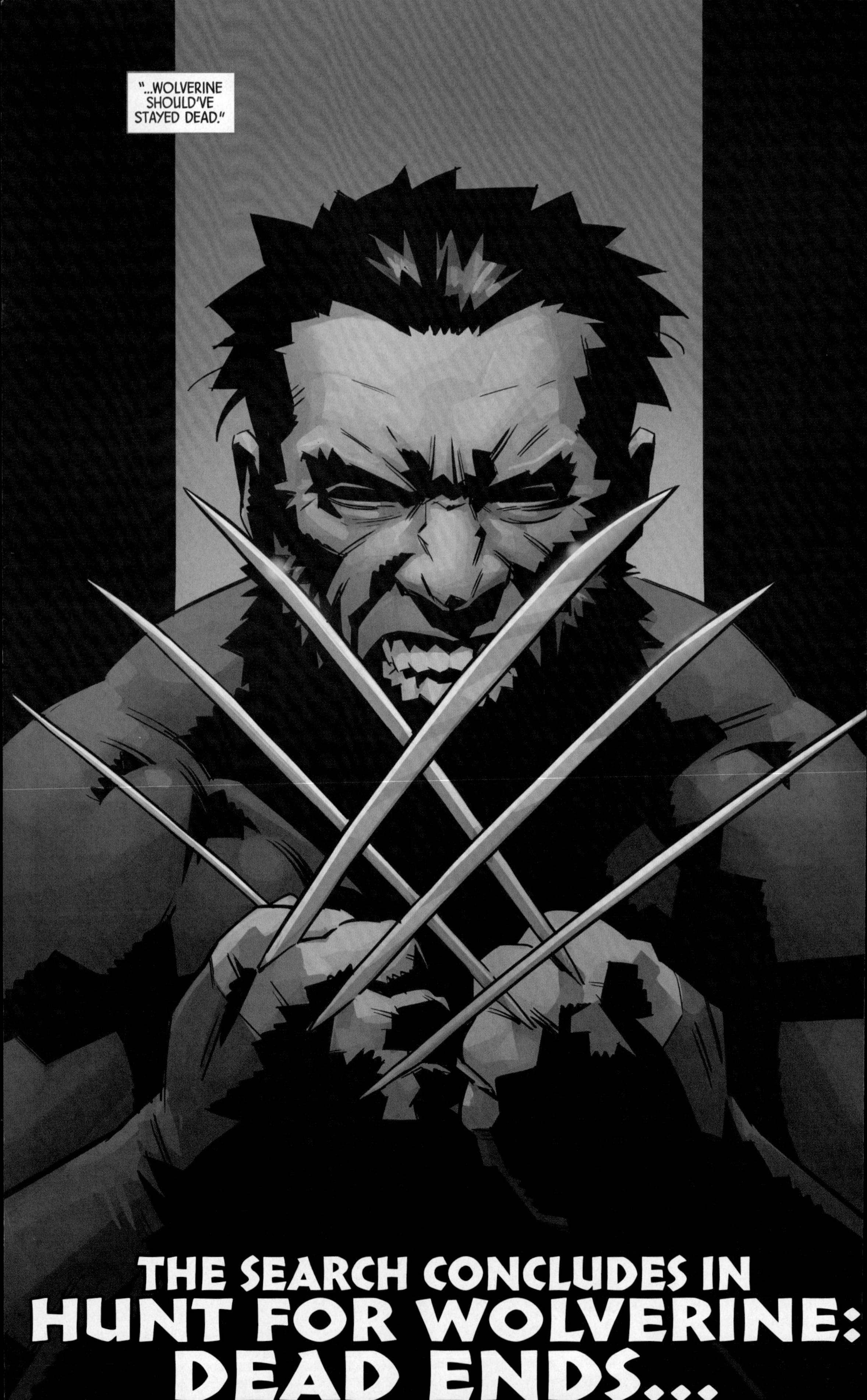
"...WOLVERINE SHOULD'VE STAYED DEAD."
THE SEARCH CONCLUDES IN
HUNT FOR WOLVERINE:
DEAD ENDS...

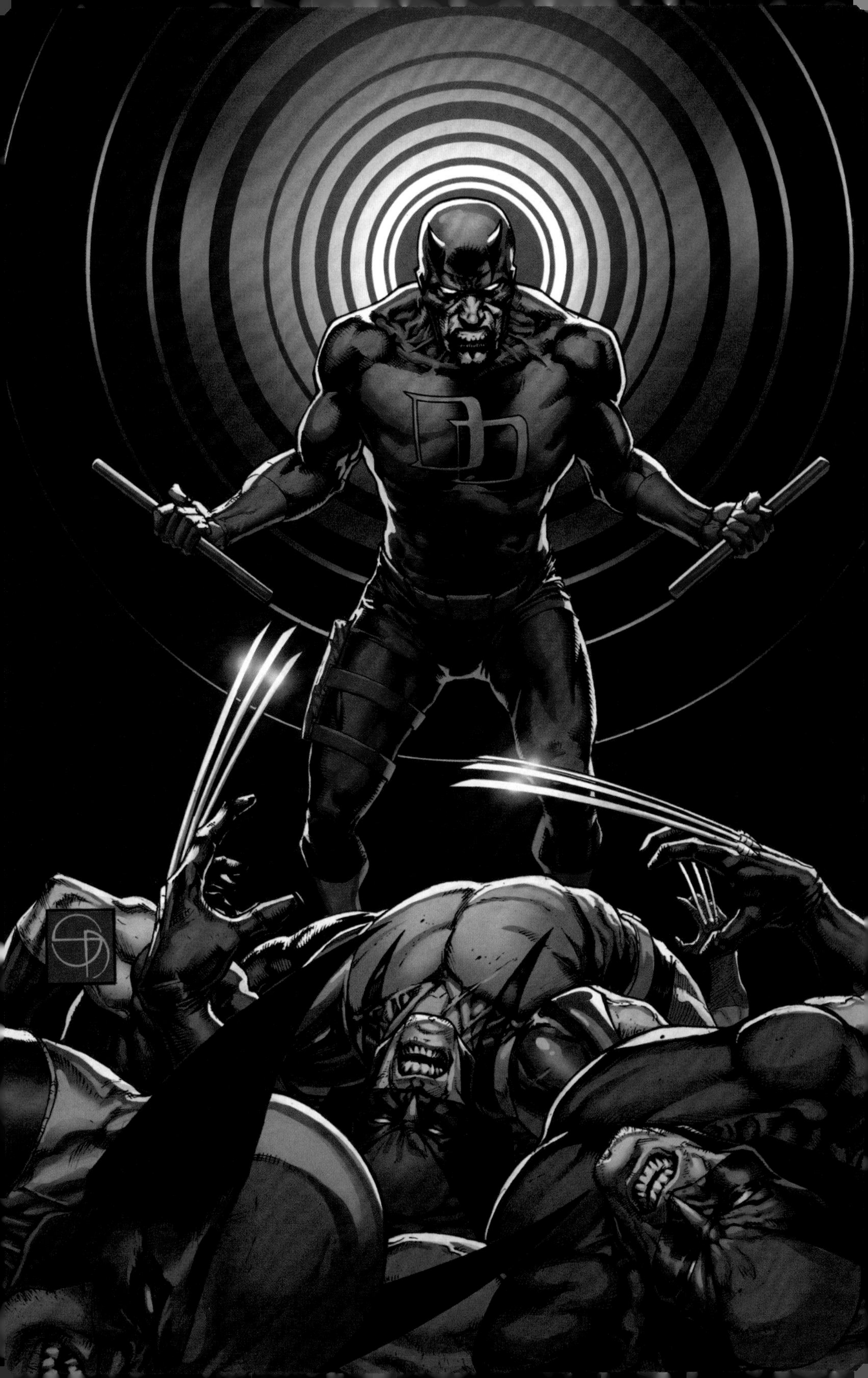

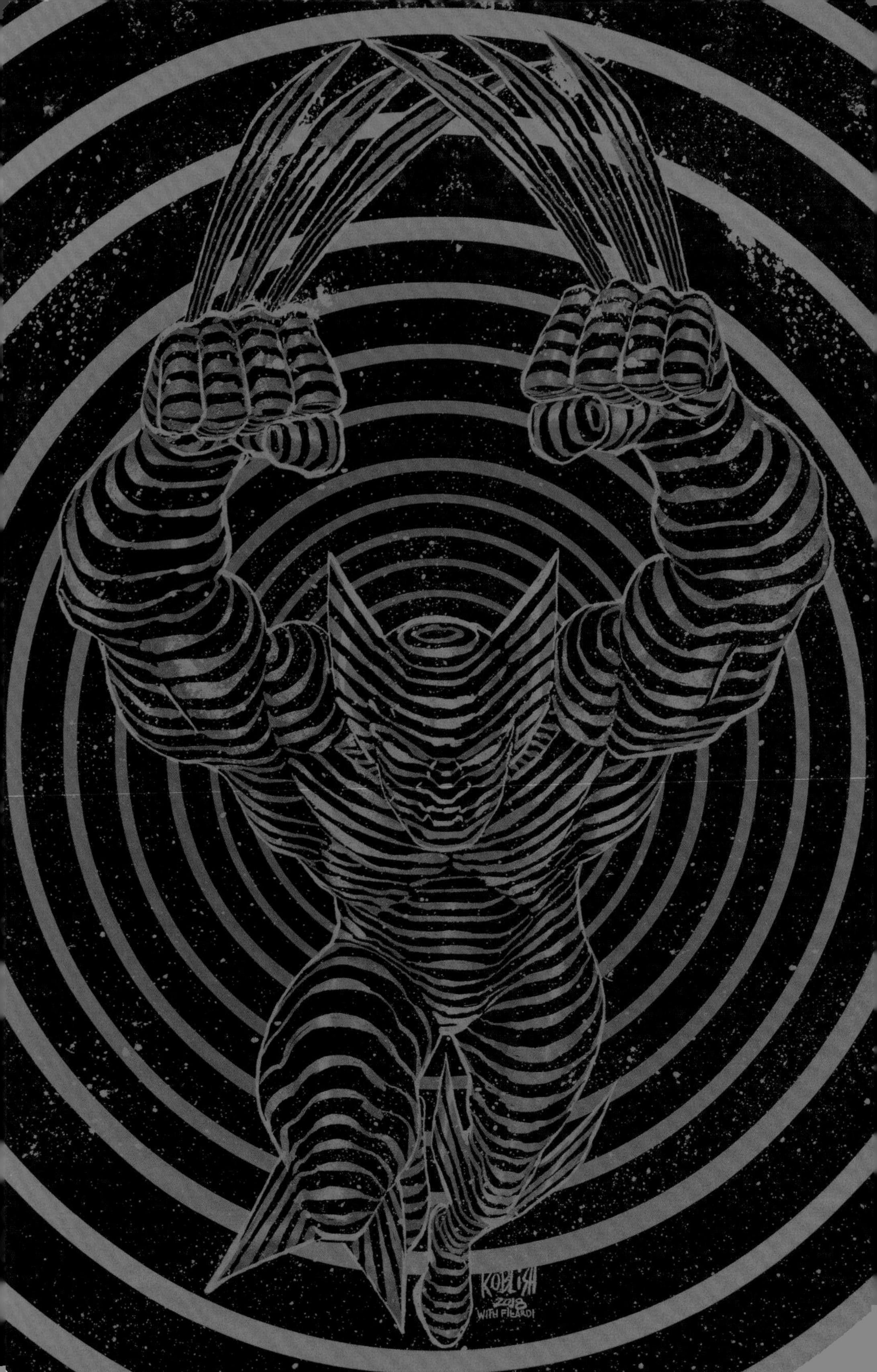
KOBLISH
2018
WITH FILARDI

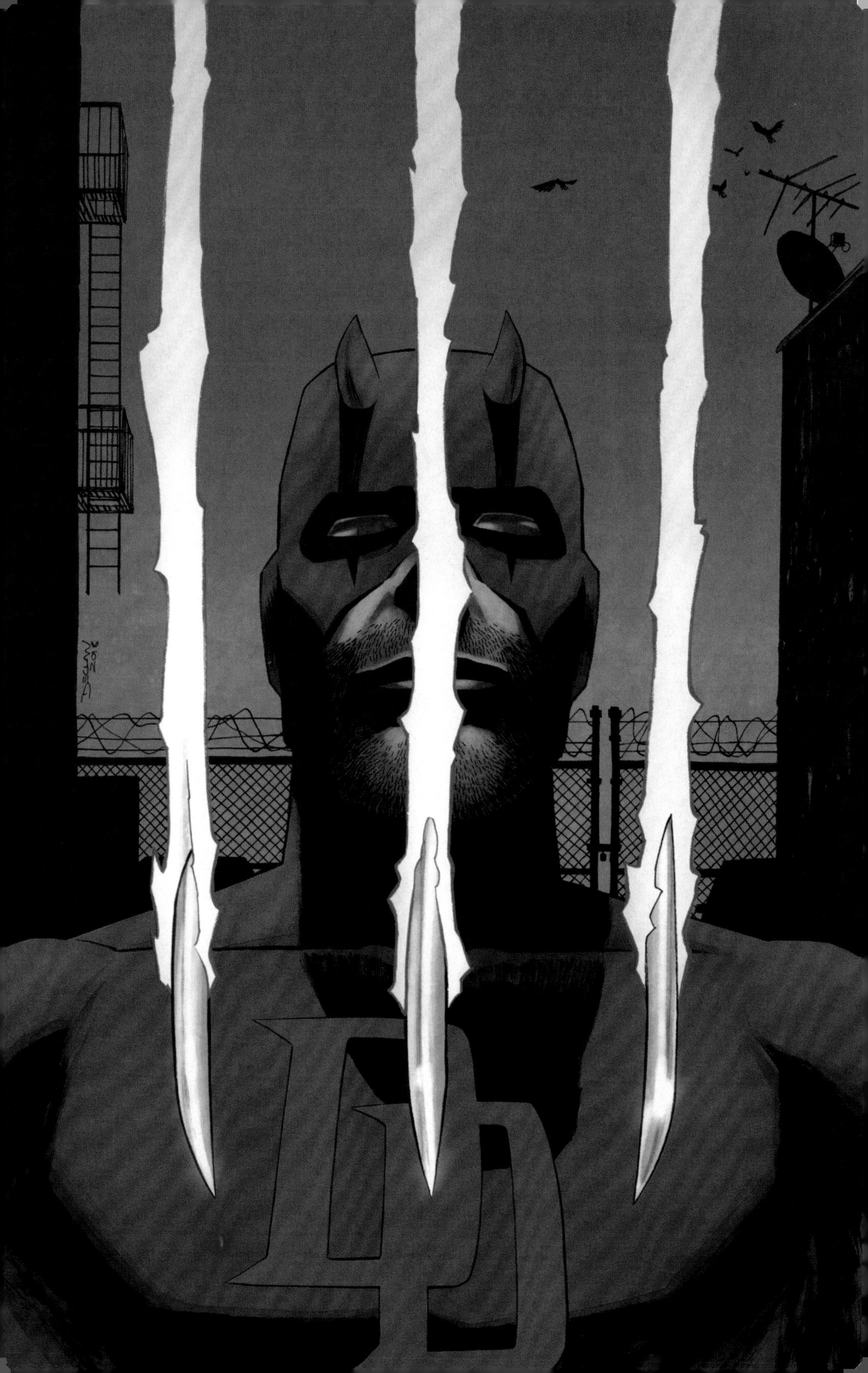

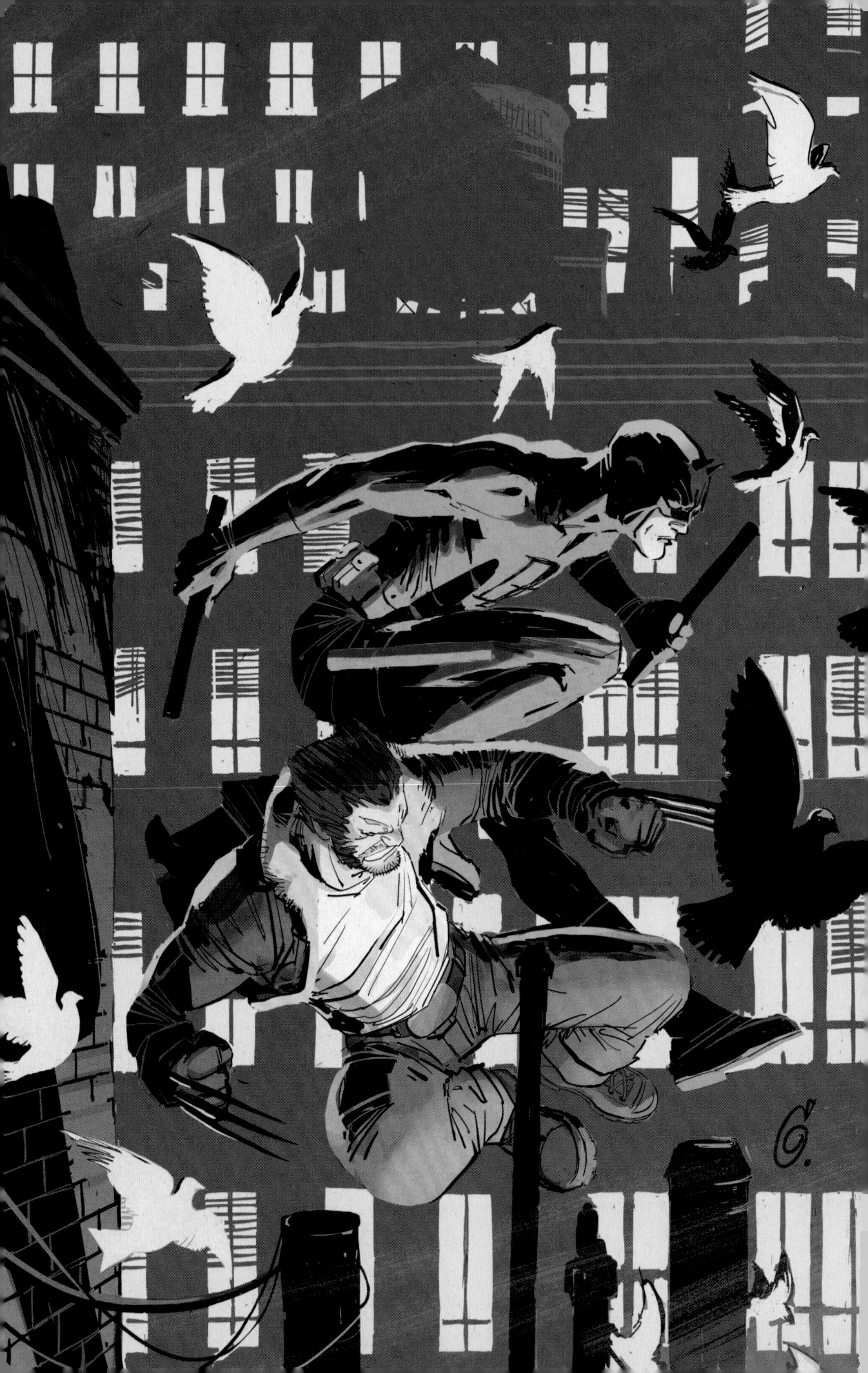

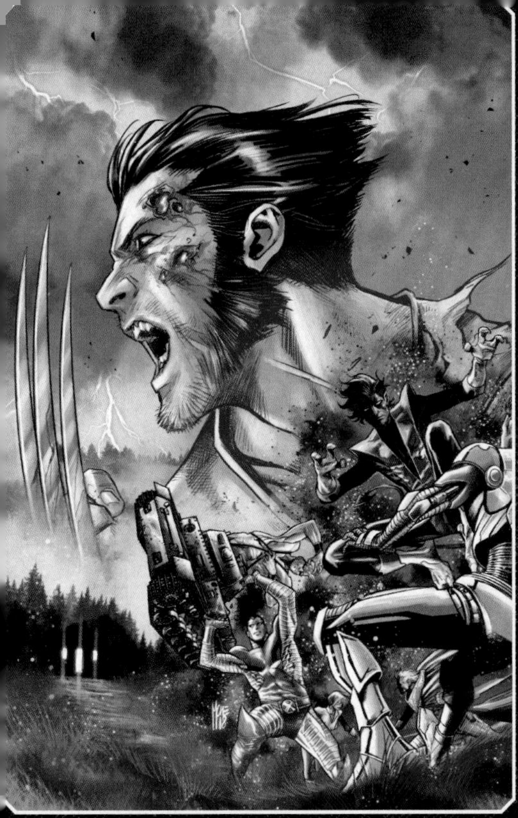

Marco Checchetto
HUNT FOR WOLVERINE #1 VARIANT

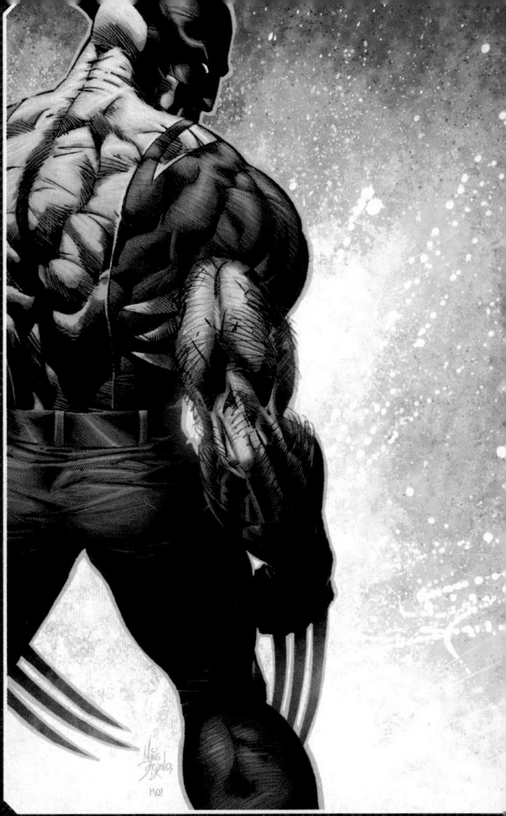

Mike Deodato Jr. & Morry Hollowell
HUNT FOR WOLVERINE #1 VARIANT

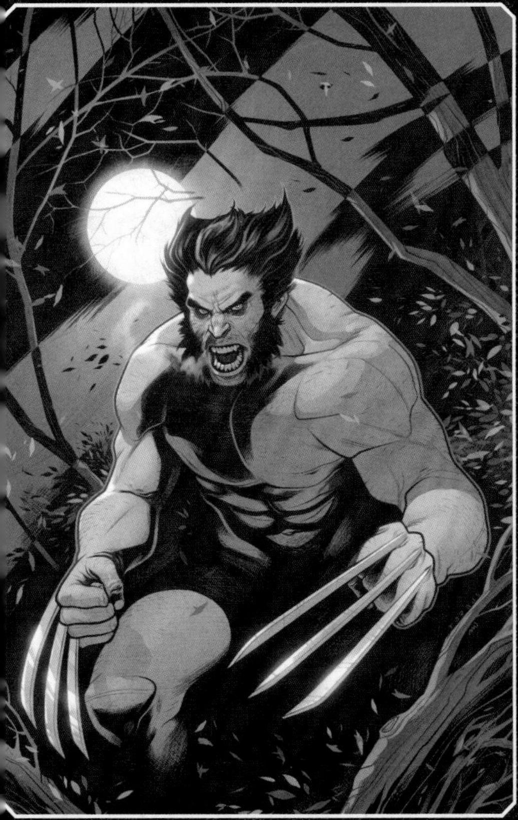

Elizabeth Torque & Nolan Woodard
HUNT FOR WOLVERINE #1 VARIANT

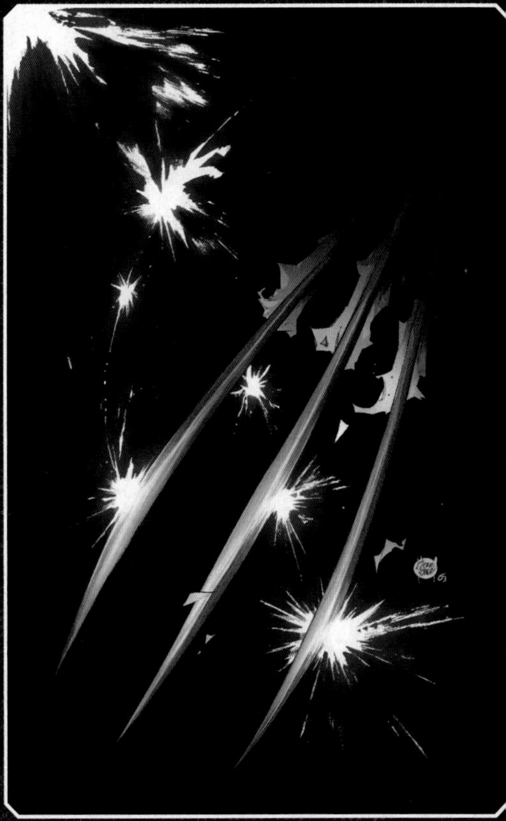

Adam Kubert & Dan Brown
HUNT FOR WOLVERINE #1 TEASER VARIANT

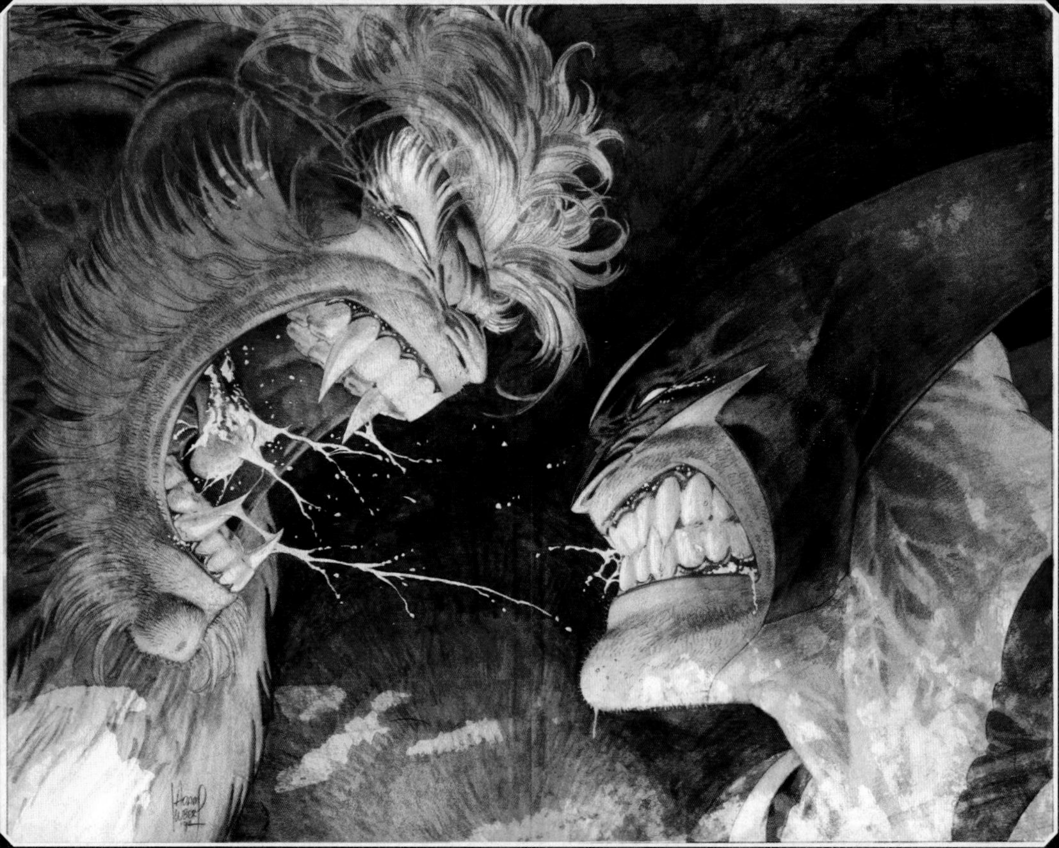

Adam Kubert & Dan Brown
HUNT FOR WOLVERINE #1 REMASTERED VARIANT

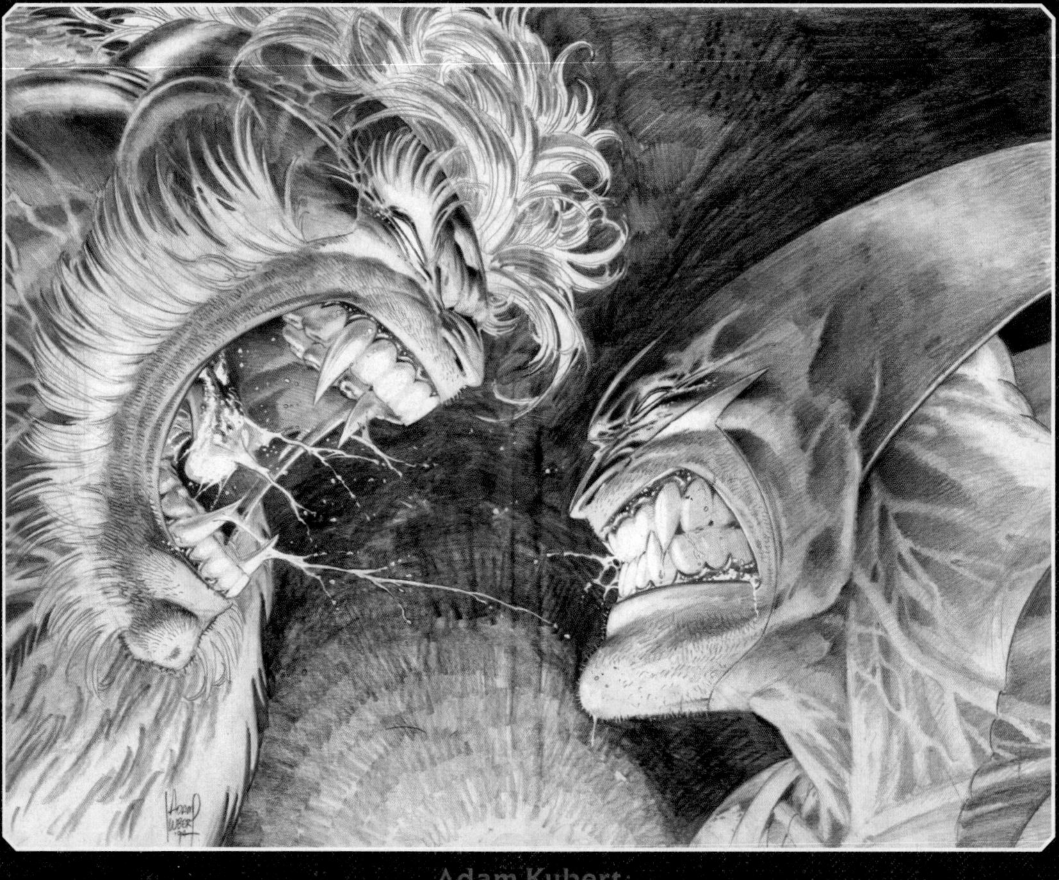

Adam Kubert
HUNT FOR WOLVERINE #1 REMASTERED BLACK & WHITE VARIANT